The Collapse of the Broadway Central

by
Michael Heslin

The Collapse of Broadway Central

Published by Three Knolls Publishing & Printing | Tucson, Arizona
www.3knollspub.com

ISBN: 978-1-941138-915

Printed in the USA

Contents

Preludes for the Gaslight

I went back last night to the Gaslight. I went down my crossword streets again to talk of love and war. I saw everyone before long. In the sacred places between Monk's blue chords we tolled our joyous bell of modernism, that calls to the faithful on Seventh Avenue South. At small tables by smoke stained walls I recorded the echoes of my Jazz Age. I hear them softly now but more clearly than yesterday. I saw so many faces I knew but I left the Vanguard early because I didn't see you there. Coming down to Sheridan Square I turned my collar up and stood by the spiked fence talking to the General. Was it I who put a desperado's kerchief around him that Halloween? It might have been but he seemed a stranger for it now. Hey buddy, he said, how goes the battle? I said I'd let him know. The papers would be coming off the trucks soon and Christ Almighty at the news hut opens up. Christ Almighty, he's a little cranky, has a poem on cardboard he composed himself: No Change, No Directions, No Nothing. If you take too long getting a dime from your pocket Christ Almighty says c'mon c'mon c'mon c'mon c'mon. Ask Christ Almighty to break a twenty and Christ Almighty says Christ Almighty, what you think I'm a bank here? He and the General are neighbors but not close. I understand, I am between them sometimes. Nobody asks the General how to get to Washington Square but they ask Christ Almighty all day long. Christ Almighty says never heard of it but the General would like to be asked for he had the habit once of leadership. He wants to raise his arm and point. So he asks how goes the battle and waits to hear how do I get to Houston Street or the uptown express. So I asked what I could never ask Christ Almighty: how do I get home? You can't ask a soldier that, he said. I suppose not I realized. I went over to the news hut, shuttered for the night ahead. I read the poem that all ghost notes know, that all ghost notes buried in the riff know by heart: No Change, No Directions, No Nothing.

A woman moving in the dark breathed in my ear. Come have eggs with me at the Pink Tea Cup, she said. She pulled me there behind her hooded cloak. Her father is a justice of the peace back home I'm told but she is a witch with moon sliver eyebrows. Cheesecloth pouches of spice hang from her belt and she sprinkled fennel and rosemary on our eggs. Somehow she has my copy of Mexico City Blues and we read choruses over our coffee, side by side. She is incantatory and her place is five flights up. There is a closet door over the kitchen bath covered with the holly wreaths she weaves. Coriander, her familiar, hisses at me. Holding a pinch of tea, perhaps leaf of my imagining, she changes men into swine, into yearning beasts with indiscreet memory. Her lure is tart lipstick, anise and wine. My longing is to sleep on her breasts and lie in the curl of her arms the night through. There's no heat in her room, no record player, but her tidal origin brings comfort. A candle lights our way to the roof and by the parapet wall she spreads her cape to sail into the ether, beyond the penumbra of the Staten Island ferry. I kissed her in my midwestern way, missing her garden of herbs and catching the top of her ear. She pushed me away but in point of fact I was just going over the Gaslight a minute with an infinity of doorways to pass.

As I was crossing Sixth Avenue (will I ever be done doing so?) the Wizard appeared. He's been making an unsteady living at the Figaro cheating at the matchstick game from Last Year at Marienbad. He says it keeps him in espresso and is less tiring than running beside tour buses dressed as a beatnik. Gee, I wish I'd taken you to one of his pacifist Punch and Judy shows. Judy is a suffragette who convinces Punch his club is an extension of his arrogant male ego. They read pamphlets and sound like Fabians. In the end a Bertrand Russell doll in a high starched collar says Punch and Judy have achieved a spiritual marriage of true minds. Everyone liked it the first week but it got boring because Russell took over and Wizzy used him to make up insulting lies about our friends. The last performance was rather sad. Russell was drunk, his little Edwardian suit disheveled. He turned on the Wizard and called him a failed artist. Embarrassed, filled with pity and terror, I left in search of an Orange Julius and a soft pretzel. Yet Wizzy carried on. Back when he was a beat poet I wrote that he looked like an agnostic praying mantis. Secretly pleased, he said I was too visionary to work for a newspaper. He did not mean it and neither did I.

It wasn't your duffle coat but still I turned my head. The toggles were unfastened and it was my heart's desire to fasten them. That's how it is at the big game in November. You hold her close and ask if she is cold and if her poor thermos is empty. The atmosphere of those Saturday afternoons when you kissed the ice crystals from her hair remains. Her upturned face and casual flip were proud of you, proud of your ideals and prominence on the student newspaper. Now I wanted to stop this other girl before she reached Bleecker Street and say: pardon me, miss, do not mistake me for one of those free love bohemians but it would be a pleasure, nay an honor, to fasten the unfastened toggles of your duffle coat. Familiar, yes, her profile recalled Betsey, a girl I met at Newport. Betsey liked the Brothers Four but not John Lee Hooker so much. There was you see much talk of authenticity at the festival. Some acts were said to be dubiously authentic, some very authentic, and a few so excessively authentic it was unbearable. Betsey had a boyfriend, as earnest and pink as a ham bone (though am I not as white as parched corn?), who bemoaned Pete Seeger's struggle between two masters, Moscow and the banjo. Isn't it ironic, he said, that this most authentic of Americans should kowtow to the Party Line. Such, he continued, is communism's fatal spell. Heck, I said, I didn't know that. Betsey was so pleased with her boyfriend she sipped from his lemonade. But now the girl who looked like her was hurried past Bleecker by the out-of-town wind that turns love cold. She fastened her own toggles and I beheld her fly away.

As I was slipping down Minetta Lane she called to me from her fire escape. She needed a nutcracker and remembers I can open walnuts by pressing two together in my hand. (We are all known for something I suppose.) She gave me coffee and I could see her eyes were red. I assumed it was a man she was crying for but no, it was her new casting photos. They made her look like Theda Bara or as she put it a chipmunk with a hangover. Attempting gallantry (and the Ohio born can only attempt) I said they made her darkly mysterious like Monk's... she said I was darkly stupid. I drank my coffee and listened to her bracelets jingle as she stubbed out red-tipped cigarettes. (Where are they, those who wore bangles and lipstick while the city slept?) She's tired of the theatre, of trying out for Albee and Beckett and only getting call backs for commercials. I showed her a play I wrote with a magnificent part for a certain someone. They're all hicks, she said, I don't do hicks. It was hard being thrown over by her because she projected many images. It was as if I'd slept with all her roles without knowing her true voice. Having an early rehearsal she asked me to go so I put on a Monk record I'd given her. I hoped to hear a piece of Blues Five Spot for the road but even with eyes closed I knew she was shaking her head. I said I was just going over the Gaslight a minute. That's it, she said, that's it in a nutshell. Yes, it seemed to be true. You should have put some hookers in that play, she said. I'm sorry, I told her, we don't have them in Monacacy Court House.

I poked my head in the Cafe Reggio on the chance you might be there but saw the Wizard instead. He was waving from his favorite table, the one below the portrait of Cesare Borgia. Evidently he had a live one for his pocket chess set was out and he was poised to employ his famed abstract expressionist defense. It assumes various forms but the simplest and most successful is a yawn and the lazy interrogation: isn't that Jackson Pollock over there (or Betty Boop or Cannonball Adderley)? As his opponent turns to look Wizzy moves pieces on the board or adds and subtracts according to whim. Enthusiasm gets him into trouble, like the time he was caught playing with three knights. It's a miracle, he said, grandmasters will make a pilgrimage here. He had to move onto another coffee house until things blew over. (Since life began we have been moving on to one coffee house or another.) Some are angry with him nonetheless. A poet returned from India not long ago and spoke of his time in an ashram there. The Wizard, not a very enlightened person, felt left out. He juggled pastries in a kind of Egyptian snake dance he thought vaguely Eastern. He was ignored. In frustration Wizzy forced his way through the admiring throng and proposed a Zen riddle that begins with a traveling salesman's car breaking down at night near a lonely farmhouse. So the poet bestowed upon him a gaze of such benevolence and warmth Wizzy shrank back as if he'd been kicked. But now he was calling me to his chess table where I was introduced to his opponent as Edna St. Vincent Millay, the famous writer. As we shook hands Wizzy rearranged the board. The man said timidly he'd always believed Edna St. Vincent Millay to be a woman. Really, Wizzy said, I suppose you also think Evelyn Waugh is a dance hall girl? Mr. Millay here, he went on, is the soul of sensitivity who ventures out on certain nights to take moon baths on Gansevoort Pier and to pay my espresso bill. I took the Wizard's check to the cashier. Immortality does not come cheap but here, by the rolling river shore of an Italian cafe, I knew the Edna St. Vincent Gambit was mine alone.

There was such a crowd on MacDougal I could not get over. (Have you ever felt, have you, that you could not get over?) The Gaslight was near but it seemed hundreds of people were rising from the Cafe Wha? to fill the sidewalk. The man from Aesthetic Realism pushed me against a car. In reality opposites are one, he said, art shows this. I did not know what to say and I stood upon a bumper in search of you. Everyone was with someone for love is a twice told mystery. Someone behind me said they tried to join the Peace Corps but all they had left was New Guinea and off-Broadway. Let's go have a beer, said the woman with him, I need to read you my journal. I am meaningless, she whispered, you are meaningless, these grapes are bitter, who is Monica? Seeing an opening I worked my way to the corner but was carried to the park. The Have Your Picture Taken With A Beatnik man was snapping his fingers. I'd never seen him so busy. By the fountain voices demanded: why are you so defensive? Why do you refuse to recognize the value of analysis? I just read your column, said another, and disagree with it completely. Why do you refuse to recognize that Ochs is not merely a folk singer, that Ochs is Zola? A man reading aloud from the paper cried that's him. Why do you refuse to recognize that there can be no literature that is not truly lived, that has not been sweated out, as it were, through the pores of the working class? I said these were all very interesting viewpoints but I was just going over the Gaslight a minute. I ran down Thompson to West Third. My breath was short, I didn't know why. The painted figurehead above the firehouse was in a Whitmanesque mood. I have heard your heel taps in Ohio, it said, and seen you scoop froth from her malted with your finger. Yes, it was true, that was me. As I chatted with the figurehead a fireman looked through the glass. You're strange in a way I can't express, he said. I know that too, I said.

I knocked because there was light in her transom. I'm sorry, she said, I don't want another bourgeois love affair right now. More than many, she was much taken with Auden's lament: If equal affection cannot be, let the more loving one be me. But is it a lament and are we sure of even that? Please understand, she said, it's not your cowlick or boyishness, it's not even the apple pandowdy your mother bakes. (I don't have a cowlick.) These things were hard for her to say because she needed to be generous. She was afraid I'd come to quarrel with her, to be difficult as we often put it, when it was only that I was passing. This was but a pause in my restlessness and the night is long. I saw her as she once was before speed and altitude carry us away. I must keep flowing outward, she said, and not be dragged down. (Like mine, hers was a walk-up apartment. When you have an elevator you tend more towards optimism.) I've heard that women, out of kindness or habit, deflect argument by calling their virtues faults and this may have seemed the easiest way to get rid of me. She was writing and I had misjudged her tension. What I'd taken for anxiety and concern for myself was simply annoyance. My visit, easily confused with our wintery romance, was unnecessary and that was all. I invented emotions for her, compatible with me, a little pain but never a wound. I said I would go, a lamp was shining on me full. (Why do we have such lamps?) I believe she had a horror of me; had her mouth truly been on mine? What's happened to you? Sleepwalking, I said, it keeps you up all night.

I sought to go where it was not so brightly lit, beyond the glow of the Surfmaid bar. I saw Raymond from Dauber & Pine sliding towards me. Re bop, he said to me, and I wished him re bop too. Raymond keeps his head down, addressing your belt buckle in a legato way. Squares have made his life a living hell and eye contact with a square, even for a moment, profanes. He is most bothered by squares who come in the bookshop for biographies of great white men and semi-classical poetry. (By semi-classical Raymond means not improvised.) We get along because there are degrees of Ohio squareness he can't penetrate, mistaking them for unique hip quirks of my own. And I know Monk's middle name is Sphere and Raymond appreciates that. Hip as he may be though he is quite shy around girls. On Grove Street once I introduced him to a woman as a very down, very progressive tone poem, the living embodiment of Epistrophy. He was pleased and this night too he was in clover, having just added to his continuing chronicle of the single greatest moment in jazz. This had to do with Ornette Coleman's plastic saxophone. (Raymond did not specify where it happened because a single greatest moment in jazz belongs to the ages.) Ornette was concluding a lengthy open ended blues. His solo wandered far but then, forehead corrugated with inspiration, he blew a final transcendent note. Raymond felt an electric quickening, an ache within, a spasm, a sadness, and at last a restful stillness. It was 3:23 A. M. and the bartender was asleep. The owner was counting receipts and there were four customers in the club. It was, Raymond assured me, the single greatest moment in jazz. Another time he told me of a single greatest moment and I foolishly asked how he knew. In his face I saw the disturbance I'd caused. I don't know, he said. I'd turned the key, heartlessly, to his loneliness. This time I was respectfully silent and I could tell he approved. I said I was going over the Gaslight a minute but hoped to catch Monk's second set at the Vanguard later. He inquired as to the square situation as far as the corner and I said it looked all clear to me. With thanks he wished me bo reep and I said bo reep to him too.

I stopped for a drink at the San Remo and she stood behind me at the jukebox. Hey Hemingway, she said, you look like the coat rack in a funeral home. She was an older woman to me once and the only one, besides you, who was born in the neighborhood. I told her I was tired and needed to rest. I said the same the night she took me home to her apartment of pull chains on Fourteenth Street with the meat trucks passing below. That was always her home and she'd never been to the Half-Note or read the paper I worked for. She called me Hemingway because his name was in the paper when he killed himself and they said he was a writer. As I held her in the room where the meat trucks rattled the pull chains she told me she was forty and said don't worry, it's not catching. I said it did not matter but it did and her embrace felt cold though she was warm with the blessing of anthology. I did not come back and now I was confronted by the lights and mixed years of the jukebox. Was pushing a letter and number simpler than the pursuit of a lost thread? If you arrive one day to see yourself bound on a grid, the coordinates you will plot, the references you make, may be the A-9's and K-12's of a glowing Wurlitzer. Forgive me for living so long on the strength of one honest sorrow. Listening without love is a skill that art despises and love without unveiling is a mirror. They were moving chairs for closing time. Say Hemingway... I turned and faced her. Sorry, she said, I took you for another party entirely. That's all right, I said, and I went out.

I heard a man say he'd never heard it so loud. It's like, he said, a simultaneous poetry recital with free form jazz accompaniment. Hardly, his date countered, what you hear are the shock troops of the new moral order, the retreat from conformity, a drift towards anarchy, and the ceremonial slaying of society's sacred cows. A cab driver, rolling his window down explained: hootenannies are reactionary and passing the hat is a spineless concession to capitalist profiteering. His passenger rolled her window down and said folk singers and their ilk lack class consciousness, encourage sentimental posturing, and extol worker identification with product. A painter sneered cabaret socialists, coffee house revolutionaries at them. Artist, they sneered back, cast off your chains of individual expression. The travel writer, notebook in hand, said: The finger-popping, free-versifying denizens of Manhattan's fabled tenement Montmartre are well worth a visit. Attired in black berets and dark glasses (known as shades to the initiated), they inhabit picturesque cafes, modeled after real European ones, where they discuss the latest existential-isms while imbibing cup after cup of fiery hot espresso. Sometimes even girls get into the act. Don't worry about money (locally called bread or moolah, ya dig?), a few cents and a yen for deep thinking are all the admission you need to one of these exclusive dens. Insider's Tip! If you want to be taken for one of their own be sure to pepper your speech with the latest cool expressions, such as: Jeepers, 23 Skidoo and (wildest of all) Don't Tread On Me, Roscoe. When you do don't be surprised if that big Daddy-Oh himself, Jack Kerouac, stops by your table to say: Welcome aboard, you way gone cat! Happy Hunting, Hipsters!!

There were colleagues from the paper, talking and laughing. I hid in a doorway. If they saw me I would have to explain and an explanation is such a deadly thing. And their familiar voices recalled to me the fear I had run from, that I would meet me in my unending return. The police came through on one of their periodic sweeps because the neighborhood has become a magnet for undesirables; a haven for the rootless youth of the outer boroughs; a teeming bazaar of pizza parlors and marijuana cigarettes called joints; a rendezvous for homosexuals of all kinds; an urban crossroads of sub-cultural currents; a swelling crescendo of conflict between old world restraint and the New Permissiveness. I heard shouts in the street: Wagner Vows Action... Clean-Up To Begin Following Monk's Last Set Saturday Night... Top Cop Knocks Pot Shop... Clergy Fears Teen Brainwash... Folk Singer Swallows Harmonica... Bronx Mom Moans: MacDougal St. Stole My Child... Cafe Au Go Go Co-ed Coos: I Lost My Homework There. Looters Rampant, Guard Mobilized, Martial Law, Order Restored. The police came through on one of their periodic sweeps and swept my colleagues away. I came up out of the shelter with the moon in my eyes and saw nothing that I knew.

In green fatigues, she was the first I'd seen of her tribe. My back to the Gaslight she asked for a light. In the match flare I saw her face, small colored stars beneath her eyes, petals painted on her cheek. Where had she come from? She offered me a hit and said down there, indicating perhaps Chinatown, Delaware or the Dry Tortugas. She was sloppy and had poor posture and was imprecise. They used to come from the Ivy League and Big Ten to act and write and work in publishing. They carried portfolios and had very definite opinions of Mozart and the Guggenheim. They drank mixed drinks and not beer from a bottle. They would talk, at the Cedar Bar, at Chumley's, at the White Horse, at that spaghetti place with the homemade wine. They turned the jazz down low and talked. They made more coffee and talked. The sun came up if it dared and they talked. Therapy, color field painting, marriage, infidelity, Fellini, sex without love, love without sex, who did what to whom, when they did it, would they be willing to do it again, hostility, death, the Sunday *Times*. Talked to a crisp, yes, but you could always squeeze more out of it like an old tube of anchovy paste. You see I'm unsure of myself with someone who does not tell me she identifies strongly with the woman in Persona or that Simone de Beauvoir has written her life ten times over. Ambiguity is one thing, not saying anything at all is another. I asked the girl in green fatigues why she dresses the way she does and she said lots of pockets. I like lots of pockets too but we're not really getting anywhere. It's not something you can work into a system and have with your coffee like pound cake. Color field painting, oh good night. We might have been in downtown Cream of Wheat for all it mattered. No, it didn't matter where she was. I was just going over the Gaslight a minute but she was not. She was looking for a head shop.

I was looking for the singer, on the ground where I had first seen him. You remember how he made a talking blues from Robert Frost's Birches? That was the darndest thing I thought. He sang Merle Travis songs and Bye Bye Blackbird. You remember, don't you? We were together and I wished I had worn my raincoat so I could put it over you when we ran across the park. Was it that time at the Gaslight or another where the woman passing said her world was modeled on surrealism? I'd been about to say the tables packed together reminded me of the dodgem cars at the county fairs where I grew up. Pretty poor stuff I guess, not like comparing yourself to paintings anyway. Shallow as a pie pan, I was trying to impress you always. The singer came outside and I said I want to write about you. Raspberry is my favorite flavor, he said, and I'm five eleven soaking wet. He was the genuine article all right, in boots and dungarees and an old leather jacket. My hair was sticking up in the back like corn tassels, I tried to slick it down. The singer seemed like someone I could talk to, the kind you don't meet every day. I said I'd like to meet a girl in the rain in my windbreaker and go to a cafeteria and drink hot chocolate and watch her make a ponytail real quick with a rubber band and hold the tips of her fingers across the table. Yes, he said, I would like that too. I told him I used to go to the Gaslight with a girl. He was interested. Tell me about her, he said. Perhaps I told him too much, was that my mistake? Trying to be fancy, of course, I said her skin was a little brown, a little lighter than a caramel apple. And her eyes were green, so green. By the lamppost he started to sing and I knew without hearing the end that it was already done. I walked away. But I felt what a good thing it is, when it's late and you're between here and there, what a good thing it is to hear a song sung so clear for no other reason than love. Yes, for no other reason than love.

I heard voices at the corner of West Third and went to investigate. It was an early morning neighborhood tour and the guide said they'd arrived at one of the most interesting and historical of our local nightspots, the Cafe Bizarre. Yes, the Cafe Bizarre, Home of the Folkswingers, Where the Beat Meet the Elite. This building, she confided, was once the stables of Aaron Burr, one of the most fascinating figures on the stage of our nation's history. Vice-President under Thomas Jefferson, he was involved in a fatal duel with his political nemesis, Alexander Hamilton. Yes, a bullet at ten paces in Weehawken ended the life of the dashing arch-Federalist but Aaron Burr's fabulous career came to a close on that field of honor too. I could see the guide had them hooked as she closed the circle about her. And some say, she hushed, that on dark and stormy nights when the moon is full (as it often is here) the ghost of Aaron Burr himself can be seen presiding over the festivities. Ah, she continued, I see some you don't believe; well, I can only say strange and wonderful things have been known to happen here in storybook Greenwich… Just then the Wizard stepped from between two parked cars. He had a Marianne Moore tricorn hat on and a lace handkerchief tied around his mouth. Boo, he said, I'm the ghost of Aaron Burr. Dancing and whirling, Wizzy went into a combination sailor's hornpipe and Watusi. He was pulling out all the stops but I don't think he was very frightening. The tour group shuffled their feet and stared at the sidewalk. The guide went on bravely, asking if there were any questions. Yeah, I got a question lady, Wizzy said, and you'd better listen up. Why doesn't your blood run cold at this sight, a man whose time has come and gone in the gray light of morning? You're not scared, he cried, and I am. Wizzy was beside me and I put my arm around his shoulder. My nerves are completely shot, he said, it's the espresso. Yes, I agreed, too much espresso. Huddled against me as we walked away he turned to throw back one last melancholy boo at the half-light figures. It was not a boo like I'd ever heard before. The Wizard doesn't live far from you and I helped him up the stairs. He said he was sorry to have taken me out of my way. I said it was no trouble, I was just going over the Gaslight a minute. I always come this way, sooner or later. He was sleeping when I left and I lowered the shades so that tomorrow would not disturb him.

When I met you on Sullivan Street and you told me you were married I believed you did it to make me jealous. It was an illumination I had. I suffer from them sometimes. We went into a cafe that was opening but you wouldn't have coffee, only water, because you were on your way to church. It is not as much fun to talk when one person is having only water. It made me shy. It was funny to realize that as I looked for you from place to place you were home asleep all the while. I hope you didn't feel awkward too. I chattered about Monk and the jazz promoter of whom I planned to write but stopped when I saw I was not on your mind, like the milk and sugar you did not require. Did I ask questions in an automatic way? I hope not but I wouldn't put it past me. I was determined to black out your attraction, like the light we switch off so others cannot see inside. Yet I never included the serenity behind your beauty in the reckoning. The goal I set myself, to forget you and all you meant, proved as elusive in the end as a dream of one syllable. It was never within the immediate reach of waking. You have become, more than if you had loved me as I wished, a permanent part of my voyage. I was keeping you from church. Outside the moon was in the sky, like our childhood moons in their sleepy nightcaps. I waited and looked too long, watching you. Some things are the same. In Ohio once I came upon a doe in the woods. A birch was fallen across a stream, a grackle cried above my head. My foot slipped, there was a splash, and she moved off towards Houston Street, far from me again.

Did you ever dream lucky baby and wake up cold in hand?
-   Cold in Hand Blues

When Worlds Collide

The phone rang at 185 Bleecker at ten to six, a Friday. Further away there was a bell ringing on MacDougal Street, early vespers bell. Fletcher heard one, the other, went back to unconsciousness without regret. The bell ceased, the phone continued. That was worse. The bell had taken the sharp edge off the phone. While the bell yet tolled it might be a morning somewhere like droplets on a milk bottle, a red barn across the field. The telephone meant that other world, a hot night on the metro beat, Manhattan. There was, as Duffy had said, something to New York like waking up with a whore.

Fletcher swept his arm around, knocking the receiver to the floor. He was sleeping on his sofa, sleeping in his clothes. He didn't taste good, sour in the stomach, a tongue stinging on teeth. It wasn't the smartest idea, a grievous mistake in fact, to drink from a canteen belonging to a guy with skull and crossbones on his eye patch. A basic black eye patch would be dissuasion enough, the skull and crossbones indicated he was Bluto and you Olive Oyl. Yet your bony elbows and knobby knees did not hold much interest, it was your soul he craved. He wanted you to be like him, a not uncommon thing. There was speed or worse in the canteen and there you have the simple half-life of summer's decay. Fletcher felt like soft burst fruit thrown from a car window. He scraped the receiver up to his face.

"If you're not with a broad you're fired." It was Scanlon at the paper. "Tell me, don't sirens sound sweet to you no more?"

"What is it?"

"The Broadway Central fell down and went boom. Jesus, Rush, pick your head up. That's not the Macy's parade out there."

Fletcher did not pick his head up. "So?"

"So I would enjoy having a member of my staff at the scene who at least knows what the mayor looks like. In other words it would please me like money from home if you would get the hell over there, pronto. Kapish?"

"I'm sick, John."

Unavailing. "So was Oscar Wilde and he never missed a fire yet. Stop in the Shipwreck and find me squire Mahaffy. I want pictures. Now get."

Scanlon deflected further reluctance by hanging up. Fletcher nodded his head, yes, and dropped the phone. Polite as always his employer, delightfully pleasingly brisk.

There were sirens and an undercurrent of muffled car horns. Fletcher got up like a drunk and achieved the other side of the room without falling. An accomplishment worth listing in his resume. He had a corner, top floor apartment with windows overlooking both Bleecker and MacDougal. The Bleecker windows were on the fire escape, kept locked. He spread the curtains on a MacDougal window and pulled up the sash. Sunlight and late afternoon heat jumped at him like a spat of hot grease. Lying in the dark had been a slow baking, this was the grill.

And the horns were no longer muffled. Fletcher looked south through the humid haze to Houston. A commotion his mother would call it, all hell breaking loose otherwise. Scanlon was not prone to exaggeration but the thought occurred this had been a trick to arouse his reporter from slumber. It was not. A mounted policeman was on the sidewalk and going east like insurrection was in the wind. Something was up.

On the toilet Fletcher removed his trousers and brushed his teeth. He'd thrown up everything he'd eaten since high school and then some. No frat house beer blast had ever left him so impaired. His urine smelled evil and the toothpaste tasted of wood putty. Gripping the towel bar, a convulsive retch spread from stem to stern. You are what you eat proclaim the pure of gut and perhaps it was true. Dosed at a rock festival would not be their epitaph. Comatose on his bathroom floor - yes, that nugget would make the rounds pretty quick at the class reunion.

He rinsed his face, then floured with talcum powder. He had tousled midwest hair, it did not much require a comb. He put on clean chinos and a polo shirt. Reasonable people wore shorts in this weather, Fletcher not among them. But the disorientation continued as he searched for his keys. He did not remember being dropped off, or opening his door, or removing his shoes. He'd come back with Becker from the SoHo News. Becker was a decent companion but perpetually carnal. Fletcher explained in the car, spasmodically, that he was sick, probably dying, but Becker was more concerned with acquiring what he called toothsome hitchhikers. The sequential slowing and stopping as prospects were scanned on the highway added notably to Fletcher's nausea. The decision was two girls young enough to cling together in the back seat. They slept most of the way from Elmira as Becker cursed his luck. Fletcher hardly noticed. He was passed out with his head on the glove compartment.

His house keys were in his shoe, a tassel loafer. Two minutes since he'd looked out the window, he was not making good time on his wobbly legs. In the bedroom he poked at the bureau top for change. There was not much to go with two wrinkly dollar bills. He crammed it all in a pocket with pencil and small spiral notebook and tried not to look at his desk. He looked. His typewriter was missing, stolen over the Fourth of July weekend. It still hurt like breaking up. An electric Remington, his college graduation gift, he'd worked with it since then. There were three paragraphs he'd sweated over for an afternoon in the carriage. They took that too and the carbon though he supposed his copy only went where he would have put it eventually.

Fletcher was on the street a minute later. A reporter in a hurry never waits for the elevator. Just as well, his building didn't have one. The sidewalk felt unruly and he stopped to steady himself. Five blocks from Broadway traffic was backed up west to Sixth Avenue. It was indicative when cabbies were out of their cabs, flipping through the Post on their steaming hoods. Nothing vehicular was moving. Potbellied men in undershirts were gesticulating the news at storefronts, their palms separating in the universal signature of explosion. Fletcher wondered how you said ka-boom in Italian. A priest was sprinting east in his cassock but more delightful to Fletcher's bloodshot eye a WCBS camera crew was stuck behind a garbage truck. They were scrambling their equipment out of a van to hoof it like the rest of the working press.

It was cool inside Shipwreck Kelly's, like always. Astride the saloon doors Fletcher peered into the inviting gloom. No Mahaffy, no life to speak of. Little stirred except the dust laden ceiling fans and their motion was perceptible only to the initiated. Barney who dozed by day and by night at the end of his mahogany bar was a shadow. Fletcher hesitated. Pointless probably to enter and question thus… seen the shutterbug Mahaffy this third day of August, Our Year of Nixon, nineteen hundred and seventy-three? Barney was less explicable than the oracle at Delphi and protective of Mahaffy who did not charge for First Communion and Confirmation photos. For his part Mahaffy said he liked the Shipwreck because it was darker than his darkroom and he was putting some of his drinks on Logan's bill while Logan and Maggie were out of the country. Logan's bill was kept under the coin tray in the cash register and taken out occasionally and checked for prints.

Fletcher felt better. Not less sick but better. As he crossed Sullivan Street heading for Thompson the crowd was moving with him like a piece of the continent. Motor traffic had declined from logjam to chaos and a hook and ladder wailed in its imprisonment. As he passed between the Washington Square Village Houses expectation was high and climbing. Elsewhere in the land preparations were underway for good rockin' tonight but here at the last gasp of Fun City New Yorkers were streaming towards what they trusted would be box seat rubbernecking. It was infectious. Fletcher's six feet loped through the muggy soup du jour surrounding him. A healthy sweat, he'd forgotten being at death's service entrance a short while before. An emergency shot of adrenaline had saved him.

But the view up West Third was the usual one as Fletcher cut across north at Mercer. The small theatres and cabaret that clustered at the rear of the Broadway Central hotel seemed much as usual too. The back wall, save for the customary broken windows, was intact. Then Fletcher corrected himself. It was not disappointing that destruction was not in evidence, it was a relief. You weren't supposed to feel that way, so wolfish news hungry, yet his pumping heart was dissatisfied. The actor who played McMurphy in *One Flew Over The Cuckoo's Nest* was lounging in the midst of pedestrian turmoil on a car fender. Fletcher had seen the show three times. Once would have sufficed but the paper received free tickets that made for a cheap date. Amanda, a Ohio relation grand touring before college, sent a Times Square postcard home to say cousin Rush had treated her to a fabulous Broadway production and to dinner afterward at an equally fabulous and terribly interesting real Broadway nightclub. The production was Cuckoo's Nest and the nightclub was Spink's, the bar of the Broadway Central. Amanda's geography was generous to include lower Broadway in the theatre district and dinner was a euphemism for drinks and peanuts (she also had a some Cheez Doodles in her bag) but it forestalled Ohio from calling out the militia.

Pie, as he was known west of the Hudson, was the writer in the family and thereby given latitude in the eccentricity line. Amanda admired her cousin even as she found him mysterious and forbidding. Fletcher could not understand this as he understood himself to be about as mysterious and forbidding as potato salad. She called him Rush as opposed to his childhood nickname because it was more grown up and she was earnestly trying to be so in his presence. Under the influence of Harvey Wallbangers and the overall native grubbiness of Spink's she accosted her cousin with... I bet you think I'm a virgin, don't you? Fletcher smiled like a department store dummy, the kind in men's sportswear, but Amanda let him wiggle off the hook. Well I am now, she confessed, but que sera sera you know. This was unleashed with the kind of fatal gaiety known to the last stages of tuberculosis while Fletcher continued to grin incompetently. As they say out where you can see the stars Amanda got tight as a tick and Fletcher was able to waltz her home with her dreamy head on his nervous shoulder. He put her to bed and Amanda concluded her fabulously interesting Greenwich Village weekend with a real hangover.

A Ninth Precinct cop Fletcher knew led a charge of police sawhorses to the back of the hotel. The general public, precipitously and undemocratically booted from the sidewalk by this flying wedge, clogged what little movement remained in the traffic dripping south on Mercer. New Yorkers converted to gawking hayseeds was an arresting sight but he ran the short half block to Broadway. If something was happening he had to plug into it soon before additional laps in August's olympic pool of humidity dropped him panting in the gutter. As he reached the corner at Third and Broadway an ABC reporter was setting up for a live shot by studiously dimpling the knot in his rep tie. Fletcher was disgusted with himself. The six o'clock news had beat him on his own street. That he worked for a weekly that wouldn't appear until the following Thursday did not matter. He was offended in his territory like another man's arm around your sweetie. Professional pride to an extent, print journalism taking it on the chin again, and then there was that fifteen dollar tie.

Once around the corner Fletcher forgot about the tie. He knew Broadway between Third and Bleecker as well as any street in the Village. Not far back he'd dated an artist who had a high windowed loft looking across at the hotel. She complained about a man who spied on her with binoculars while she was painting. (Fair to say she sometimes painted in what back home they call the altogether.) If she was still there she didn't have that problem now. The front of the hotel, eight stories of stone, plaster, staircases, bathtubs and birdcages, was lying on Broadway from lamppost to lamppost, from fire hydrant to No Parking sign. All that was rubble spilled across the street to the manhole covers. What was left of the sun was in Fletcher's eyes, he closed them. He'd been here before, that former self he sometimes resembled in a way. The artist had pointed to the window where the binoculars glinted and he'd thought, yes, that was my floor.

His first thought, this question... why would anyone blow up a welfare hotel? In an earlier day, regardless how you came to the Village and regardless why - whether you were there to hang up your shingle or search for that shingle - if you didn't know someone with an apartment well enough to sponge off until you found your own place you probably put in your time with a hotel with weekly rates. Fletcher was no exception. Until it was his good luck or misfortune, his view varied, to stumble upon the rent controlled, self-basting humidor he currently enjoyed Fletcher lived a transient soup and crackers life. A room at the Broadway Central was his last itinerant stop. It was $16.00 a week and echoed like a gymnasium when the windows were open. There was a bar of shaving soap on the bathroom sink when he moved in. He thought that was a nice touch until the tenant next door came and asked for it back.

It was not a welfare hotel then but an old fashioned New York hostelry grown undistinguished with the years and the passing of the carriage trade north towards Central Park. Vanderbilts and Astors lived one block east on Lafayette and they liked it well enough to remain until something greener offered but the Broadway Central, the Grand Central Hotel once, could not go with them. It was stuck down there between Bleecker and Third, in the bleachers of the cast iron district, where the breeze on a warm day carried the sting of printer's ink. By the time Fletcher arrived in 1960 with his typewriter and ream of onion skin the Central was on the approved list of secondary Village accommodations. If not so faded fine as the Earle on Waverly Place, putting you smack in Washington Square and with wallpaper not reminiscent of succotash, it was less stuffy than some others. (He never got past the front desk at the Valencia on St. Mark's, police detectives were blocking the way.) The Central was also cheaper and not as particular about cooking in your room as some others. He'd been invited to leave the Albert on Tenth Street due to a misunderstanding about his hot plate and some suspicious eggs on his dresser. They were not so fussy on Broadway.

Fletcher jumped a barricade feeling like he'd never been sick a day in his life. He had a likely looking fire captain in his sights when the fire captain was grabbed by a police captain and they went nose to nose in a jurisdictional dispute. The uniformed services were putting on a good show but the fire department had the higher ground.

"Make sure your boys keep the area clear; my men are going in."

The police captain was biting on pipe. "Nobody goes anywhere until my bomb squad says so. Got it?"

No, he did not get it. The fire captain began spitting his words in individual gobbets. "There was no bomb here for Chrissake. This is structural."

It was a body and they were fighting over it. Caught up in the crossfire Fletcher muttered to himself just like the bumper sticker... I love New York. But there was someone calling his name, twice before he turned to look. It was Becker. "Got anything?"

Fletcher shook his head. "What about you?"

"Not much. Nobody is talking bomb. Gas maybe." Fletcher looked regretfully after his cop and fireman who were taking their love affair to the commissioner level. A gas explosion, somewhat better than a water main break, not so good maybe as a nor'easter, hurricane, or untimely blizzard. When ugly buildings fall down most readers flip to the sports. New York has ugly buildings like it has pigeons. And they fall down. "Anybody hurt?"

"Got to be, got to be. Look at this, it's fucking Berlin."

Fletcher's eyes went to his feet. In searching for details he had ceased to recognize the destruction. He was standing on a loaf of Wonder bread and he stepped away as if it were alive. The rush hour traffic helicopter was beating over them. A hundred cops, as many firemen, the emergency medical service, twenty reporters from print, radio and TV. A half-hour ago they were doing something else and now they were all over the field, in and out of it like gophers. Looking to ask a question to get an answer to peg his working hat upon, Fletcher hadn't noticed ascending ten feet of hotel living crushed together on the street. He climbed up on it like king of the hill, seeking, the way he'd been told, the story on the other side.

Becker tossed away a broken picture frame, his mind far from urban archaeology. "Those girls were pretty cute. I think the older one liked me."

Fletcher had to think, then recollection. "What older one? They were both about twelve and that's with makeup."

"Come on, they weren't twelve. High school at least. And I deserve something. I took them all the way to Rego Park."

"Where's that?"

"Queens, where else? And you were a big help. What are they going to think when I've got a corpse beside me in the front seat?"

"You should have told them I was Gregg Allman."

"Not me, I don't lie to chicks. You don't look like him anyway. Maybe I could have got away with Bob Weir. And they were worried about you. Me too. Just because I work for a newspaper doesn't mean I have no compassion."

"It doesn't? Since when? I'd like to tell my mother."

Becker, chewing gum, moved it around. "So I gave them my card. They've never been in the Village so I said give me a call and I'll show them around. What is it with these kids? They'll hitch all the way to a Dead concert in north bumfuck but they won't get on the subway to Manhattan? What are we, monsters?"

"The jury remains out on that one, Paul."

A man getting his suit dusty worked his way over the crumpled hotel marquee, press pass in his teeth. A cop shouted at him. It was Hickman from the Daily News. He waved cheerfully to the cop and dropped down beside Fletcher.

"Hell of a way to make a living," he said. "Got anything?"

"Not me; but Becker here has an interview with two Mouseketeers."

Hickman looked sideways at the shorter man. "Becker, you need a hobby to keep you out of trouble. Have you ever considered newspaper work? You might find it interesting. How was Watkins Glen?"

"The Allman Brothers took the checkered flag," Fletcher said.

"And this pussy went and got himself dosed."

"You don't have to travel for girls like that, Rush."

Hickman was a little older, a general assignment guy. He'd help anyone out and Fletcher had to sometimes fight the urge to call him mister. Fletcher shook his head. "Not that kind. Something in some wine I drank. Bad LSD maybe."

"Is there good stuff?" Hickman looked at him sympathetically. "A sweet Buckeye like you, Rush; it should never happen."

"Anything doing over that end?"

"They're waiting for Lindsay. As soon as Hizzoner declares an investigation into this tragic but unnoteworthy event we can all go home for the weekend. And don't worry, Becker, you'll recognize him. It's Friday, Lindsay will be the one in the white dinner jacket."

"He'd better not try to nonchalant this," Becker said. "I think there's bodies buried in there. What about you?"

Hickman looked aloft where the front of the hotel had been. It was like a cut in a mountain stripped for mining. He gestured with his chin at a closed truck parked across Broadway on Great Jones Street. It had the seal of the city's hospitals on the side. "I think somebody agrees with you."

"What's that?" Fletcher stared too.

"Don't you downtown boys recognize the Bellevue coffin wagon?"

Suddenly there were sirens of a particular urgency. A two car motorcade and police motorcycles howling from Lafayette.

"Sounds like the mayor's home," Hickman said. "Time to be shooting lame ducks in a barrel. I saw your man Rothberg around somewhere, Rush. Maybe you can skip the bloodletting."

"Thanks, I think I will."

Hickman exited backwards, his eyes wide on the gaping divide in the building line. "Sometimes these things happen for a reason. When they don't there's no story."

"Can a building collapse be an act of God?"

Hickman was moving away "God gave up on New York City real estate a long time ago. Got a pair for the Mets Tuesday night. What say?"

"Yeah, sounds good. I'll call you at your shop."

Becker watched Hickman spin and trot towards the microphones throbbing at the mayor's car. "He always get those passes for the ballgame. How come he never asks me to go?"

"He's shy," Fletcher said.

Grunting, Becker left to join the inquisition. Fletcher kept his distance. He watched the tall Ivy League frame of the mayor bow out of his Chrysler and bend to catch a word from his press secretary. Lindsay had been mayor for 7.5 years and in a few months would not be. He looked as if it couldn't come too soon. His administration began with a nasty transit strike and was almost concluding with a no star hotel pouring its welfare clients out onto Broadway. Now ensued the usual thing. The uniformed services, though the cops in particular hated him, hustled to be seen on camera showing the mayor over the finer points of the disaster. Lindsay's overall popularity was down around near beer but he still looked good on television and his freshly shaved brahmin manner tended to make even the most bona fide five o'clock shadow sad sack in his vicinity look statesmanlike. It was a transfusion no print reporter could touch. They just made you sound stupid by quoting you.

Fletcher went to work for three hours. The diversion of the mayor's arrival provided a few minutes alone with Fire Chief Hagan. He then talked to a subway engineer who had just come up from a sidewalk grating where the BMT runs below Broadway. The engineer looked no more surprised than a bookmaker ever does. The hotel manager was available but Fletcher ignored him on purpose. He talked instead to the director of the Mercer Arts Center whose theatres might fall down next. He talked to some of the actors in El Grande de Coca-Cola who were worried about their jobs. (Good sidebar that at least.) He played a hunch. Two men were standing together on the east side of the street so adroitly inconspicuous they had to be something. Fletcher crossed to Great Jones to come up behind them. He gazed with touristic thrill seeking up at the building but they weren't buying. That was all right, he knew they were building department inspectors. They had no comment and said it so eloquently as they walked off he didn't have to write it down.

As the street lights came on the emplacement of the city's relief agencies was complete. A supervisor from Social Services gave Fletcher a breakdown of the welfare recipients carried by the hotel. She was using the present tense but wouldn't much longer. There were over a hundred cases and she had accounted for half. The Red Cross was checking names against the desk register. As the news spread some of the missing joined their fellow refugees on the street. A volunteer told him the Red Cross allowed a three dollar daily stipend for food while new housing arrangements were made. The Red Cross sandwiches were American or Swiss wrapped in cellophane; he was tempted but he still had a place to live. A hot dog wagon had rolled down from Astor Place for the occasion. The hot dogs were sold out. He spent the change in his pocket on a pretzel and a Sprite. He was sweating and he wasn't getting anything. He sucked pretzel salt from his lips and thought three bucks for food wasn't bad.

Mahaffy turned up. The Irish twinkle in his eye was actually a squint. Late as often but he was good with a flash. He'd gone to the *Local* to borrow money, was asked how his hotel pictures were, replied they were great, left immediately to see what was going on. He put Fletcher's Sprite can to his forehead in lieu of a ice pack. "How come nobody told me? This isn't cold."

"It's August. I tried for you in the Shipwreck." Fletcher sometimes surprised himself and others when he talked like a New Yorker.

"Logan put an advertisement in the Staats-Zeitung how he's no longer responsible for my debts public and private. It was in English too, that costs more."

"See that bald guy with the file folder?"

"Did one of your playmates do this?"

Fletcher retrieved his Sprite can. "He's the manager. I want you to take his picture and make sure he sees you taking it."

"What, full frontal banality you want? Don't bother me with the mug shots. I feel like Brassai right this minute."

"Just tap his shoulder so he has to turn around to you, okay?" Fletcher saw a police sergeant he knew coming up from Bond Street. "And check your film first, Joe."

Mahaffy was hurt but it had been known to happen. "You sound more like the old man every day," he called after Fletcher.

The police sergeant, named Mackey, was as broad as he was solid. Fletcher approached him at an angle, blew gently on his badge, polished it with his thumb. "Say, Mack, did the late lamented here have a house detective a guy might get to know?"

As gently but with fingers like pincers Mackey removed the wrist from his chest. "Not for years, not since the welfare went in."

"What did they do about ice water complaints."

"They had rent-a-cops and they called us. A house dick can't do much these days. They ain't etiquette as your friend used to say." Mackey had loved Duffy too.

"There used to be a guy, uh…"

"Kuntz you're thinking of. An okay guy."

"An okay guy? You mean an ex-cop?" Fletcher looked to the uptown distance. "Kind of beefy, bad teeth, heavy smoker. Bad leg maybe."

"Christ, Fletcher, don't you people have anything good to say about anybody? He limped on account of a bullet in his leg. Most likely put there by some scumbag disadvantaged your weekly sewer service wraps a halo around."

Fletcher deemed their conversation at an impasse. He changed the subject. "As a matter of gravity, how come a good part of this hotel is now flat on Broadway instead of being up where it belongs?"

"You think there's a story here? You must be hard up." Mackey looked disdainfully over his shoulder. "A building collapse, that's all. It got old, it fell down, it could happen to you. Nice seeing you, Rush. Give that old prick you work for my regards."

"First thing, it will cheer him up."

Fletcher watched the sergeant stroll off towards a group of like minded civil servants. "It could happen to you," he hummed, "if you're young at heart."

Back on the sidewalk the hotel residents were jammed around the police barricades hoping they would wake up soon. Most of the transients were already gone, having no reason to stay. Some maybe got out with their suitcases; some didn't need suitcases, they didn't have a change of clothes. If a few got away owing two or three weeks that wouldn't cause management distress, they would have skipped anyway. Another room was available somewhere, there being little honor amongst cheap hotels. You might be a deadbeat on Broadway but you were a week in advance cash crosstown.

Some residents had furniture, food in the hall refrigerator, baby clothes. There were welfare mothers, old people on pensions and Social Security. There were intermittent working people like the counterman from Leshko's on Avenue A who had a fight with his family and spent the last three years watching TV in his room at the Central. There were steady working people like dishwashers and the maintenance men and the ticket seller with the cat's eye eyeglasses from the Eighth Street Playhouse. Aside from the welfare families they were people alone for the most part and that's how they assembled around the police barricades. There were junkies and perhaps the women they lived off who were often junkies too. Coming from Ohio you might not call that a couple but it probably was. Some of the ungracious insane, many who shout imprecations at an indifferent universe, wandered in tight circles. Others were simply disoriented, like earthquake survivors. In a no longer rural society floods and tornadoes get a lot of play on the AP wire but the Broadway Central wouldn't run beyond New Jersey. All news is local. Twisters flattening the righteous in Wichita is a notable twist of mother nature but New York City, full of sinners, is nobody's backyard.

There was a woman Fletcher remembered. Dressed in black Queen Victoria material he would never have identified her without his mind located in 1960. She called him "young man" and said if anyone required her she would be in the "card room". So far as he knew no one ever did require her and if there was a card room he failed to discover where it was. He was too busy burning up ribbons in his Remington and looking out the window. She'd been at the Central all these years and Fletcher was dismayed a moment on her behalf until recognizing that since leaving the hotel he'd passed the same period of time in one apartment. They were birds of a feather it might be but now her nest was blown down.

A loud rumble ensued and some of the crowd flowed back in fear of an aftershock but it was a compressor groaning to life. All was now under the lights like a night game. The fire department was spotlighting the hulk and acetylene torches were at work. Fletcher had not budged at the noise, he'd seen the compressor being prepared, and neither had the old woman in black. She continued, her gloved hands on a sawhorse, to stare ahead at her lost home. He should have spoken to her but he could not. He walked behind the lines listening to what was said. It was not what you would commit to memory or talk about in the newsroom. A fat guy with a wheeze, he looked like the go-fer in a plumbing supply, told a cop who wasn't listening how he was paid up for the whole month and now what. He paid bang on the first like always and here it was only the third, would they give him his money back? He said it over again with no variation to a fireman and a minute later was saying it again, this time to a meter maid. The fat wheezy guy sought relief and guidance from authority, any authority at all. Everybody likes to talk bad news and the margins of life are composed of filler who only get to talk it about themselves.

He wasn't picturesque this fat wheezy guy, you wouldn't put him in a play. *The Hot L Baltimore* was at Circle in the Square, not far from Fletcher's apartment. He hadn't liked it, maybe because his date didn't show. Maybe she'd already seen it with someone from another paper who also had passes. The Baltimore was a rundown hotel full of odd characters, many amusing or attractive in some manner. Fletcher thought it was shuck. In his experience people living in run down hotels weren't like that. They were like the fat wheezy guy who was about as attractive as a peach pit. That's the problem with the theatre, Fletcher complained with his arm around the empty seat beside him, it isn't like real life. How true, the seat replied, how profound you are. He had a feeling if you wrote a play about fat wheezy guys even fat wheezy guys wouldn't go to see it.

Rothberg was calling. Fletcher whistled, raised his hand. Something told him he was done for the night. He could go around again but there wouldn't be much in it. Empty city buses were herded on Great Jones down to Shinbone Alley. Residents were waiting to board, some looking back, some not. In the half-darkness the hotel looked plainly ominous. It was like a wreck at the bottom of the sea. Rumors were circulating. They were being taken to the armory on Twenty-Fifth; the Plaza was offering to put them up; there would be cots on an out-of-service Staten Island ferry. Fletcher didn't think so. The welfare mothers at least were bound for whatever welfare hotels had the influence to get them. There was good money in welfare, no questions asked. You had the full faith and credit of the city behind you. The others, like the woman in black, get placed here and there. It will cost more and they won't like it as much but will have the consolation of knowing no one is sleeping in their old room.

Fletcher's old room on the sixth floor was mostly in the elevator shaft. He used to hear the whirr of the cables through the wall. It wasn't an unpleasant sound because it was New York. Rothberg was waiting in a doorway on the west side of Broadway close to Fourth. He had Lindquist with him, they were smoking a joint. Rothberg was professional but tended to get high as soon as a job was done. There was no talking to him then. Lindquist was new, he was hanging out a lot with Rothberg, didn't seem to care for Fletcher. Maybe he felt Fletcher was in his way. A column would be good, as soon as he could get it. He said after hours, loud to some and soft to others, that Fletcher was a burn-out.

"Scanlon went home," Rothberg said. That made sense. Rothberg would not be smoking if there was a chance the chief might catch him. "He wants us in early tomorrow, you included." Fletcher nodded. Early meant ten o'clock, not much before that.

"What did the mayor have to say?"

Lindquist answered though Fletcher hadn't asked him. "The most unbelievable bullshit, that's all it was."

A blue pencil to that, Fletcher thought. Avoid redundancy, bullshit by its very nature is unbelievable. "Seen Mahaffy lately?"

"You won't find him now. He got five bucks out of Lindquist."

'It wasn't a loan, I owed him from lunch."

Rothberg choked on his inhale. Mahaffy was not accustomed to eat lunch or any other meal regularly. He might steal a sandwich from your desk but only to hold it for ransom. Borrowed money went around easily on the staff, you'd be short on the rent or have your Con Ed shut off if it didn't, but Lindquist was getting to be a banker. And covering for Mahaffy was suspect; bankers, Duffy warned more than once, always call in their markers,

"How was Watkins Glen, Rush?"

Fletcher didn't know where to begin so he didn't. He saluted goodnight, walked back to Third Street. He looked over the hotel a minute, watched a welder at work and the sparks fly heavenward. The buses were loading. He thought he saw the old woman in black through a dark window but wasn't sure. Maybe, maybe not, like everything else. Tired of waiting for something, for anything, he left to write up his notes.

An Actor Prepares

Fletcher had a noise like Rice Krispies in his ear, his right ear. Being right handed it was the ear he leaned in with in conversation. He shifted around on one of the orange plastic scoops that served as Scanlon's office chairs to hear Agosto. He was not interested but it was a staff meeting and you were supposed to listen to your colleagues. They pretended to listen to you. Agosto went on at length, stridently righteous as usual, but Scanlon did not seem to mind. He had a comfortable reclining chair and a fan on his desk. If he had to sit on a plastic scoop in a corner of the room where air currents did not venture he would have cut her off long ago. Yet at long last he raised his traffic cop palm.

"After Labor Day," he said.

Scanlon disliked saying no directly, he holidayed instead. No matter what you were attempting to sell him on he'd put you off until the next natural break in the calendar. Secular or religious, Fletcher had heard them all. Like the time on the phone he told a freelance to wait until Ramadan was over, looking suitably pious as he did so. Scanlon didn't know Ramadan from the seventh inning stretch but nobody else did either. There was always a reporter with a story burning a hole in his pocket but equally true there was always another holiday up the chief editor's sleeve garters.

Labor Day was a favorite. He'd come out with it early in the summer, before the Fourth of July if need be. Maybe that wasn't fair but kinder maybe than saying your piece stank like wet dog's hair any time of the year. And as the long hot days accumulated the succinct mumbo jumbo "after Labor Day" came to mean something more than go away, you bother me. (And if you pressed that is precisely what he would say.) It was the cry from the depths of a man surrounded by boilerplate on a broiling August afternoon. There were New Yorkers, Fletcher had seen them, who stalked the unrelenting summer streets with figurative dynamite strapped to their chests and a not so figurative fuse in their teeth. "Don't interfere with me," they implied, "or I will blow us all to hell." Come winter perhaps they were the mildest of men. Scanlon was not that bad but the heat made him churlish and with Duffy gone there was no one to hose him down. These days it was better to let him swelter in peace. But perhaps Fletcher had foregone asking for much. It amounted to the same never mind in the end. There are hot nights in this town, Duffy had been wont to say, when I'd give my left nut for ten minutes under a harvest moon.

Ignoring Agosto's vocal distress Scanlon turned to the fan to dry his nose sweat. The grousing grew louder, purple in tone.

"I said after Labor Day, Rose."

More emphatic this time the boss. He had a soft spot for Agosto but she was pushing it this morning. Fletcher ignored her when possible but she seemed more overwrought than normal. A Puerto Rican lesbian, she'd been on staff for two years and had moved from a kind of affirmative action intern to a real presence. For many she was a thoroughgoing pain in the ass and didn't make up for it with any special ability. Scanlon tolerated her, no one knew just why. Everything in his background, everything you knew about it at least, suggested he should not put up with her loudmouth complaints. But he hired her and continued to back her up. It was Duffy however who encouraged her. They were both from the Bronx and though Duffy was born in 1910 and Agosto in 1950 their similarity was evident to him. Duffy told the *Local*'s business manager who called her a cha-cha queen to get out of his office. (Benson used language like a bookkeeper. Cha-cha queen was the expression for a homosexual Spanish male. Those who knew the difference didn't bother to correct him.) Agosto called Duffy Mr. Duffy. She called most non-Hispanic, non-black men gringo. She called Scanlon the gringo.

This morning she called him a shithead. Fletcher winced from where he sat in his orange scoop. It was years, five or six, before he'd been able to call Scanlon by his first name. He worked up to it late one night in a bar, pretending he didn't care if Scanlon fired him for excessive familiarity. Scanlon didn't, maybe never noticed, maybe still didn't. Now here was Agosto, all five feet of her in haute linebacker couture, rumored to dictate her copy into a cassette player (not true), who couldn't type (also not true), who bitched (well, yes she did), demanded (without question), set conditions (undoubtedly) and quit every other day (probably exaggerated), here she was calling her liege lord a shithead and departing in a stomp or as much as ninety pounds (approximately) can stomp on a mushy August morning. The appalled city editor was on the edge of apoplexy. Certainly no one ever said that to Horace Greeley. (Note to self: did shithead as an honorific exist in the nineteenth century?) Fletcher disguised his laugh by massaging his cloudy ear. Indeed, Scanlon was an awful shithead sometimes.

There was a half a buttered roll on the desk. There was always a half eaten buttered roll on Scanlon's desk. You'd think once in all these years he'd finish the other half. He never did. Before long the wad of roll remaining and the Zeus Brothers coffee shop wax paper it partially nestled in would become curled in that week's collection of desktop refuse. Needing something, Scanlon pushed out his arms like a boy at the beach trying to keep waves from a sand castle. Sometimes the desired object came to hand, like a coffee drenched file of clippings or indecipherable index cards, but just as often it was churned deeper into the adhesive mass, gluey with eraser dust, pencil shavings and gummy buttered rolls. The sticky weather made it all that much more enticing. "It's on the chief's desk" was not a response intended to calm a suppliant reporter who needed to know his story was bound for greatness if not immediate immortality. Just like the busybody he was, Scanlon read everything that went in his paper.

"John," the feature editor said, "you're screwing me."

Not meant literally of course but received anyway with a round of hollow chuckles. Baines, the city editor, blinked appreciatively in his blinky manner. Here was safer ground, they could all join in the fun. Paige Phillips, the feature editor, "miss back of the book", was a woman too but she was not, most definitely not, the passionately intractable Agosto denouncing her prince before all his courtiers. Scanlon and Phillips were at war but it was a quiet affair, fought with smiles and insincerity (bluster for him, coyness for her) with only the infrequent ack-ack of annoyance leaving a hint of cordite in the halls. The Wall St. Journal said they were "engaged in a battle for the soul of the *Local*" but this was romanticized hooey from over where the troglodytic roam. The paper's soul, if it had one, was as ill-defined as any other animating principle. Getting your finger on it might find said principle squirming off in another direction. Scanlon did not like to say no to women (he'd been married three times) but had no trouble letting them go (divorced thrice). If he felt Phillips getting out of hand back there in featureland he'd fire her on her birthday and if that day was also Christmas all the better. Phillips knew that as well as anyone. The war was quiet because it was mainly inside Scanlon. Or to put it into Duffyese... the chief couldn't be sure but she was right.

This was Scanlon's sixty-eighth summer in New York out of a possible sixty-nine. The year he missed, his sixteenth or eighteenth, Fletcher had heard both quoted, was passed in unspeakable toil at the Providence Record. One of his duties was carrying bottles of Prohibition beer to the whorehouse, an activity that might have left him cynical if he were not already. It became one of Scanlon's deepest beliefs that what could be bought in New York could only be rented in Rhode Island and that this more or less obtained throughout the rest of the world. Except for a couple of honeymoons Scanlon hadn't been significantly off the isle of Manhattan since the war.

His father was a newspaperman, far enough back to have interviewed Lincoln's assistant John Hay when Hay was McKinley's Secretary of State. That wasn't difficult then when indoor plumbing was not the norm. You sat outside a politician's office until he had to go to the jakes. You had the time because news sifted slowly. There were still men around who'd covered the Civil War. They themselves moved slowly, no reason to hurry, for what story could ever touch the one they'd cut their teeth on. Scanlon senior worked for Hearst and like a number of men in his day once he went to Hearst he never worked anywhere else. Fletcher's Scanlon grew up believing that William Randolph Hearst was the greatest man since Jesus Christ rode into town, leading to dis- enchantment when junior learned this was something less than the case. But his father was dead by then so it could have been worse. They had a distant relation, a songwriter, who spelt the family name with a second "a". A tune he wrote about a rose was so popular it came to be called Scanlan's Rose Song. Somewhat Irish, papa Scanlon was quite proud of this connection without rea- son to be. If a by-line had ever come his way he might have changed his own spelling for that added aristocratic touch but a by-line never did. It never came to his son either but the difference was John Scanlon never wanted one.

"I don't get Kate Millet for nothing," Phillips of the features was saying, "and she's not accustomed to having her reviews killed."

By tapping on his ear like a telegraph key Fletcher enjoyed a moment of clarity before it sandbagged up again. So he had a intimation Scanlon wasn't accustomed to hearing the word accustomed with regard to writers.

"After Labor Day," was the dry bones reply.

"Not good enough, John. Not acceptable."

"It's not a summer piece, Paige." Scanlon was big on seasonal copy. He hadn't read a book in thirty years, or so he said, but if he ever went on vaca- tion (not likely) he'd take a beach read along, perhaps Jacqueline Susann, even if going to the mountains. (Ah, Fletcher sighed from his scoop, cool mountain air.) It was though always the season for crime, that was in his bones as it was in Duffy's. They could chew over a good murder for hours. ("You mean to tell me he ran out of kerosene halfway through burning her body? What an idiot! Why don't these people think these things through?")

"A guy looks at that on the subway, Paige, it's gonna wilt what's left of his shorts."

"It's not written for men, you're missing…"

Scanlon raised one of his hamburger red hands. "I haven't glanced at the profile in a day or two, Paige, but as I recall we do have sons of Adam plunk- ing down fifty cents for our weekly effort as well as those on the - you should pardon my French - distaff side. The question is: should we be running this at all if it's not intended for half our readership?"

Advantage Scanlon. Phillips hadn't meant to say what she did, he caused her to fault. You got so caught up daydreaming what his neck would look like in a wreath of barbed wire you forgot yourself. (It happened to Fletcher until he ceased arguing and accepted the rumblings of the mighty potentate for what they were: sassafras.) For then, unforgivably, you pursued your own folly to its depths. Instead of serenely backing away from whatever dubious premise you began with you persisted in the hope of shoving it down the old man's throat. That's when Scanlon really smacked his lips.

"I suppose," Phillips said too quickly, "a column once a month about antique car collecting truly engages the majority of our women readers?"

Fletcher rubbed his forehead. "Hupmobile" didn't engage anyone but that wasn't the point. Scanlon concealed his glee by looking sorrowfully reflective.

"It's true what you say, Paige. Hupmobile is an anachronism as I've said myself more than once. But Mr. Sheehy has been here since the beginning and he's getting on. I think we can put up with it a little longer. He'll retire soon; I expect we'll be leaving together."

(Give me a break, Fletcher groaned to himself. He wished his other ear were clogged so he wouldn't have to hear this guff. The implication was the feature editor could go over to Sheehy's nursing home and push him and his pathetic wheelchair down the stairs as Scanlon didn't have the stomach for it.)

"That's not what I meant, John, please."

Of course that's not what you meant, Paige. No one in the room thought that's what you meant, least of all Chief Wahoo. And what was this "I expect we'll be leaving together" business? The hell, Scanlon wasn't going anywhere unless Quetzalcoatl dropped in through the window from University Place and carried him off for lunch.

"I know how you feel, Paige. We've kept away from boxing and football and the rest all these years but it hasn't been easy. I like that sort of thing myself but it's not in line with our readership. I feel strongly that sports coverage caters too much to men…"

If Scanlon was disingenuous before this was a plain lie. *The Local* avoided sports because that's the way he wanted it. He didn't like or dislike any of them, he simply wasn't interested. But he did hate sportswriters. He thought they were lazy bums. He thought writing about sports turned decent reporters into two-fingered sloths who spent their time prognosticating and fixing handicaps instead of digging. Covering sports was bad for your instincts because everything was right there in front of you. Not having real work to do, like stealing police records or spying on widows and bribing bellhops, you consequently began to think too much. Every sports desk in town had a lazy, unshaven bum who thought he was Walter Lippmann. Nothing made Scanlon more suspicious or brought out hackles on his hackles quicker than a writer who treated a given sport as anything more than a game. Polo, basketball, hopscotch, you name it; there was always some joker convinced it was Allah and he its prophet.

Even an innocent sports metaphor ("The Nixon administration, caught offsides in Cambodia…") left him cutting and slashing at his grimmest and most unyielding. Fletcher once tried to corner him. What about the undeniably fine writers past and present who wrote about sports on the side? He had a list ready but never got to the first name as Scanlon interrupted with a typically gnomic pronouncement. Victor Hugo, he said, lyricized about the sewers of

Paris.

What was that supposed to mean? And when did he read Victor Hugo? Each April when baseball began Fletcher craved writing about it. Surrounded by Sporting News box scores he'd lie back on his sofa and knock out fifteen hundred words in longhand. A monthly piece like that for the length of the season and maybe a World Series recap could soothe a troubled spirit. But he could never quite drop it on Scanlon's desk. Duffy would have gone to bat for him ("X that, avoid muscle bound allusions.") but the living Duffy had so often in the past it was painful to plead again like a copy boy. So Fletcher never did, filing the yellow sheets of copy in his bottom drawer.

"Then I'll make a deal with you, John," Phillips said. "Give me Kate next week and I'll get you a hockey puck as a chew toy."

Blinky Baines blinked spasmodically. That's what he liked to hear, the old one-two, give as good as you got but with an undertone of respect and clear admission of your ultimately subordinate position. Another blink of supreme satisfaction. This was the way to run a newspaper, especially if the city editor needn't get involved. In the business forty years it was possible Baines had never written a complete story. This did not mean he was not a fine reporter. He was the *Mirror's* courthouse man and he knew every judge, lawyer, clerk and fixer in New York County. In those days he seldom went to his shop. It's likely his typewriter had hardening of the arteries. He phoned into a rewrite man who worked with assurance because Baines was not of a disposition to get his facts wrong. He went with nothing until he was absolutely sure.

When the *Mirror* folded he was fifty-five and considered suicide except he would have to write a note. Scanlon made room for him at the *Local*, ostensibly as city editor though this was not like being city editor on a daily. Baines came to understand that. Over the years the staff dismissed him as Scanlon's errand boy, two blinks meant yes, three blinks even yesser. But there was a suspect political tinge to that interpretation. Baines and his chief got along because they both esteemed hard news and didn't care deeply about anything else. Scanlon lorded over one and all for the sake of efficiency but was not especially interested in having his ass kissed. If two blinks meant yes and three yesser maybe one blink meant o captain, my captain you reek. The staff believed the city editor was soft on Vietnam (being named Baines as in Lyndon Baines didn't help), guiding war stories from the front pages to favor metropolitan news. This was sometimes true. The problem was Saigon was 10,000 miles away in another judicial district. Baines couldn't check. He couldn't go to the judge's clerk with coffee and danish and say... what's up with your guy, is he tossing the election?

"I wash my hands of it," Scanlon said. "If some poor citizen shoots himself Thursday next due to it being one hundred and ten in the coal bin and your girl calling him an inadequate louse may God have mercy on your soul. I only pray he's not a subscriber."

Blink. Blink. Blink. Blinky was so enthusiastic Fletcher was certain he had something in his eye. The litany of blinks appeared to promise… you see, the chief is not so bad as long as we choose to reason together. Baines really did look pleased, happy in his ignorance of what went on at the back of the book. Fletcher joined in the mostly youthful disparagement of Baines until he revealed it to Duffy. Baines may not be the future of journalism, the assistant editor said to him, but there is nothing illegitimate about his past. Could he say as much about himself?

'Thank you, John. Your usual monogram on the puck?"

Phillips was gracious in victory in her demonstrably inexpressive Episcopalian way. She'd been there three years and was at last losing, to Fletcher's sense at least, the scent of Slumming No. 5 that had clung to her. Still you asked: why is she here and not at Conde Nast or *The Atlantic*. Or *Cosmopolitan* for that matter. The common answer, that she had a feminist itch most publications could not scratch, was obvious but not satisfying to the terminally steamy minded. Out of Vassar by way of The Chapin School she'd tried California but didn't like wearing sunglasses at night. ("Well, got to go along with her on that anyway.") She talked Scanlon into a job that didn't exist. *The Local* never had a feature editor because it did not like to say it had features. ("Don't talk to me about museums unless one gets robbed.") God knows it was a mess back there. Phillips proceeded to tidy up in a manner as clipped and patrician as her speech. She was the first woman with any real clout at the paper; it had not interested her to be an entry level girl Friday. She had a boyfriend but he was obscure, perhaps a stockbroker or a shoe salesman. Her salary did not matter, she had money of her own, one estimate being heaps and heaps. She was expanding the back of the book like middle age spread and this dictum of Scanlon's did not impress: when a newspaper is readable the day after it hits the street it is a newspaper no longer, it is a magazine. She had great legs.

And she crossed-uncrossed them like Barbara Stanwyck in *Double Indemnity*. Undoubtedly it was only this that kept Rothberg awake during the meeting. He was nearly supine in his orange scoop in anticipation of just how much thigh the feature editor was going to present him. Probably not much more. Rothberg was of the opinion, shared by few if any, that Phillips had conceived what Fletcher's high school crowd called a purple passion for him. During the June boat ride, an annual event of Scanlon's invention that all grumbled about for weeks and then thoroughly enjoyed, Phillips had a few cups of beer and by the standards of her slippery associates loosened up a bit. Rothberg assumed it was a positive sign she hadn't brought the stockbroker along but perhaps the boyfriend did not appraise a moonlight cruise around Manhattan with the scruffy *Local* staff as a plum of a good time. By her third cup of watery Rheingold Phillips was telling Rothberg how much she liked his series on the mayoral candidates. It was a sincere compliment because the series was exceptional, easily the best work the paper had run all year. Rothberg did not normally drink but as Scanlon was adamant about not having that "pot stuff" on board he had some beer too. It went right to his head and causing a short in his reception he misread Phillips' well intentioned remarks. As the tabloids put it, he'd been her love slave ever since.

Scanlon adored the boat ride and delighted to dwell on its midsummer details while the frost was yet on the pumpkin. ("See me about that after Groundhog Day.") Everyone was invited: editorial, advertising, circulation, janitorial, the wait staff at the Zeus Brothers and the paper's truck drivers. (For an autocrat Scanlon had a wide egalitarian streak.) He paid for it with money that should have gone to one of his wives and the night was lavish beyond what humble *Local* employees had come to expect from life. There was enough food, enough drink, and taxis to take everyone home from the pier. Already an institution when Fletcher arrived in 1961 he'd never missed the boat ride, a fact he did not reveal. If anyone asked, not that anyone would, he could say he'd skipped a couple over the years and memory being frail there was no one to contradict him.

"Where's your goddam Lindquist?" The chief glared at Rothberg. "He should've been back long ago."

If the Phillips victory grin was discreet it had, in Fletcher's view, every right to be. She'd taken this round (yes, sports again, but part of the American idiom, isn't it?) because Scanlon's mind was elsewhere. He'd eavesdropped the meeting with the absent air of a man waiting for everyone to leave so he might find succor with the rye bottle in his file cabinet. But it was not a drink the editor craved, he was parched for an update on the Broadway Central hotel. Some days his internal rhythm still pulsed to the demands of the old afternoon dailies. Twisting one of the cigars he no longer smoked but only chewed Scanlon did not resemble a man whose deadline was four days off.

They'd gone over the hotel collapse early for ten minutes, Rothberg and Fletcher speaking first, then Ellis Harmon who'd been covering the rescue work that morning. Pinching and rolling his Antonio y Cleopatra Scanlon listened quietly (reflective of his gravest attention) before signaling to Baines to take up the rest of the issue. (As he no longer smoked the damn things, Scanlon had switched to machine made cigars, coronas mostly. He was still gnawing his way through the boxes bequeathed to him by May, Duffy's widow.) About noon, interrupting an argument about the length of a Watergate paragraph, he dispatched Lindquist down to the Central to see what was doing. Lindquist looked persecuted, if you were not at the weekly meeting you could well become its subject, but newest on the totem pole there was little he could say. He'd been gone an hour, not unreasonable, but Scanlon was clearly impatient. Likely there was no special hook to the story for them but you never know. *The Local* had been battering the Lindsay administration for three years over its welfare policy and if a fresh club were to come to hand there was no reason to turn your back on it. Fletcher regretted not volunteering to go; it would have got him out of the meeting.

"He's a growing boy," Harmon said. "Probably stopped for a slice."

There was light laughter as the hint of stopping for pizza when Scanlon was expecting you back like a boomerang was illicit. You might do it while being sure to leave no tomato sauce visible anywhere. Harmon was all right but he was quitting. Newsday wanted a black metro reporter. They were circulating in from the Long Island suburbs to the five boroughs and Harmon was sharp, visual, a punchy alert writer. Newsday was the kind of tab that ran your picture a lot so maybe they would make him a star if he found the right angle. Harmon preferred the News but the shop on Forty-Second Street was still, as Scanlon delicately put it, "a bunch of bottlenose micks". (Scanlon considered the *Daily News*, owned by the *Chicago Tribune*, an out-of-town newspaper with an inexplicably large local following.) So Harmon was leaving, "after Labor Day". Scanlon called the city editor at Newsday, an old friend, and swore at him for fifteen minutes. It was all bluff. He'd trained Harmon, he took it as tribute that a daily was hijacking him.

Fletcher and Harmon were not close though they had worked together for five years. Harmon once jokingly called Fletcher a Cornhusker and Fletcher jokingly replied Cornhuskers were from Nebraska, he being from Ohio was properly a Buckeye. Harmon, from Bedford-Stuyvesant, couldn't imagine it made any difference. One night working late Fletcher heard Harmon saying motherfucker this and motherfucker that. He didn't usually speak that way around the newsroom. As he hung up Harmon noticed Fletcher a few desks away and smiled apologetically as if he'd been caught talking to himself in the john. Guy I grew up with, he said. Everyone has another life, Fletcher thought, and if you are black maybe you have another life and another one after that.

Harmon talked to Fletcher during the boat ride. He said he had an offer from Newday. He couldn't turn it down but how did he tell the old man? Fletcher said this wasn't a problem. Scanlon had his faults, boy did he have his faults, but he was a newspaperman and incapable of begrudging the advancement of another newspaperman. The editor was unpredictable but you could say that much about him with certainty. Fletcher was right. Scanlon yelped like a debutante and shredded three cigars before planning Harmon's farewell dinner at Luchow's.

Fletcher was staring out to sea when Harmon spoke to him on the boat, or pretending to stare out to sea as it was some tall apartment houses in New Jersey they were passing. He was pondering how his adult life was defined by the boat ride. It went around in circles and he had never brought the same woman to it twice. This year's boat ride was in a lower key, the first without Duffy. Fletcher had not brought a date. Because he'd had one unhappy marriage and two unspeakable ones Scanlon longed for others to share his condition or at least be approaching it. He would have ragged Fletcher for coming alone but knew the younger man half his age felt Duffy's loss as keenly as he did. They talked quietly much of the night, reminiscing, though neither for their own reasons would have called it that. There was no music this time, Scanlon's concession to a death six months past. It would have hurt too much. No matter what sort of band was playing a sufficiently oiled Duffy clog danced every year with less than triumphant results. It was a shamanistic thing cherished in a closed environment. As Duffy could have no successor Scanlon decreed this particular vision of unity and harmony to be at an end.

The absence of music was a relief to Fletcher in another way. He didn't have to choose it. Throughout the early history of the boat ride Scanlon always did. Possessing a genuinely feudal view of life he believed he knew what was best for his subjects. For the June, 1967 excursion, the month Sgt. Pepper was released, he selected a latter day big band outfit called the Sy Solomon Boys. They appeared to know every novelty song ever written. They were not very boyish, the opposite in fact, and made one long for accordions and klezmer trios. An hour into what Scanlon always called the voyage the staff petitioned the captain to maroon the Solomon Boys on the shores of Spuyten Duyvil. He refused, something to do with the Law of the Sea or some such nonsense. (There was much talk of mutiny.) Duffy complained you couldn't clog dance to *The Flight of the Bumble Bee*. The next day a hung over Scanlon informed a hung over Fletcher… you're the goddamn music critic, you pick the goddamn band from now on.

"He still doesn't know the Village that well," Rothberg explained; "sometimes he gets lost."

If this was intended as a defense of Lindquist's presumed tardiness it did not appease the editor-in-chief. His smile was bitter, mocking. The notion that one of his reporters did not know his was way around the neighborhood was absurd and all too true. "Let's move on," he barked, one eye on the door, the other stabbing at the clock. Fletcher knew that look. It was irritation ripening inside Scanlon like pungent cheese.

Selecting the boat ride entertainment was everything a thankless task should be. You could not please everyone, least of all the newsprint rear admiral. Scanlon was loath to let a decision slip away. He needed to influence but didn't want to be held accountable again for any sour notes. Fletcher resisted but it was never easy. (Scanlon was, for example, a great jazz lover as in the Charleston or Sweet Georgia Brown via the Harlem Globetrotters.) His triumph as an impresario came in 1970 when he booked Oscar Peterson. Even Commander Scanlon was won over. He stood by the taffrail in beaming solitude, proud of his newspaper, his people, proud of his boat ride. Moonlight became the editor-in-chief. Tall, unstooped, hair silver gray, mandibles like a bird of prey. He wasn't as Irish as he pretended to be, there was Welsh and some Cornish miner in his background and perhaps something spiritually Roman too, that air of satrapy.. He thought of canceling that year because of the invasion of Cambodia and the student deaths at Kent State and Jackson State. He did not for the boat ride was precious to him in a way difficult to understand. And his sympathies were often Wobbly, unionist. He wouldn't mind forfeiting his deposit but there was the matter of depriving twenty working-men of a night's wages. So the evening went on as planned with Scanlon, cold as a carved figurehead on the prow, tapping his foot to Oscar Peterson.

Fletcher's date, Janice, had not tapped her foot. They hadn't been going out long and when the night was done he knew they weren't destined to go out much longer. His very success undid him. Ebullient perhaps due to the praise received for Oscar Peterson he puffed the compensatory theory of boat rides too much. Janice said the whole business was a paternalistic fraud and he should be ashamed of participating in massa (and dominant father archetype) Scanlon's plantation parade. But it's only a boat ride, he protested. Look around you, she said, this is what you get once a year instead of a decent salary (She had a good point there.) The Great White Chief will be handing out Thanksgiving turkeys next, (Scanlon did, smoked ones, Fletcher could make his last until Christmas.) Janice spent the second half of the trip looking as if she were trapped on a plague ship. They broke up shortly after when she moved to Boston to join the Women's Collective. Fletcher tried not to take it personally, he felt the system was at fault.

"I've got a memo about that here somewhere," Scanlon was saying. He was probing the buttered roll debris on his desk when the door opened and Lindquist sauntered in. The slice of pizza in the young reporter's hand was as prominent as a slot machine on an altar cloth. Scanlon looked up, benignly, full of hope.

"Any bodies yet?"

Lindquist, passing large, dropped heavily into a scoop that could not fully contain him and lost control of his slice. He swore and picked it up from the floor. Sweating, his body language seemed to suggest wild goose chase.

"Nah, nothing," he said, a swallow and a fair amount of eternity later. Fletcher rubbed an eyelid. He'd either underestimated Lindquist's dimness or overestimated his desire to stay with the paper. This was not the way to get your ticket stamped for the next boat ride. Now why couldn't Lindquist be creative. He could have told Scanlon they'd found a group of girl scouts in the rubble making s'mores and reading the Kama Sutra. That would satisfy the old boy for a while so they could finish the meeting and go somewhere air conditioned.

"Nothing?" Scanlon sounded like King Lear.

"You know, it's like what Ellis said. The digging is slow because they can't use machines or something else might fall down. I heard one of the fire-men say it's a pancake but I didn't get what he meant."

Scanlon grinned toothily, not a pretty sight. Lindquist might have asked the nice fireman what a pancake was but why be inquisitive when you could have lunch instead. Maybe hearing about pancakes made him hungry. Scanlon looked from face to face like a disappointed game show host.

"A pancake, my children, is… Blink, do you want to…"

"You go ahead, chief. You got the eloquence for it."

Scanlon nodded his thanks. "Friends, a pancake is a building that falls in on itself, straight down and flat. Is this important? Well it is if you're so unfortunate as to be lying underneath. A pancake doesn't leave as many air spaces as a building that topples over to one side or falls out like a teepee. They do that sometimes."

"The Hotel Du Lac, chief."

"I was just thinking the same, Blink. The Hotel Du Lac: unsurpassed hospitality in the West Forties."

"A complimentary fire ax in every room."

"Including the honeymoon suite. The Du Lac collapsed just after the war as I recall, sewer excavation weakened the foundation. Luckily it was matinee day and all the hookers were at the theatre with their mothers." Scanlon paused for dramatic breath. "Now there was a Berlitz studio in the lobby and the building fell in on that side. Everyone got out except one boy, eight years old, a plucky kid. The whole damn Berlitz studio came down on top of him but it wasn't a pancake so there was breathing space. It took a week to dig him out. They knew he was alive because they could hear him whispering. With a doctor's stethoscope they could hear him. They couldn't make out what he was saying but it didn't matter as long as they knew he was in there waiting for them. They supposed he was praying, a most human thing to do. Well they had miners from all over the country come to help and a week later as I said they brought that brave little shaver out. Yes they carried him out hungry and dirty and speaking four European languages. And I don't mind telling you there were some hardboiled New York reporters there and not one of them went home that night and beat his wife. That's all for today, class. Get the hell out of here."

Scanlon turned to his city editor who was blinking his most maximum appreciation. They exchanged ancient lore like scribes and bartenders. Editors and staff ambled out, relieved and damp. Fletcher, responding to a wave from Scanlon, slid out of his scoop and took a real chair by the desk. He turned the fan to blow in his face. Baines, the last out, closed the door as Scanlon leaned forward with a chomp of cigar and examined Fletcher. "Feeling better, Rush? You look, how shall I put it, moribund."

"Thanks… yeah, I'm better. It was food poisoning I think."

Scanlon mulled this over. "That used to happen to me but I got a divorce and it went away. What about that place you went?"

"What, Watkins Glen?" Fletcher dabbed at his ear. "Rock festivals aren't what they used to be and it didn't take long."

"Well bless my soul, I don't know what to say." Scanlon took back his fan. "Now I hear Eddie Condon is dying, not expected to last the night." Fletcher nodded, took out his pad. "If he goes I'll want a box on page five, black border, find a quote from somebody people have heard of. Louis Armstrong maybe. You choose. Give me six double column inches under a photo. Not too sweet."

"Okay… what about the hotel?"

Scanlon spat dismissive cigar leaf juice into his coffee cup. "Not much there I'd say. Let Harmon handle it. I want him to have the front page again before he goes. It's our bailiwick but what can we do. The *Times* will pierce the corporate veil on this. For our purposes it will be picturesque as piles by deadline."

"Sure did look like a bomb for half a minute."

More dismissive saliva. "No terrorist organization short of the Army Corps of Engineers could do that intentionally. I heard it up here. I thought it was Agnew's head rolling but no such luck. Just rotten beams and subway vibrations."

"What about criminal negligence?"

"What about it? Yeah, we'll play it that way but the real estate nabobs in this town have got teeth where the rest of us sit down. No dice. Don't expect too much on that score, lad."

"I hear there was a narcotics detective on the second floor. He heard a crack he didn't like the sound of and went through the hallways yelling them out. Has a loud voice, blew his cover."

Scanlon swiveled on his chair. "A guy like that, maybe there are pairs of legs walking around today would otherwise be dead. Who will ever know a thing about it? If I was a reporter…"

"Yes, chief, do tell. If you were a reporter?"

Scanlon leaned back, addressing the air above Fletcher's head. "If I was reporter I'd go to see the hotel manager after he gets done being Lindbergh du jour.. Maybe tonight, tomorrow even better, being the Lord's day. Go out to his house, dinner time. The little woman is there, the kids with Gerber's smeared all over them. It's what every man wants in life. I'd take him outside. It's a nice street, no welfare there, everybody has their own tree for their own dog to piss on. I'd pick lint off this guy's suit and tell him he owes me a favor because I come all the way out to Bayditch or Rat's Neck or wherever the hell it is to tell him to get a lawyer. The Manhattan DA, a real merciless son of a bitch I say, has got felony charges he don't know what to do with. Maybe he wants to give them to the hotel manager as a present for being so famous. But maybe I can help him if he tells me what he knows. I guarantee you: If that guy don't shit a Dutch doubloon right there at your feet I'm a Hottentot. You might hear something useful. That's what I would do if I was a reporter."

Fletcher looked searchingly around at the walls. "John, where do you keep all your humanitarian awards? I'll give my notes to Ellis."

"That reminds me. When we have a broad pop out of a cake at Luchow's, should it be a black broad or a white broad? What does the Supreme Court and Emily Post have to say about this?" Fletcher grimaced skeptically. "Don't look at me like that. Why can't I have a broad pop out of a cake? I'm paying for it."

"It ain't etiquette in this day and age."

"Hookers have got to eat too you know."

"Make a donation. The watch will be fine."

Scanlon crunched his cigar with disgust. "Why don't I retire and turn this place over to the girls entirely? I can just smell the muffins baking in the test kitchen. And what about Harmon's replacement? I want somebody just like him."

"You give the words equal opportunity a whole new meaning, John."

"Don't be smart... who hired Harmon?"

"The best reporter you ever saw."

Scanlon looked aside, dropped the cigar in the cup, pushed it aside. "Duffy loved it when buildings fell down. His eyes would fill with tears. I mean that. Something like this lad, there are stories within stories within stories. He understood what was underneath. There was a guy used to cook at Longchamps years ago. He told me the hardest thing to do in the kitchen was bone a chicken. That was what Tom could do with something like this, get right down to the bone for you."

"Do you think he was born with it, John?"

Scanlon did not seem to hear. "You know the first time I saw him was at that fire in the Bronx?" Fletcher knew that. 'He was a kid but he had every-thing. He made me feel like a punk. People told him things without thinking. They'd look in his face and they didn't see a reporter, they saw somebody they could trust.

"Should they have?"

"What? Why are you twisting around like that for Chrissake?"

"One of my ears is stuffed up. I can't hear."

"Just as well, I was about to be maudlin. Go home, get some rest." Fletcher stood up, went to the door. "You're too old to be going to these rock concerts, Rush. The Grateful Dead, for God's sake, what kind of a name is that for music?"

"They used to be called the Sy Solomon Boys."

"Get out of here. And if Lindquist hasn't started on the second course shout in his ear I'd like to see him."

Fletcher opened the door. "Can I have a wing?" "Just tell him to get in here right now."

Don't have to shout. Fletcher stepped through the doorway but Scanlon called after him. "Rush, wait a minute, come back." A pause. "You used to live at the Central, didn't you?"

"Yeah, early on."

"Know what it used to be called way back?"

Fletcher closed an eye. "The Grand Central I think."

"That's right, but before that, before the Civil War it had another name. It was called La Farge House. Know why, Rush?"

"No, John; why was it called that?"

Elbows on desk Scanlon interlaced his fingers and propped his chin on the bridge. "The gentry on Lafayette Street," he said, "had their friends stay there. And La Farge was the name of the Marquis de Lafayette's country estate in France. That's how they used to do things once."

"Maybe they still do somewhere."

Scanlon shook his head. "This city is falling apart right around us. That fucking Wagner."

"A babe in arms when Lindsay came in is in the third grade now."

"I know, I know, you're right. We've all had a hand in it. Everyone takes a brick home for a souvenir and the walls are coming down. You love your hometown, don't you, Rush? That place that's always inside you? You wouldn't think it but I love my hometown too."

Fletcher nodded, waited a moment, there was nothing else. He quietly closed the door as he went to look for Lindquist.

Ash Can School

Eddie Condon did die, 67, at Mt. Sinai sometime Saturday. It was on the front page, bottom right. Out of habit Fletcher went early Sunday morning to buy the *Times*. His grocery on Sixth Avenue had it too and opened early but he liked the news hut in Sheridan Square so that's where he went. The *Times* was coming off the truck at half past five, warm, as it were, like breakfast rolls. Christ Almighty the vendor interlarded the book review and magazine into the freshly arrived news sections and slapped the offering over to Fletcher who clinked quarters into a cigar box. Christ Almighty grunted, professional courtesy as they were in the same line of work more or less. Logan gave him that name, it being Christ Almighty's custom to mutter this hosanna to most questions and all climatic conditions, the heat particularly. The heat was hellacious to Christ Almighty, it seared his loins. Bundling like a fur trapper in January was more to his liking, if anything was. That was difficult to determine. Unlike other news vendors throughout history Christ Almighty was not communicative. He spoke to Logan but gave Fletcher only the temperature and relative humidity.

The sun beginning in his face, Fletcher went south on Seventh Avenue and back to Bleecker to wait for Zito's to open. He buttocked against a car fender amid the overwhelming smell of bread and felt hungry. It was, as Hemingway might say, good to be hungry. Fletcher had slept well, from six the previous night to near five that morning. Gone whatever it was, that intestinal mystery, the craving for euthanasia. When he bent down to retrieve a roving toothpaste cap in the bathroom his head did not seem to rattle as he stood up. And his ear was open, he could hear Mrs. Romano sweeping the sidewalk five floors below. He felt so much better he didn't regret that the night had been merely dark and not cool. The street lights had come on as the city continued to steam and now they stood, a half axis later, indistinct in the post-dawn as a grape arbor mist clung to the fire escapes. It created a despairing continuity, like days in a lifeboat.

A promising clash of pans within the bakery and a fluttery fluorescence from the ceiling. Sound and light thus combined brought a drop of moisture on the tongue, a pang for the lost kitchen. Fletcher shifted the *Times* to his other arm, it had the heft of textbooks on Sunday, and noddingly greeted a fellow Zito's devotee approaching with a dog. They were familiar solely from this weekend encounter, a Tuesday uptown might have them pass without recognition. Their Sunday morning was ritual but unlike the communion of worshippers it could make New Yorkers awkward. The man, unquestionably an NYU teacher, had his *Times* and a small white bag from the patisserie, beyond Fletcher's means. Why - Fletcher's inquisitive gaze ran up from the soft Italian loafers to the creased cream colored trousers to the LaCoste shirt - why does this guy stay in the city in August? He did not pursue the question as it made the mind dwell on beach houses with breezy front porches and the salt sea.

Fletcher pulled at a shirt collar nowhere near his neck. On his left a woman came up carrying the *Times* and ten bucks worth of magazines. *Vogue* was on top and *W* on the bottom, maybe *Marie Claire* in the middle. She was as much younger than Fletcher as the NYU teacher was older. She had therefore missed and did not care about what made Fletcher an individual as opposed to an anonymous buyer of bread. He regretted this, who wouldn't? The first Sunday she appeared, early in the summer when the pavements were not yet featuring fried eggs easy over, he twisted his head and shoulders into a yoga stretch to see if there was a wedding ring. There wasn't but likely it was unnecessary exercise. Women in her world did not marry so young. And yet, this tugged at him, she was up betimes. He was attracted to women who arose when he did and dressed for the day. He sought company with coffee. On the breakfast talk shows of his radio youth you heard the toast scraped and spoons dropped but it might be the sophisticated married hosts who had been out late first nighting were not really hungry or really cared to see the dressing gown across from them. Mornings were sacred to Fletcher as the nights were irrev- erent and dedicated to glitter and doubt. He preferred to write in the morning and if possible to love. With the right woman, seen softly in muslin through the screen door, you might be in Eden again. Hard to say if the fashion hunt- ress on line with him was given to muslin.

An Italian couple in who knows what year of Zito's patronage redirected Fletcher's concentration. Goodness knows it needed redirection at the mo- ment. Their hesitant pause at the bakery door was met by an oldish man, young by comparison, presenting them with two bare loaves. They stuttered on, momma and poppa, and Fletcher tried to picture them on his Ohio Main Street but like three card monte players and gypsy fortune tellers they did not fit. Fletcher stood down from his fender. Now the store was prepared for all others as if the old couple were a hymeneal hymn scattering the promiscuous night. A prehistoric cash register rang once, twice, a sour gong of welcome.

The NYU teacher went in first. This was not so much deference on Fletcher's part as indecision. He'd been trying for several weeks to probe the eternal debate, resolved: is it easier to pick up a woman standing in front or in back of her in line? (Say, miss, ever notice people in New York say 'on line' and the rest of the country says 'in line'? Interesting, huh? Fuck off.) So far he hadn't succeeded at an exchange of trivialities with the early rising one. One Sunday the end of June he was remarkably bold. He had a hangover and should have stayed in bed, if not on bed, but before he could speak his brilliant opening a stranger to the Zito's dawn patrol, male, talked her up. His overture went nowhere and he received, in Fletcher's view, a tidy brush off and wasn't seen again. This served for Fletcher as well. Through the subsequent Sundays he had yet to speak a crumb to her.

He might ask where she bought her *Times* as it did not come from Christ Almighty. The vendor had an orderly mind and sections were arranged in proper sequence. Her Business and Finance was next to the sports, an outrage the Schopenhauer of Sheridan Square would never tolerate. It didn't look like the late sports either as there was no headline for the west coast Yankee game. Conceivably she'd picked up the Saturday night's bulldog edition by mistake. It might be she didn't care though he disliked to think so. It was the sacred and profane again. A newspaper lost its immediacy on the kitchen counter over-night even if you didn't look at it. The old cop-delivering-a-baby-in-a-taxicab chestnut sometimes carried the newspaper swaddling angle, dear to printers all over town. Hot off the press was precisely that, an unread newspaper is sterile, just the thing for emergency obstetrics in a Checker. The defunct Journal-American appeared to specialize in this at one time, their own sanctimonious sheet assisting at the nativity. Presumably they did not herald births brought forth upon the competition.

A bulldog edition of *Times* once brought him sorrow. The summer before JFK was killed he was seeing a girl named Grace who called herself Psyche. Not a bad stage name perhaps but she was the receptionist at a moving and storage company on West Street. She read a lot. Psyche, she said, was the personification of the human soul as embodied in a beautiful girl. Fletcher more than agreed. He loved the name Grace, hated calling her Psyche, but it does not pay to argue small matters with women you are trying to get into bed. So he called her Psyche but in an undertone he hoped others would not hear and she would find sensual. She did not it seems. They were out on a Saturday night, a movie (Hollywood, the personification of the soul didn't have much taste in films) and then a few hours at the White Horse. She liked to drink, Black Velvets. Her moving and storage company company was an old fash-ioned concern with a six day week. She was unwinding. He could sense her unwinding right into his arms. Leaving at midnight their condition approxi-mated what the average man believes to be balance in what is otherwise en-tropy: he was sober and she was not. She was downright unsteady. Geography was in Fletcher's favor as well. The White Horse, on Hudson, was near her place on Barrow while he was light years away on Bleecker. Unfortunately it wasn't raining. But by any decent reckoning of neighborliness (neighborliness is what they would call it in Monacacy Court House) she would ask him up. It was such a long way to Bleecker and MacDougal. The candy store on her corner was open and she stopped for the Sunday paper. Fletcher breathed in the night air. He was going home with her and in the morning they would drink coffee and read the *Times*. It was like a vision out of the Arabian Nights. When he brought his eyes down from the flying carpet Psyche had bought two newspapers. She gave him one. Goodnight, she said. Ten years later Fletcher still would not buy the bulldog edition of the New York *Times*.

He took home a yellow semolina loaf, doughy to the touch. For all his time in Manhattan, one third of his life, he'd never developed a taste for hard crunchy bread. Even bagels he could not always negotiate. Was he indeed soft in the center like the heartland? The woman with the defective *Times* swept into the bakery and swept out again with enough bread for two or three. Fletcher had noted this excess before. Boyfriend? Roommates? Did she make bread pudding the way her grandmother had? If he looked at a woman like that and thought of bread pudding it was perhaps time to look into analysis. He couldn't afford it. Maybe she was in analysis and working on contentious issues concerning her father. So she had temporarily renounced men. Becker would say as consolation they were lesbians. They don't worship at our church was his way of putting it. It was a mild analgesic, like aspirin, and seemed to take some of the pain away.

Bleecker Street smelled like beer, a bit like marshland. A larval state for later in the day when it stank of a rising summer pestilence. Crossing Minetta Fletcher saw a sofa on the sidewalk that was in some respects better than his own. The upholstery at least was not a pattern of renegade parameciums and it did not sag as much. Getting it home was the difficulty, who could he call at this hour? He'd have to let it go, a choice item like that would not last long. He walked on, sour graping over his shoulder: it probably has bed bugs, fleas, heartworm. In any case he was too old to be still furnishing his apartment from discards as he always had. Upon relocating from your hotel to rent controlled iron lung your first task was to discover the bulk collection day for the surrounding streets. If that was say a Wednesday you would be sure to find by nightfall Tuesday a variety of wardrobes, bed frames, dressers and davenports set out for your inspection. He learned to bring a flashlight and lowered expectations. The ambitious called the sanitation department for collection days in better neighborhoods and then set out with borrowed station wagons. Even people on Park Avenue throw out furniture when no one is looking. If you had a few dollars left from that last check from home you could encourage a building superintendent to let you shop in their basement. Fletcher acquired a Britannica that way, stacked volumes of which he used as extra chairs.

At his apartment house, the sofa forgotten, Fletcher climbed the stairs slowly. There was a new sublet on the fourth floor, a woman, she'd tacked a bullfight poster of all things on the wall by her door. He continued to be shocked by it, feeling he'd walked into the wrong dorm room. A bullfight poster was so unfashionable he was tempted to knock and congratulate her but they hadn't met. Mrs. Romano said she was a nice girl, meaning she could be anywhere from twenty to fifty and did not wear tights. Mrs. Romano did not approve of tights. She was not pleased with Manolete either, the walls should be bare so you could see how clean they were, but she said nothing. She did not want the new tenant to think the building was unfriendly. It was not. Short of bringing a casserole to her door Fletcher did not know how to welcome his new neighbor. If she was from Indiana she might appreciate the gesture, if from the Upper West Side she might not. In any case she did not want to be welcomed to the building at six in the morning. He ascended another flight to his own door.

Maxwell House had not been on sale all summer. Fletcher was midway through the third of three cans he'd bought on special in June. Soon the journal entries take on an increased tone of desert island despair - coffee getting weaker every day - no hope in sight - ah… Marooned in August. If he were given to jotting down prospective titles that might be worth a jot. He shined up two nectarines in the sink and cut the semolina loaf into even strips. The fruit was said to be organically grown. A sixties guy he knew, Judd, brought it. He was gone to Europe and beyond, no plans for returning. He came by the *Local* to shake hands and divest of shared bearings and directions. He was Fletcher's age, just divorced, cynical with a side of paranoia. Judd labeled Watergate, the investigation and hearings, a sham. He said it was a put-up job by all concerned so Nixon, back seemingly to the wall, could declare martial law. Then he could revive the war, close the campuses, bring apartheid to the United States, lock up what was left. If Fletcher did not see it maybe he was starry-eyed with wonder at what a great job the holy press was doing with the story. Were they? Yes. Weren't they going through the motions in a salted mine? He could not say.

But Judd had not come to argue. Aside from the fruit he had a gift, a photograph Fletcher had never seen before. It was of the two of them and a friend, Meg, at the Central Park Be-In, Easter Sunday, 1967. They were sitting in the Sheep Meadow in a heap of water colored Daffodil Power paper plates. Judd and Meg were moderately naked, Fletcher wore chinos and a beige short sleeve shirt. An airborne Frisbee was behind their heads. Judd's wife Sal took the picture. They were freaks then, becoming radicalized later. That's why Fletcher had never seen it for following the change in her political consciousness Sal did not trust Fletcher whose hair, except when he was saving on haircuts, did not reach the tips of his ears. He was never invited to their apartment on Avenue A though he did have a beer with Judd now and again. Calling old friends crypto-fascist came easily to Sal. It seemed to be a case of over-achieving and might have happened to Meg too but she died too soon.

The photograph, 3 x 5 in a dime store frame, went on a shelf over Fletcher's desk. He looked at it but not as deeply as she deserved. She might look back at him out of those migratory eyes and say: you've forgotten me, haven't you, like everyone else? He had. She was the only suicide in his life and he kept her locked away like madness in the attic. She also might say: you never slept with me so you think you're not to blame. Yes, the thought was there, dumbly inevitable. Meg was all the things you hear at the Sylvia Plath memorial service: brittle, intense, underweight, combative. A man making the list might not include brilliant. Someone complained to Fletcher she was too smart in bed. He pretended not to understand but had a feeling he did. He was never drawn to her physically. She might say something caustic. She might say something caustic about him to another woman.

She left New York not long after that Easter Sunday for she had some independent money and the on and off habit of photography. Fletcher received postcards from expected places, Marrakech and Amsterdam. There was a notably incoherent one from Spain that she signed three times. She was back in '69 when the cat was out of the bag at home, when the peace movement had become an exercise in B-side self-expression. She had a boyfriend everyone hated, some kind of multinational journalist she'd picked up like a feral animal. They moved into an infested squat on East Third next to the men's shelter. No one could grasp it, she didn't have to live there or with him. She gave a few parties, claustrophobic and unhealthy. If you didn't dislike the thieving, esperanto boyfriend on arrival you did when you left. She became inward. You didn't see her much and were sorry when you did. The men she knew worried in a calm, untroubled way but for women there was something like anguish. Meg was declining, disappearing; they felt it inside them like the onset of life. Except this was the outset. A woman stopped Fletcher on the street. She was in tears about Meg and hardly knew what she was saying. Fletcher knew cops, all kinds of people. Couldn't they find someone to beat up the boyfriend so maybe he would go away? It was possible to laugh because he was dispassionate but the woman friend could not be. Meg had sores on her arms but didn't do those kinds of drugs. She was squalid and manic at the same moment. You'd see her racing along Eighth Street to buy cigarettes at a store fifteen blocks from her apartment. In the middle of talking you'd hear a sound and realize it was her teeth chattering. Everyone had a story about her, a patch from the creepy quilt. The boyfriend burned a Hell's Angel on a deal and had to leave. There was no change. Finding her on the fire escape, not really distinguishable from old clothes, was more than most could handle. So you kept away, contradicting your heart. There were parents who claimed her, she was back in two weeks. She called at all hours so you unplugged your phone. You said she was breaking down, you said she could not connect. When Fletcher returned from the Chicago 7 trial she was dead. She jumped in the East River and not for a moment was she buoyant. And now her picture was close to sentimental, like a child in a sailor suit, because she came apart while it was all going to pieces.

Fletcher ate his breakfast, drank coffee, went through the *Times*. It had been a slow Watergate week, little revelation. Nixon would have to give up the tapes soon just to get back in the headlines. The hearings were increasingly exchanges between counsel that was good for lawyers but made for dull reading. The office pool for Nixon's beheading had over three hundred dollars in it, held in sacred trust by the old sagamore himself, Chief Scanlon. Three hundred would buy a new typewriter but Fletcher was unable even to hope he would be so lucky. Nixon despised the press and they despised him right back but Fletcher supposed there were betting pools on his departure even where the Moral Majority worked. Taras, the Ukrainian night elevator operator would probably win again. He'd won the World Series pool the year before knowing less about baseball than he did impeachment hearings.

His coffee was not strong enough. Fletcher read Alden Whitman's Eddie Condon obituary. Workmanlike, it came out of the file. You had to wonder, you had to wonder if you were morbid or a reporter, who the youngest person written up in the *Times* obit file was. A solemn business that would be, portraying youth in the past tense, as you do your own. A few weeks before, at Max's Kansas City, Fletcher looked over the front room crowd. He felt like a crick in the neck a greater gap than usual between those newly arrived and those who no longer stayed until closing. There were so many now in their mid-twenties and they seemed like teenagers. He'd noticed it less at Watkins Glen but the festival was an aberration, the last footprint of the beast. The club scene was a better barometer because it was more about intimacy, about searching.

The Broadway Central was front page for a second day, an accomplishment for a welfare hotel in a city dominated by corporate interests. Fletcher was off the story so he read the *Times* account without prejudice. The lessee was fined in July for an unrepaired structural violation: "unauthorized work on a bearing wall within the building". Yes, that would not have helped any. But "the lessee"? Already the actual owners of the hotel were receding from the picture. The city was proceeding with a condemnation order, its inspectors having declared the building unsafe. Lindsay was closing the barn door after the polo ponies had heigh-hoed away. With any luck the demolition people would finish their work before any more monkey business was discovered. No residents would be returned and the Mercer Arts Center would be forced to move. Fletcher had mixed feelings about that. He was tired of Cuckoo's Nest and *El Grande de Coca-Cola* but in the romance without finance department they were more aromatic than a walk to the Fulton Fish Market. Yet Amanda had enjoyed that. The smell, the crying gulls, the hum of cars on the grid of the Brooklyn Bridge, the blood and guts smeared aprons of the workmen. She said it was all very realistic and she was right.

There'd been a letter from his cousin in Saturday's mail. He put the *Times* aside and read it again. At his suggestion she no longer included Greenwich

Village as part of his address. Her grand tour concluded, Amanda was coun-
seling at a camp in Michigan until school began. His mother's side of the
family, a sturdy bunch, always had to be doing something. They would not
accept that a girl should loll away those exquisite weeks between high school
and college cruising hamburger joints and fleeing the state police down back
roads. Amanda's branch, the Stedman clan, was especially obnoxious in this
regard. She was given a choice between the summer camp and some dreadful
library project at home in Dudley, something like varnishing the shelves or
sneezing through boxes of the Ohio Historical Society bulletin. For the Stedmans pioneer stock like themselves were obligated to get the wood cut and
stacked before the usual harsh winter set in. In other words they were always
storing up nuts of one kind or another. Amanda bore it all cheerfully, believing
perhaps that everyone everywhere was this way. No wonder she considered
her cousin Rush a rebel.

Camp was an absolute panic, confided Amanda; the kids were from
another world. She probably did not mean they were extraterrestrials. More
likely her brief New York intoxication induced her to find the counselors and
inmates of Camp Kleenex on Saginaw Bay a trifle behind the times. And
maybe they were, the times changing the way they do. She had a right to feel
so if she chose but never mind, there was something more troubling about the
tone of her letter. A shadow of dissatisfaction lurked in the aquamarine ink of
her fine and cursive handwriting. (A flabby thought, not well expressed, but
he was uncertain how to put it.) He hoped he wasn't responsible. Amanda had
been so looking forward to beginning Ohio State, his own school, in the fall,
but now... now what? Now she sounded disenchanted, frustrated. These were
not words Fletcher wished to use in connection with his tender cousin. He
didn't want her like the other Stedmans; he liked her questioning and slightly
off beat, as long as she was in context. The idea of her at OSU was comforting, like a milkshake. Sure, she'd feel circumscribed there to an extent but it
wasn't all that provincial (well, kind of) and she could always take her third
year in Europe, lots of students were doing that now. He'd write, call now
and then, see her at the family pow wows. Yes, he knew how she felt but she
should stick with it: form those lifelong friendships (Fletcher had but one from
college), do the core curriculum, major agreeably, cultivate the examined life
on the side and generally validate his own experience. In the end she'd look
back and say it was all worthwhile. He did, sometimes.

Amanda did not say it plain but implied between the curlicues that she
did not see the point in pursuing drama or the fine arts in Columbus when the
real thing was available five hundred miles to the east. (Five-fifty, Fletcher
mumbled, he'd made the drive often enough.) People were so tyrannical
about education these days, never considering it might not be for everyone. If
Amanda thought people - read Stedmans - were tyrannical about college, wait
until she discovered how tyrannical they could be on the subject of moving to
New York to dip her toes in depravity and godlessness. Fletcher could hear his

49

name resounding in distant domestic circles and his mother asking: you didn't turn that foolish girl's head, now did you, Pie?

That was putting it strong it was true but at the very least his mother might fold her arms at him and her folded arms were a terror to behold. He never should have taken Amanda to the fish market. The letter's second half was disturbing as well, containing a mildly rapturous recount of late summer romance with someone named Robert. He's the nicest boy... well, hardly a boy really, he's twenty. Fletcher was suspicious of camp counselor love affairs. They normally ended in weepy bus rides home and forlorn trips to the mailbox. Amanda may have been better off in Dudley varnishing the library shelves. She admitted she should not be sharing these things with her cousin but he was the one person she could write to who would understand. Her life was only beginning, everything was new, it was all so exciting. There was so much to say but she had to close... Duty Calls!!! She ended on an ominous note. Perhaps she would see him sooner than anyone expected.

Fletcher chewed his bread, drank coffee. Sooner than expected... now what did that imply? He expected to see her Labor Day weekend at the annual family gathering, a tribal rite essential to his internal calendar. If the June boat ride initiated a dormant period coincident with his work the September jamboree as it was called concluded that inactivity. He always attended, taking Greyhound if he could not borrow a car, and he went alone. (The jamboree was an event you should not inflict on any but a spouse.) He'd stay a week, spending the extra days with his parents if Monacacy was not, as they say at the Olympics, the host city. The jamboree rotated from year to year amongst four towns and extended family groups, all within fifty miles. His mother was in charge the year before, exhausting herself in the process, this September would find them deep in Stedman territory. As he grew older Fletcher came to understand that the jamborees, which he loved, would not exist without women. They did the work while the men played softball. That might be why he returned to New York spruced up. He ate the achingly familiar food and touched all the bases.

So he was looking forward to seeing Amanda that weekend. Fletcher was an only child and he enjoyed his cousins, the younger the better. He kept up personally with some and heard about the rest through his mother, a tireless source of family tidings. Amanda was a universal favorite, had been since she was a toddler. Her own crisp sparkle was the main reason but it did not hurt that she was the least Stedmanish of the Stedmans. (The stork that brought her, his mother said, must have needed glasses.) Everyone liked her, not everyone found her parents and older brothers as sympathetic. Alone among Fletcher's relations in the Four Towns the Stedmans had pretensions to wealth and pride. It was not ostentatious wealth as wealth goes but it crept up on you like a rash at times. The cruise ship menus on the coffee table and the Lincoln in the driveway said all that was needed.

Mrs. Stedman, nee Haines, was first cousin to Mrs. Fletcher, nee Rushing.

They were the same age but all similarity ended there. When she was eleven Amanda ran into an emotional wall with her mother. Mrs. Stedman, Minnie by name, declared her a willful, impossible child whom she could not recognize as her flesh and blood. Mother and daughter fought, rarely reaching accommodation. It was 1966. Maybe it was hormones, maybe the zeitgeist. When school ended Amanda was grounded for the summer, Mrs. Stedman even marking the street corner trees beyond which her daughter should not pass. It was not a happy solution. Fletcher's mother, Ella by name, was not impressed or pleased. Keeping young girls around the house like that, she said, was a low road to somewhere you didn't want them to go. Ella casually drove to Dudley, casually dropped in on the Stedmans, casually visited the prisoner in her room, casually packed a suitcase, and casually drove off with Amanda back to Monacacy Court House for a visit. It was extraordinary interference and Minnie Stedman hit the moon three years before Apollo XI. When she returned to earth the two cousins ironed it out because Minnie understood from past attempts there was no arguing with Ella Fletcher even if the subject was one of your own kids. Why I thought you would thank me Minnie Haines, Ella told her. (Fletcher was shocked at his mother's cunning.) Amanda spent the summer in Monacacy (a much nicer town than Dudley all would agree) roaming where she would. Fletcher, broke as usual, took his vacation at home that year. He spent much of the time with his young cousin who found him fascinating, perhaps like an exotic parrot that knows Shakespeare. He would have liked a sister when he was young but now he felt more deeply for his mother. Out of love he could not explain he imagined taking part of himself to give her another child.

Fletcher finished his breakfast. The best part of the morning was gone. Soon he'd be in the middle of the week's worst afternoon, Sunday's. Reference books beside him on the sofa he wrote four hundred words on Eddie Condon in longhand on a clipboard. It took two hours and would have gone faster on the typewriter. He wrote it from Scanlon's point of view (he found this almost too easy of late), like someone who'd grown old with the century, who went to nightclubs that were now in many cases the sites of office buildings. Condon was a guitarist who did not extend himself much. He "comped" as they used to say behind the soloist and made memorable wisecracks. His music, his trade actually, was indelibly pre-war with a whiff of raccoon coat about it. Fletcher pretended it was his Jazz Age but of course it was not. It was enough that it was anyone's.

Becker called. Now he was sick, he said. He described his symptoms. Fletcher told him to suck some limes, it sounded like scurvy. Becker complained that no one took his ailments seriously but it didn't matter, he was really calling to see if Fletcher had set anything up yet with Mona. She was an ad seller at the *Local* for whom Becker had formed an indecent passion. A mite spooky was Mona. She did most of her work on the phone, a good thing as she dressed like a vampire. Becker seemed to like the vampire type, consistent for a man who kept a post office box and who changed his phone number every few months. He became smitten with her, if that's the word, at a New York Dolls concert at the Continental Baths (they were both there on business it seems) and then again on the boat ride. (I'm the cabin boy, Becker explained to Scanlon who did not recognize him.) He'd been bugging Fletcher ever since to meet her some night after work. Presumably Becker could then happen along and the rest would follow as the one night stand does the tequila. But Fletcher kept stalling. He found the whole approach artificial, even unethical. He did not know Mona well, she chain smoked, he was not as a rule attracted to vampires, and there was more than some possibility she would say no. He pointed this out. You don't understand, Becker pleaded, she doesn't wear underwear. Surely this was argument at its most persuasive. And he owed Becker more than one favor and Becker would do the same for him. On the other hand this was lust, not the search for a life partner. That's your problem, Becker persisted, you don't appreciate lust. Fletcher relented and said he would see what he could do the following week.

Fletcher reheated coffee, realized his milk was spoiled and he was out of sugar, and wrote his weekly column. The time included two long looks out the window and some sit-ups. He led with Watkins Glen and tried not to be downbeat though he had not much positive to say. He'd covered the commercial aspect previously and try as he might he was unable to squeeze much out of The Dead, The Band and The Allman Brothers. They were groups, organizations nearly, already with a past too long to inspire much comment. So he was left with the festival itself: the audience, the traffic, the meaning of life in August. That's what got him sweating and staring out the window. The sit-ups did not help either. It was a column loudly proclaiming: I am a stiff and you can't fix me. He hadn't the energy to try. The cool morning, semblance of, was behind him and he was left with coaxing more efficient revolutions from his cranky fan. His bare feet were gluey to the painted floor. Reading his copy over he didn't like it less, didn't like it more. He feared that he did not care. He was tempted to blame the weather but the weather might ask if he would do better in November with a patter of rain on the window?

Noon. He brewed iced tea and called Elke. He let it ring six times and hung up, not quite convinced she was not there. German, Elke worked for UNICEF in their Christmas card division. They met the year before concerning a feature Fletcher and Mahaffy did on city park murals. It wasn't a bad job of work. He had a fondness for handball court art, urban and ethnic. She called about a mural in Chinatown two teenage brothers did, hoping to license their design. Nothing came of it, too political no doubt, but Fletcher showed her around south of Canal. She didn't know the city well and he took her to a dim sum in an alley off Elizabeth Street that had the triple recommendation of being secluded, colorful and cheap. She was a striking woman, mid-twenties, amply educated, formidable perhaps but it may have been the accent. Fletcher was at ease because it was out of the blue, she wasn't a date. Not so the second time. She called a week later and he went up to her midtown world. UNICEF House was on 42nd Street and they hit a few historically seedy bars on Third Avenue. She seemed to enjoy them. They finished in the automat, starkly lit, drinking coffee. Fletcher was far from at ease. He wasn't seeing anyone and he wished with the suddenness of whiplash that he was seeing Elke. He could not begin to think what she felt. He didn't know any European women and couldn't find his balance. Each time their thoughts meshed, or seemed to, there followed a trans-Atlantic thud. On the street he offered to carry her heavy book bag. A German man, she said sharply, would never do that. Well, he wasn't German, was he? He was from south central Ohio, Norman Rockwell capital of the universe. In the bars she was lively, in the automat subdued. Perhaps that was the European response to caffeine. She did not understand American men, she said. There was no friendship with a woman, it was all about sex. Fletcher nodded his head, not knowing whether to agree or disagree.

He thought about Elke through two glasses of iced tea before taking up his French lesson. There were language records from the library, featuring voices who could not get work dubbing movies. Scanlon's convenient memory was dodging around the NYU French classes he'd promised. That did not augur well for Fletcher's assignment to Europe. He felt overmatched by the usual impenetrable reasoning, just like with the war. They argued for years about a posting to Saigon with the same result. Sometimes it was money or Scanlon's insistence that Fletcher could not be spared. That was baloney no matter how you slice it. Duffy tried to change the publisher's mind but it was also Duffy who preached loyalty: your paper comes first to the last column inch. Sick of discussion Scanlon said finally... if you were any kind of reporter you'd know the real story isn't over there, it's here. There was truth in this but the words stung. Fletcher stayed with the home front and didn't ask to see the war again. And now it was over except for the shooting. Scanlon said he would make it up to him but this was baloney too. There was the time when the freedom to write as he wished was exhilarating; now it was merely addictive.

The sun crossed over the top of the apartment house, that sun drenched tropic isle that New Yorkers call Tar Beach. He left off his French, the not very animated recorded voices putting him in a doze. He dropped back on the sofa, a mistake. It was two, two-thirty, he should go out for a walk. His mother was concerned, he didn't get enough exercise. She had a notion he took taxis everywhere and rode in police wagons to the scenes of scintillating crimes. His father preferred to believe he spent his days playing gin rummy in smoke filled rooms. (Ohio's great contribution to the presidential roster, Warren Harding, was put forward in the original smoke filled room, dad.) Fletcher closed his eyes, deepening his mistake, and mumbled French verb forms. Elke spoke it effortlessly. The last time he saw her she came to the newsroom.

Scanlon, poking into Fletcher's personal life in his seignorial fashion, vaulted from his office to be introduced. Fletcher grudgingly obliged whereupon his employer, having had a very liquid lunch, erupted into horrid French in the happy belief that she was. Elke got it all despite Scanlon's scenic New York accent and replied amiably, a bit too amiably Fletcher felt. Scanlon winked in the manner of powdered Casanovas the world over and said he'd learned all his French one weekend in a Marseilles hotel room. This garnered a brighter smile from Elke than anything Fletcher had said to her. Fortunately Scanlon was called to the phone or Fletcher might have pitched him out the window. The next week she went home to Munich for an extended stay. She was back by summer but they hadn't met. The two times they spoke on the phone she was distant though a better word might be uninterested. He was not important to her and would not become so. It was a hard thought to sleep on.

Rising gasoline prices woke him, it was six o'clock. Fletcher blinked at his wristwatch, hoping it was not the next morning. It wasn't, still Sunday. Wearing a wristwatch at home is a hallmark of the college grind. He washed his face and swallowed more mouthwash than was necessary. Why would anyone dream about rising gasoline prices? He put on shoes and left. He was in such a hurry to get out he didn't look at the bullfighting poster. It wasn't bad on the street, a breeze blowing, warm but smelling rain. Down the street at Ishmael's he had a falafel and a Coke, sitting at an outside table decorated with a small can of shellac and a paintbrush to indicate to any passing city inspector that this was not illegal outdoor seating but simply a temporary home for a small can of shellac and a paintbrush. Ishmael was from Algeria and had more history in his face, Fletcher felt, than Mount Rushmore. It was a good falafel and Ishmael liked to shake hands with his regulars. Fletcher paid and tried to walk off his annoyance. He'd wasted the afternoon, daydreaming, falling asleep. He hadn't worked on his Nation review or looked over the notes for his book. It was worth kicking himself about. He walked north through the park and up to Union Square. That didn't satisfy. He went further, looping around Gramercy Park, taking Irving Place back to Fourteenth Street. A Fourth Avenue bookshop was open and he browsed a few minutes in the sidewalk stall, coming away with a well thumbed Michelin Paris guide for a quarter. At Cooper Square he turned east to Broadway and stopped at Eighth Street. There was an internal combustion snarl, unusual for Sunday. He knew what it was, no reason to look, but he went back to the hotel again.

It was getting dark at the Broadway Central. Flares were lit, the borrowed stage lights were on. The digging was continuous and the silent begrimed faces of the hard hatted men were taut with weariness. There were some audience looking on, not much. Within the barricades a man stood sketching on a pad. Fletcher studied him a moment but then noticed a statuesque silhouette at the outer rim of debris. It was Scanlon. Fletcher dipped under a sawhorse and as a cop started for him he hurried to his editor for protection. The cop stopped. It was doubtful the police commissioner would tell John Scanlon to move along.

Scanlon did not turn his head.

"A hell of a thing, Rush. They just brought the first body up."

"They expect more?"

"I would think so. If it had happened after midnight it might have caught who knows how many. As of now I'll give you odds on five or six."

A stretcher covered with a sheet was passed over the rubble by two white-shirted EMS attendants. Fletcher raised himself on the balls of his feet.

"Old poor people don't weigh much," Scanlon said. He looked at Fletcher. "You seem better. Put something in your stomach?"

"On my salary? Eating is for the Time-Life crowd."

Scanlon ignored this. "We have the same instincts the two of us."

"I was on my way home," Fletcher said, shaking his head.

"No? Then why do I find in Mahaffy's file several remarkable candids of our hotel manager's unremarkable physiognomy?"

"Mahaffy is on what is humorously referred to as your payroll. Ask him."

"I did. Our hotel manager has a gold tooth, a sign of culpability recognized even by the ancients."

"Cans't thou recall sire telling me it is Harmon's story?"

Scanlon waved this aside. "I was merely commenting on your ability, Rush. You must pardon an old man his backward glance."

Sheesh. "Well, while I've got you in a reminiscent mood, if that's what it is… what about Paris?"

The expression did not budge. "Of course, of course; we'll talk about it after Labor Day." Fletcher stiffened. "Rush, what do you want me to tell you now, with Harmon leaving? This isn't the right time. Come on, I'll buy you a drink."

"No thanks, John, not tonight. I have to work on my book."

Scanlon turned away as Fletcher knew he would. He did not care to hear of projects not connected to the paper. "Good night, lad."

Fletcher walked off on West Third, leaving Scanlon as he found him, sepia toned and alone on the corner.

Church of the Strangers

Scanlon was on the money. Overnight the clouds blew off and Monday morning came up hot and still. It stayed that way. By early afternoon rescue workers were relieved every thirty minutes. They staggered across Broadway and dropped in the narrow shade of the loft buildings. A sanitation water truck sprayed them and brown streaks ran down their shirtless chests. Some were heavily muscled and brown and others had soft indoor skin. It was too hot to eat. They closed their eyes, smoked, chewed gum. The sun beat, there was no hurry to the seconds and minutes. The men went back to work.

A man named Grecco cleaned his Ray Bans. He came from Philadelphia on the train Saturday morning wearing a suit and tie. He still wore the tie. The fire chief told the mayor: the best in the business is on the way. Grecco was an engineer and his business was digging. He dug safe if need be. When he saw the wire service photo of the hotel on an inside page of the Inquirer Saturday morning he saw a pancake. He called and said if they could use him he was ready. The answer was yes and four hours later Grecco, a civil servant, was heading downtown in a taxi from Penn Station.

The Department of Buildings said why do we need this guy from Philly? When something falls down it looks like you haven't been paying atten-tion and people notice. They were looking for the building department plans for the hotel. They'd been looking since the previous night and could not find them. An inspector had to tell Grecco. He was sorry, the inspector said, sometimes the pre-1900 stuff gets misplaced. That's all right, Grecco said, I don't need the plans. Standing within a semicircle of city officials Grecco had questions, answered them before anyone else could. Original construction? 1840's. First re-construction? Late 1870's. Extension to Mercer Street? 1914-15, no later. Grecco walked once around the perimeter and sentences begin-ning "judging by the exterior masonry…" trailed away. He'd never seen the Broadway Central before but after ten minutes he could talk about it for hours.

In the gondola of the cherry picker Grecco looked down as the boom swung him as high as the fourth story. Above the slope of the stone and plaster the hotel was a breached fortress, a courtyard open to one side. Grecco wheeled in the sky, noting plumbing lines and window frames, splintered joists and eye beams. Water service was shut off but the pipes, snapped at unions and elbows, continued to leak. The drops fell forty feet to disappear in sunlit dust. Grecco signaled, the crane operator brought him down. Hagan was waiting. They had never met. The white haired Chief, close to retirement, extended his hand.

"How's it looking up there, Joe?"

"It's an apple cart, Chief."

"I got you. We've been taking it slow."

Grecco nodded. Work was stopped midnight Friday when a section of the lobby floor caved in. No injuries but the crew was jumpy. They resumed at dawn but when the call came from Grecco Hagan ordered another halt until the engineer arrived. Grecco did not need to have it spelled out. They were turning it all over to him.

"Make haste slowly," he said to Hagan. "No sudden moves but steady. We'll lose them any other way."

"You think anybody is breathing in there, Joe?"

Grecco looked where eyes had stared and fingers pointed for twenty hours. "As of right now I'd say yeah."

Hagan thought so too. "Tell me what you want."

"Three crew chiefs, your best. When they say stop the men have got to stop. And they're in for the duration. If I train them we're here until it's finished. They may never do this again but they'll do it right here."

"I'm not looking to pay any condolence calls for these guys."

"Everybody does what I say, Chief... nobody gets hurt."

They were ready in an hour. Grecco wanted a card table, sketch books, magic markers. He took off his suit jacket and draped it on the chair as he sat at the card table. He drew diagrams with thick red and black strokes. On another pad he drew the foundation with a No. 2 pencil. Once, twice, he put the magic marker or pencil down and held a hand to his forehead. Recently he'd begun to have headaches and nights when he could not sleep. When he was young he drew churches and theatres and ballparks without people in them. Behind him they were saying: who does this guy think he is, the Exorcist? Grecco was fifty-three. He'd spent his part of World War II in the South Pacific placing explosives in holes he had dug. Out of a response he could not unlearn he looked at piers and bridges to see where he would plant his charges.

When Grecco heard (he heard by asking) there was a narcotics cop in the hotel when it collapsed he asked to speak to him. In his mind, on his sketch pads, he'd assembled the rooms, hallways and stairwells. He knew the exits, they were there when he closed his eyes, and the time available to reach one. Given a choice you run out where you came in, most people would. By his warning the narcotics cop provided that choice and it was most everyone Grecco was interested in. He couldn't dig everywhere. Too little time, too much risk. He needed to dig where he would find living people and what he did not know and could not create on his sketch pads the cop saw. There were five missing, four residents and a porter, three women and two men. They were somewhere. It was possible, it was what he wanted to believe, they were somewhere together.

The cop was young, the way Grecco had been in the war. He put his arm around the cop's shoulder and said that was good work yesterday. The cop said he felt the hair stand up on the back of his neck. He was on the fourth floor and heard a crack and then glass breaking. He went up to the eighth floor and knocked on doors, kicking at them, shouting get out, get out. He told them not to use the elevator. He came down floor by floor, his voice getting hoarse, feeling the building shake. Coming down to the lobby a woman pushed her son ahead of her. She tripped and the boy smacked his head on the bannister. The cop stood the woman up and carried the boy. They made it onto Broadway. The cop was starting back when he saw the marquee buckle and the walls caving. He stopped where he was. Grecco asked why he was going back. The TV room, the cop said. He'd been in and out of the hotel for weeks. Every day the ones who didn't have a TV went downstairs to watch the six o'clock news. Old people mostly. The TV room was in the basement. He wanted to check it. He didn't get the chance.

Grecco went to the mayor's assistant coordinating resident relocation. The assistant had the guest register and descriptions of the missing. Grecco looked over the names. Four of the five had been approximated by the hotel manager as old timers. A husband and wife, the Sterns, were more than that. The porter was the odd man out. Spanish, about forty, Grecco would have to think about him. He could be anywhere. As for the others the engineer had his clue. This was what he'd wanted from the start, a point of concentration on one side of the building. They began digging for the TV room.

That was Saturday afternoon. By early evening Grecco had worked confidently, unobtrusively with each crew. He didn't wear a hard hat, he never had in the war. Someone gave him a sandwich, he didn't notice what it was. He drank coffee and was satisfied. About eight o'clock a patrol car from the Bronx brought a middle-aged, frightened Spanish woman to the card table. Her name was Sonia Rivera, she was married to the porter. Her English minimal, she feared she was being arrested or Leon had been. He didn't always come home between shifts. He might sleep at the hotel, it was a long time on the subway to the Bronx. They had no phone, she didn't know he was missing. Grecco asked her to sit down. He spoke a little Spanish. He held her hand and did not seem like a policeman. Only then did Mrs. Rivera become aware of the destruction around her. She covered her mouth and began to weep. Grecco said they were looking for Leon to help him. The other hotel employees could not tell him much. They knew Rivera's duties, what he did each day, that was all. Rivera was a porter, Grecco could work out where his job led him. The other employees knew nothing Grecco could use to picture where the porter was at ten minutes to six Friday night. His shift ended at five. He could have washed up and changed in fifteen minutes. What did he do then?

Mrs. Rivera said he kept a radio when he was working and took it up and down. That was good, what else did he do? He smoked cigars, she said, but the manager told him not to smoke anywhere near the lobby, he didn't like the smell. Where would he go to smoke, the alley, the roof? She didn't know. Grecco thought about the bar but shook his head. It was closed between three and six; the night bartender was two blocks away when he heard the crash. Where did Leon sleep? She wasn't sure, somewhere, it was the same place he cooked. He told her once he fell asleep with rice boiling. Grecco looked at her intently. He cooked? There was no Spanish restaurant near, she said. When he finished work he was hungry and he made his dinner on the stove.

It took ten minutes to get a confirmation. They reached a desk clerk at home. Oh yeah, he said, there was an old stove in the laundry room. Rivera cooked on that, smelled pretty good sometimes. The laundry room, did he sleep there? That's right, he had a folding cot in there somewhere. Anybody else be there? Shouldn't be, the desk clerk said, hotel residents didn't have laundry privileges. Hanging up Grecco thought that was just as well. He knew where the laundry room was, not hard to determine in a nineteenth century structure. It was in the sub-basement, vented by an interior shaftway. The shaftway would have been useful but it was filled in. Large sections of the central staircase and the floor below it were on top of the laundry room. Grecco thought about Rivera washing his hands, changing his clothes. The water boiling, the rice and beans a fixed time to cook. Mrs. Rivera, her back to him, sat at the card table. Some privilege the porter had; Grecco figured her husband died hungry.

They worked through Saturday night. Grecco did not expect results before Sunday at the earliest. He put a team on the laundry room but it was pure excavation, as impersonal from his point of view as watching a dog bury a bone. He tried the subway tunnel, he explored the sewer main along Third Street. Blocked both ways, nothing remained but to go at the laundry room from above. It was not promising. By midnight the shoring supports he'd ordered for those walls still upright were in place. Much of the bulkier debris had been carted away and the dumpsters arranged on Broadway overflowed with plaster and bedsprings. The Broadway Central, never a pretty place, was not a romantic ruin either.

Sunday morning Grecco went to mass at the Church of the Strangers on Mercer. It was not his faith but he needed to remain near the site. The homily was about the hotel and the courageous men struggling to rescue their brethren. Grecco did not listen closely. It was an old church and he raised his eyes to the stained glass and the vast remote arches. If it all came down he knew where it would fall. A pastime, a fascination of sorts, he looked at many things like that. Not for the first time he considered what if it began to fall - if the church walls cracked and the columns tumbled like the last days of Pompeii. If that occurred before his eyes, if it all began to fall how long would he watch as a creator watches before he is buried too.

Outside the church a man met him. At first Grecco took him for a standard type, a disaster follower. They are not like firebugs but can be a nuisance. So he hurried his step. Disaster fans thrive on details and Grecco hadn't the time. But the man was not fawning as they often are. He said without fanfare he could see through walls. Grecco stopped. The man's name was Donald. Grecco asked if he was psychic and Donald said he preferred seer. Donald was a little ragged, a little down and out. It didn't matter to Grecco. A few centuries in either direction and Donald might be respected and well to do. In his own time he was a crazy deadbeat. Maybe he lived in a hotel like the Central. He was not the first. Another man had appeared Saturday calling himself an accredited dowser. He did not provide a source for his accreditation but said he could find water and precious metals with his forked stick. He could also locate lost objects. Grecco had him chased when he handed out business cards.

Donald was not self-promoting. He had sat quietly on a standpipe across Broadway Sunday morning with his head beamed on the hotel. He did not wish to call a television station. They would, he knew, deride his gift and mock him with raised eyebrows and humor. It was necessary to speak to the man in charge. Grecco led by example, Donald judged him receptive. But Donald was psychologist enough to know he should speak to Grecco alone. He tagged along to the church he waited patiently on the steps.

"This is mostly superstition," Donald said, pointing to the cross.

"Perhaps," Grecco said, "but what can you tell me?"

"Look again, that is what I would tell you."

"Do I require a seer to tell me that?"

"Arrogant. Arrogant. You can't afford to be."

Grecco was rebuked. There was the empire builder he believed and there was its opposite. He did not usually notice the heat but the bedraggled man was sweating and Grecco was forced to wipe his own face with his shirt-sleeve. "I would be grateful for any assistance you can give me."

Donald was mollified. "How many are within?"

"Four." Grecco lied. "I believe they are all together."

The seer turned wearily away. "You don't trust me. I can't help you." Grecco held him by the arm. "All right, Donald, how many do you see? Are they living or dead?"

"Like everyone you are right and you are wrong."

"Riddles don't help. Tell me how many."

"Five."

"You may have read that in the newspapers."

Donald did not wait to be caught again. "Arrogant. I can't help you."

"You have a responsibility as well as me."

"Don't compare us, master engineer. Five is all I will tell you. Five. Yes, I read in the newspapers if that's what you want to believe."

Grecco regretted speaking as he had. He should have listened and said thank you. The little man was gone as quickly as he'd appeared. Grecco heard his name called but it was not Donald this time. One of the foreman was running from the hotel. They were taking in water.

Seepage from an underground stream, it was not much of a problem. Grecco returned to his card table. The situation needed further study but now he was a celebrity. There were television interviews, one national, and reporters preparing their Monday stories. He heard his voice on the radio, technical and precise. He was the definition of low key and he was presented as a man who took no chances. So he seemed to be. He had personality in spite of his attempts to ward it off. In a day, as he went about his work, the focus became his life, his methods, his skill. He leaned back from his sketch pads and answered graciously whatever was asked. He felt relief, a sense of well being. The truth was, he stated, the primary work was done. They could only hope for the best. A few more hours and it would begin to tell. Patience and steadiness were the requirements now.

Grecco was giving an update to 1010 WINS when the first body was found. It was eight o'clock Sunday night. The temperature had dropped and there was a breeze. They had cut into the hallway leading to the TV room. Thomas Arndt, resident, was bunched at the base of the stairs. His neck was broken, the impact knocked the dentures from his mouth. He was carried up, pronounced dead, identified. Cameras flashed on the stretcher carrying him to the ambulance. Grecco stood apart, his face almost expressionless. When the ambulance left he stepped down to inspect the cut. Mr. Arndt used a cane; on a given day he'd be the last to reach the TV room. Two of the workers were upset, sickened. They were welders who had volunteered, not police or firemen. Grecco excused them. He took replacements from another crew and told them to take it easy. Their safety was everything now. After looking at Mr. Arndt, after examining the cut, after watching the wheelbarrows roll out hundredweight chunks of brick and mortar Grecco no longer believed anyone was alive in there.

After midnight he was alone. The late news programs were over, the morning editions were going to press. A radio reporter cruising in his car stopped for a minute, then drove on. He'd heard only the abrupt static of the police frequency and the clink of pick and shovel. Grecco stared into the interior. By degrees the well being he'd experienced disappeared. He felt uneasy. He did not think of the work now as progress. They'd bring out the rest of the dead, as scheduled, sometime Monday. Earlier, before Mr. Arndt, he'd said to the fire chief: we'll reach them in twenty-four hours. Now there was no reaching them, they were beyond it. One o'clock, two o'clock. The weather changed again. It was clouding over, possible thunderstorms was the August cry. That undercurrent of tension. He paced and could not account for his sensation of life when the crane held him over the ruptured hotel. These thoughts were his own. There were no questions or demands to share them. His own heartbeat at this moment drowned the low beat of a drum so near him.

He was missing something. The sketches did not tell him anything though he flipped through them over and over. In the rising humidity the pages stuck to his skin. The hours wasted, he thought, when he might have been planning. Restlessly he checked the men and paced back and forth on the cleared area of Broadway. His breathing was tight and he felt alone. He asked for the narcotics cop again. It was someone he knew. They were two hours finding the cop and there was light in the sky before the two stood talking under a dimming lamppost.

"The bar," Grecco said, "why was it closed?"

The cop, taken from sleep, had to think. "The bar in the hotel, right. They clean it in the afternoon, doesn't open till later."

Grecco's breath was short. "Why then? Why in the middle of the day?"

Another pause, the cop stepped back, feeling pushed. "It's a dive most of the time. Drugs, dealers, all kind of trouble. But night time they got young kids coming in, musicians, all that hippie stuff."

"So they close for a few hours and clear the place out?"

"That's right, yeah. And the prices go up."

"The cleaning: who does it?"

The cop relaxed. "She's all right, I saw her. She went home Friday early because she couldn't get the bar door open. It was jammed or something."

Grecco looked sharply at the hotel. "The door, you checked it?"

"Mr. Grecco," the cop said, "I was undercover here. Waiting to make a buy. I'm not the night watchman."

"Yes, yes, it's all right. It's not important." Grecco patted the cop's shoulder. He didn't know what he was thinking about. He'd gotten this recruit out of bed for nothing. And then he described Donald carefully, completely.

"Sorry, Mr. Grecco. It isn't anybody I've seen around."

The engineer nodded and let the cop go. He slumped in his chair at the card table. Five, that much was sure. And he knew where those five were. Turning to a fresh page he sketched the TV room and laundry as they'd look when reached. There was no question of error, his own instinct told him that. And it was too late to begin again. He left the sketches unfinished. He scrawled a line through them and turned to a fresh page. He drew the Third Street corner of the building, the glass front of the bar running to Mercer. The street entrance was locked during the day, you entered through the lobby. Grecco took up a felt pen for shading. He drew faster, it was nearly light. He looked up for perspective though the bar was flattened in front of him. He wrote Broadway Central in an arc on his drawing with a fleur-de-lys at each end. And he drew a face in the window.

Nine o'clock Monday morning Leon Rivera the porter showed up for work. Since leaving the hotel at five-thirty on Friday he'd been in Brooklyn with another woman. They never left her apartment and he never talked about his job because he didn't want the other woman to know where he worked. Grecco was told. He turned slowly in his chair and when he stood up the card table toppled and the drawing of the bar fell on the ground. He seemed groggy as if he'd been drinking and he stumbled to the laundry room dig. He called out the crew. He asked for more men. When they were brought he set the augmented crew to work on the bar from two directions. There was no explanation but he was obeyed. When a reporter asked about the change he was waved off. Grecco said he had no comment to make.

The heat came on as the skies cleared. The workers were relieved at fifteen minute intervals. They staggered across Broadway to drop beside the loft buildings in search of shade. Grecco sat stiffly, inactive. He'd closed his sketch pads. He cleared his Ray Bans of the dust and grit blowing over them. He stayed in the sun, receiving reports, approving, not moving. As the day was waning they broke into the TV room. The Sterns were there and a woman named Flores. They were in chairs, crushed where they sat. As their bodies were removed Grecco looked once, distantly. The bar absorbed him. When it was fully dark he took off his sunglasses and buttoned them into his shirt pocket. He waited, knowing it would not be long. The digging went quickly and at midnight they carried her out. She did not seem hurt and her clothes were not disturbed. A doctor leaned over her and the gathered men made way for Grecco. From where he stood her face was in shadow under the lights. It was calm and pale. The doctor looked up.

"It was a close thing, very close."

"How long?"

The doctor hesitantly, silently shook his head. "Not long at all."

"How long?"

"Less than six, four hours at the most I'd say."

Grecco looked at her and decided he would not look at her again. "She wasn't supposed to be there," he said. At the card table he put his suit jacket on. "She wasn't supposed to be there," he said again. There was no one near him.

Everyone who longs to do something well has visions.

They sometimes fail.

The woman he did not save was Vix.

Dummying The Page

Wednesday morning Fletcher saw Mona in the hall outside advertising dressed less severely in black than usual. Even vampires, he assumed, have their pastel days. Applying the theory of color receptivity he didn't lie. Did she remember Becker from the SoHo News? If so said scribe would like to see her again. Yes, she remembered Becker from the boat ride. He was the one looking up her skirt most of the night. Mona did not appear to treat this as a disqualification. Fletcher was relieved. He'd told the truth and got away with it, not an everyday occurrence in the boy's book of life. He said they could meet Friday night, maybe go down to Becker's neck of the woods. She said that was fine and left with a pouted puff of French cigarette smoke. No, not the sort it seems to give the woods a wide berth.

Becker, however, said it was not so fine. Fletcher called at lunch expecting a pat on the back and 'atta boy, feeling he deserved nothing less. Instead Becker complained it hadn't been set up so he could bump into them somewhere. Fletcher insisted this was stupid, to wit, no one would believe it. Becker said it did not matter if anyone believed it, that wasn't the point. An exasperated Fletcher asked: isn't it better she should know you wanted to see her again and have her respond positively to that? What, Becker uncorked, you actually told her I wanted to see her again? Of course I… are you nuts, don't you know anything about women at all? Evidently not, Fletcher returned with what he hoped was stinging irony. It probably wasn't. He'd lost all patience with the conversation. It was his own fault for playing Cupid, a ridiculous occupation for a grown man. It was the sort of thing girls did.

Fletcher might have said but didn't, thinking of it only after angrily hanging up (there was an illustration of the French expression for this in one of his textbooks), that Becker would not have met Mona except for the boat ride. They made more money in SoHo but didn't have a boat ride, an activity that brought out the buccaneering predator in Becker. He promised Fletcher to keep one step ahead of Captain Bligh if allowed to sign on. Scanlon did not appreciate gatecrashers, least of all from the SoHo News, an often frisky and uninhibited weekly whose existence he would not recognize. Spyglass in hand - a war souvenir though which war was not specified - Scanlon spotted Becker wolfing shrimp cocktail and roast beef sandwiches with free lunch abandon. Greek fisherman's cap on head, a gift from Pete Seeger, the editor accosted Fletcher with the sort of nautical chat he employed afloat. Mate, he said, who is that lubberly bilge rat filling his scuppers at my expense there in the bow. That's the stern chief, Fletcher said, and he's my date. Scanlon handed him the spyglass. You need this more than I do, he said.

So unquestionably he'd already done quite a bit for Becker and this was the thanks he got. Eating at his desk Fletcher grumbled through his cheese and crackers and Granny Smith apple. A grave suspicion clouded his reason, that Becker would back out Friday and leave him to trip the dark fantastic with Mona alone. He was short of cash and worse yet she might think he'd made it all up, attributing to a third party his own dubious passion. Or was that perhaps too convoluted for the advertising department? The thought disturbed the taste of his apple. This was much like admitting to a fantasy outside the gates of fantasy land.

Luckily Becker had gonads where his brains should be. He called to apologize as Fletcher was glumly examining the Product of New Zealand label on his last bite of Granny Smith. He said he was sorry, he was having a bad day. Fletcher said sure, merriment was not evident at the *Local* either at the moment. Becker's voice grew hushed. (Fletcher knew his shop, very cramped. The old fashioned horseshoe desks had five or six chairs to a side.) How did she look? She looked like Mona, Fletcher said. Becker made a sound like a percolating coffee pot. Really, was she wearing a bra? Fletcher wished his other line would light up. I didn't notice, he said. How could you not notice a salient feature like that, Rush? Because I was looking at this yellow ribbon in her hair. Fletcher trusted this information, the prosaic yellow ribbon and light colored blouse, the rest was black, would splash cold water on Becker. Maybe she's not the hot ticket you think she is, Paul. Becker was undaunted, his voice a trill. You'll be the first to know, buddy boy, the first to know. See you Friday, he added. Fletcher hung up, chucking his apple core into the trash.

Across the newsroom floor Scanlon was howling. Oaths and imprecations seldom heard outside the fires of hell were audible through his closed door. And he was swearing at himself, there was not a soul in there with him. Less senior staffers cowered by the water cooler or slipped down the back stairs to visit with the girls in classified but Fletcher was not concerned. He knew Scanlon was not dangerous until he began throwing things.

Years earlier, when their offices were still on Fourteenth Street next to the Academy of Music, Scanlon inhabited a genuine managing editor's holy of holies. Venetian blinds on the interior windows allowed him to gaze or not to gaze on his contented serfs in the newsroom. There was a glass fanlight above the door, beveled and strong. One evening in unexplained fury Scanlon heaved his John McGraw autographed baseball at the fanlight. The fanlight, being of Gilded Era construction, promptly bounced it back to him between the eyes. The blinds were up and the entire newsroom had a good view of his discomfort. There was perhaps a snicker or two. This scarcely improved his mood and yelping like blinded Polyphemus Scanlon staggered after the baseball.

It was his most cherished possession, having belonged to his father. The game to be sure bored Scanlon as all sports did but it was in his nature to venerate that which was hallowed to others. He kept the baseball perched on a golf tee wedged into a crack in his reference bookcase. This irritated Duffy whose objectivity did not extend to the New York Giants of the McGrawera. (As a baseball worshipper Duffy was ecumenical, granting his favors to the Dodgers and Yankees as well though he preferred the National League rite.) He said it was blasphemous to keep a ball of that sanctity, Christy Mathewson's signature adorned it too, on a golf tee. Scanlon scoffed at the suggestion, he liked to have this jewel of his patrimony handy in times of stress. This evening in Fletcher's memory the editor, chaotic with rage after being battered by the return of his first pitch, wound up again and hurled the ball through the more delicate newsroom window. Free of shattering glass the horsehide traveled forty feet, curved around a pillar, and clipping the copy boy in the shoulder about knocked him down. There was a shocked silence until Duffy looked up compassionately from his desk. Take your base, he said to the copy boy.

So storm as Scanlon might, Fletcher was not too concerned. For one thing old Pharaoh no longer had the John McGraw baseball. It was buried with Duffy in his grave. The night of the wake Scanlon arrived drunk and planning to get drunker. He stood weaving at the head of the open coffin wondering where to put it, the baseball that is. Other writers and editors of their generation, none of them quite sober either, crowded round with advice. Scanlon, magnanimous in grief as otherwise, told them to butt out. He was my friend, he said, and it's my baseball. This kicked off an argument about who had known Duffy longer, one shrouded in the mists of time and alcohol. Looking over from where she was greeting mourners Mrs. Duffy wondered what

this bunch of drunks was shouting about over her dead husband's bier. She pushed through to see a weathered baseball rolling from Duffy's crossed hands into the coffin lining. Scanlon was plaintive. May, he said, it won't stay up. Mrs. Duffy took the baseball and slipped it into a jacket pocket of Duffy's blue suit. There John, she said, that's for the best now. The gathered men agreed and had another drink.

Rothberg stopped at Fletcher's desk. He was chewing a Milky Way bar. "What's the old man carrying on about?"

"WBAI." Fletcher meant the radio station. "Their Media Watch spent a half-hour at eleven o'clock saying we soft soaped the Broadway Central."

"Who told him? Scanlon hasn't listened to the radio since LaGuardia stopped reading the funnies."

"One of his wives I think, that's how he gets most bad news. And we've had some calls." Fletcher looked rueful. "I've been fielding them."

"What do they want? It was a takeout for God's sake." "Sunday's News did a better job than we did. He knows it."

Rothberg was not distressed. "He read it, he ran it, it's his omelette. He can shout all he wants. Ellis went right up to deadline on that piece. He was hanging around that guy from Philadelphia, what's his name, Grecco, all day Monday."

"I know. But Scanlon fiddled with it."

"So what else is new? He fiddles with everything."

"But all he cut was the last paragraph. Harmon told me."

Harmon's takeout on the Broadway Central brought the story forward from the hotel's collapse late Friday afternoon until the end of the rescue operation Monday night. It was workmanlike and thorough, long on quotation, short on description. *The Local* went to press Tuesday and Fletcher read the piece at his desk Wednesday morning. There was no fault to find except to say it might have run anywhere and gone down like beer and pretzels. The problem was the *Local* was not just anywhere.

Fletcher did not like the front page photo either. He'd seen Mahaffy's pictures. His shots of the hotel residents lined up against police barricades were good. They didn't need captions, there was despair and homelessness on every face. Scanlon did not pick one of them. He went with a murky side view of the fallen marquee. It had the drama of a fireman inspecting a vacant lot. Fletcher expected more inside, didn't get it. The story jumped to page 59, two half columns beside the electrolysis ads. And there was no jump head, no secondary headline to catch the reader, standard *Local* practice. And the picture there was less forthcoming than page one. The front of the hotel again, cropped in such a way as to be indistinguishable from the average demolition on a New York street. There was nothing human, nothing declaring this is why the *Local* is here.

General feeling of letdown. Duffy used to say a weekly was like football, you had to wait seven days to scrimmage again. When Fletcher saw Harmon he asked what happened. Harmon said nothing happened, he seemed to resent the question. Yes, he raised the significant issues in the last paragraph but Scanlon chose not to keep it in. Scanlon was the editor wasn't he, he made editorial policy. Just wondering is all, Fletcher said. Harmon was not bothered, maybe had every reason not to be. It was his last *Local* by-line. He'd been battered by Scanlon's unceremonious blue pencil before, why make a fuss now when he would be gone by Labor Day? Fletcher told Harmon the takeout was fine, the photos were blah, that's all he meant. Yet he was more disappointed than that. Five dead: four elderly residents and an unknown young girl, a Jane

Doe. Five dead and they had missed it. He wasn't sure how or why but they had missed it and Scanlon must know it too.

"Scanlon is cautious," Rothberg said. "If he cut any criticism of the city or the building department he's waiting for all the facts to come in."

That was accommodating. If they waited long enough they might all die and go to the *Christian Science Monitor*. "Terrible pictures."

"Well we're not New York's picture newspaper. Not with Mahaffy."

"Mahaffy turned in great stuff. I saw it. You can't…"

"Listen, Rush; let's take Phillips out for drinks Friday."

This did not register right off. "Phillips?"

"Yeah, miss legs. Come on, we'll take her to Bradley's."

"Can't, I'm busy. You don't want me along anyway."

"You're right, I don't. But I need you to ask her to go."

Fletcher swiveled to answer the phone. "*Local*, news desk. No, not back from lunch yet. Yeah, I'll tell him. Thanks." He scribbled on a while-you-were-out pad. A return swivel. "When did I become Miles Standish around here? I mean John Alden."

"Maybe because you're so straight, Rush. What's the word, upright? If you ask her she'll never suspect anything."

More *Double Indemnity* for God's sake. "Suspect anything? What are you planning?"

"Nothing, nothing. I want to get to know her better. You know, like how tight she is with her old man."

No wonder Rothberg used a thesaurus. Referring to Phillips' button down boyfriend as her old man was a little off the mark. She'd undoubtedly describe him as her escort. "Not this week, Ed, I can't do it. I'm seeing Becker and Mona from advertising Friday night."

Rothberg sat up from the desk where he'd been nearly reclining and spat something partially Milky Way in the waste paper basket. Fletcher looked sour. He could never fathom why someone would spit in someone else's waste paper basket but it was an aspect of journalism he'd learned to live with.

"Mona from advertising. Mona the ghoul?"

"I prefer to think of her as runaway Amish," Fletcher said. "And today she has a yellow ribbon in her hair. I like that."

"You would, Rush. Your evident sincerity must have been a big hit in high school. Too bad girls don't give a shit about that anymore. But that's your problem. How about Saturday? Sunday brunch? I'd love to walk Phillips home after a pitcher of mimosas."

"Might be a long walk - she lives in Connecticut."

A woman waiting at the elevator fixed her stocking. "I love the heat… Connecticut? Doesn't she have something in the city?"

"I believe the expression for that, Ed, is *pied-a-terre*."

Rothberg whistled an expiring balloon. "Really?"

"Possibly a tad rich for your blood but don't let me discourage you."

"Don't worry, you won't. She still has to put her bra on one cup at a time. Set it up for any night you want."

Generous of you, Rothberg, princely in fact. Fletcher considered further reluctance but recalled that he owed this particular lovestruck swain no favors. It would be simple enough to forget about it. Departing, Rothberg looked back over his shoulder. "Nice work Becker's place did on that Union Square redevelopment deal. Beat us right in our own sandbox."

Fletcher nodded, not wanting to think about it. If it had not been for the Broadway Central he might have been thinking of nothing else. It was what he had to look forward to. As Rothberg returned to his desk Fletcher saw city editor Baines advancing with that unmistakable feeding time for the chief look in his eye.

"His lordship wants to see you, Rush... forsooth."

This should be pleasant. When Scanlon committed a boner it was his beloved custom to summon a suitable and congenial tiller of the soil and beat them over the head with it. Relieved and feeling better he was then fresh for further editorial mayhem. Fletcher answered the summons slowly, negotiating the newsroom clutter as if it were a cow pasture. Scanlon in a pet, as they would say back home, could be very trying indeed. The drawbridge was down. Fletcher went in, choosing his usual orange scoop in the corner. Scanlon ignored him, that was usual too. He would stare out onto University Place drumming his fingers like a tenderizing hammer until you were ready for the pan.

But he was ready before very long. "News about Agosto, Rush. She's quitting."

"Quitting? Huh... where's she going?"

"That's the hell of it lad. She's not going anywhere. She's just leaving me for no reason."

That could not be the real story. Fletcher had slid forward on the scoop with shock. He pulled himself up. Newspapermen didn't throw over jobs for no reason. All right, Rose Agosto was not exactly a newspaperman. She was more like a yappy mascot you wished another fraternity would kidnap. But her name was on the masthead; Fletcher felt a chill. Giving up a serious newspaper job, it was like hearing about incest.

"It's unprofessional, Rush. That's all I have to say."

If only that were true but of course it wasn't. This little affair was likely to reverberate in Scanlon's cosmic outlook for weeks and they would all suffer. And calling Agosto unprofessional was the purest clarified lard. Old Fuss and Feathers had been hooting for some time that it was precisely Agosto's unprofessionalism that made her so spontaneous and exciting. You never know what's she'll do next, he'd say while gleaming until he was almost cross-eyed. Well now he knew, she'd quit, unprofessionally.

"We'll talk about her later," Scanlon suddenly announced, looking as if he'd tossed off a jigger of venom. "Why is Harmon taking so much flak on this hotel story? Seemed all right to me, eh?"

That was neat. The buck stops outside my door. "The calls I took said we weren't aggressive. We treated it like a sewer main break."

"It hasn't any legs to speak of."

Can't let him get away with that. "Hasn't any legs? Come on, John, it's a gold mine. Class issues, housing, welfare, maybe bribery. Campaign contributions from the real estate industry. There's six different ways we could go at it. Harmon's heart isn't here anymore. I understand that. Let me do the follow-up, chief. I've got some ideas. Harmon told me he raised the issue of responsibility in…"

"I cut it," Scanlon said.

Frank, forthright; okay. "Do you mind telling me why?"

"Nothing mysterious." Yeah, who said there was. "I inserted Harmon's paragraph into the editorial for page five."

"But we didn't run an editorial."

"Right. I'm holding it pending further information."

"We don't need information, John. We have five bodies."

"Where was Mahaffy when the bodies came out Monday. He blew it."

Swift change of subject. "I don't know. But what about his good stuff from Friday night? What we went with looks like somebody dropped their Instamatic on the sidewalk."

"Too personal most of it. Those head shots, bleak. An invasion of privacy. You know how I feel about that. You should too."

Will wonders never cease. "What happened to the editorial?"

"I'm naming names, need a little time. You've been writing about long haired musicians for so long you've forgotten what facts are. This is what I want you to do."

Fletcher stood up, came forward. "I'm ready to go."

"I want you to find Agosto and talk to her."

Expecting Christmas morning Fletcher came down the stairs to find it was moving day. "I don't want to talk to Agosto."

"Good; find out what's eating her. Get right on it."

The assignment of a lifetime, like Stanley after Livingstone. Scanlon snarled into his intercom, bringing the interview to an end. Fletcher went back to his desk. Agosto lived where, he didn't know. Calling personnel he was not surprised to hear Avenue C. He dialed the number, no answer. This was true all afternoon. Each time he dialed the number he wished he were calling Elke or a source at the White House. He had a contact at the Department of Buildings, one of many Duffy heirlooms he'd inherited. But Duffy had never challenged the old man and he could not either. There were more complaints about their coverage, warming up as the paper circulated. The story might not be Fletcher's baby but he had the diaper pail. At six he was undecided. He wanted to head home, listen to music. He'd gone to the Mets game Tuesday night and drunk too much beer and then Hickman took him to an Irish bar on

Roosevelt Avenue where the News reporter fit like a batting glove. There were blue collar bars like it in Youngstown in Ohio, he'd never been to one like it in New York. The slight fog behind Fletcher's eyes had not lifted all day.

Downstairs on the street Steinmetz from circulation was coming across from the Zeus Brothers with a container of tea. Fletcher almost bolted but he was too tired. There was something about the circulation manager and his orange pekoe with lemon that made you glad you drank coffee. In his forties, he lived with his infirm mother in Stuyvesant Town and walked home several times a day to check on her medication. Conscientious, he worked late to compensate. He was pleasant but made you feel depressed. Partially this was because he had joined the paper in its first year. (Right out of Baruch Business College on Twenty-Third Street, he walked there too.) He hoped to become a reporter and Scanlon told him learn the ropes all around, we'll start you in circulation. Wanting to please Steinmetz made the mistake of being good at it and Scanlon never let him out. But there was another reason why he made you uncomfortable but it was years before anyone put their finger on it. Fletcher and some others were talking and Buckley the cartoonist said: you know what it is about Bernie Steinmetz? He looks like he's been defrosted. He did.

"Evening, Rush."

Fletcher nodded. "Bernie."

And there was something else: Steinmetz took subscription cancellations personally. If the cancellation was due to natural causes, death, senility, or blindness, removal to another realm or divorce, he could live with it. Difficult but these things happen. And sometimes separation and divorce, creating another household, brought a second subscription. This made Steinmetz happy. He'd tell his mother: the Bergers on West Twelfth Street are finished, she's gone back to her maiden name and moved to West End Avenue, subscribed for two years, still a year to run on his. So there could be silver linings but cancellations brought about by *Local* editorial policy or columnist viewpoints were more than he could bear. And as Steinmetz apparently never read the paper he had trouble understanding what readers were angry about.

Fletcher had unintentionally brought him grief of this kind. The year before, filling in at the film desk, he reviewed *Sleuth*, the Joseph Mankiewicz adaption of the Broadway play. He didn't like it. Olivier was fun but the smooth mechanics of the play needed an oil change on the screen. In other words it creaked. And because the name Margo Channing was facetiously used in the credits (Fletcher disliked private jokes) and having little to say he padded the piece with a few shots at *All About Eve*. The appeal of the 1950 Mankiewicz picture, considered his best, eluded Fletcher. He said so. More than that he said the script was overrated, the lines were merely well delivered. And that's what got him in trouble. He was contradicting himself but it shouldn't have mattered, it was only the last paragraph of a throwaway film round-up attributed to Joseph Klieg. (In the paper's early days when it relied heavily on reader contributions a number of whimsical to dim pseudonyms were employed. Joseph Klieg was by far the least annoying. It was, for example, Fletcher's accession to the music desk that finally retired the unlamented Hy Fidelity. And off-Broadway was the preserve for many years of a Pommery Brut though no one knew quite why.) Most film reviews were the work and by-line of Polly Michaels who was not on staff. She also wrote for Ramparts and other left wing journals but she liked the *Local*. The paper let her stretch out. There was some friendship between her father, not a newspaperman but an old union lawyer, and Scanlon. He left her copy in peace and paid her top dollar. And she was worth it, there being more than a few who bought the paper principally for her. But she was often on assignment and would skip weeks at a time and she would not have touched a movie like Sleuth with chopsticks.

Steinmetz stopped, paused, checked the front of the building to see if there was anyone coming out. "Rush," he said, "is there anything wrong?"

Fletcher tried to recall if he had done anything lately to make Steinmetz unhappy but no one had been sufficiently mad at him to cancel their subscription. He was perhaps getting soft or gun shy. The ad hoc Committee For The Perpetual Uplift Of *All About Eve* had given him one fair drubbing. He'd been called a twerp on the radio, a guest on the Long John Nebel show said he wrote like a teenage child. The letters arrived, as abundant as those usually written to the North Pole. (I want real letters to Santa this December, Scanlon once pleaded, who wants to write them? Fortunately no one did.) *"Your vapid prose,"* ran one, *"can't hide behind the skirts of Joseph Klieg." "You wouldn't know a great movie,"* said another, *"from a trombone."* (This got around and resulted in Fletcher receiving a plastic toy trombone at the staff Christmas party.) *"It doesn't surprise us…"* (the royal we in a letter to the editor is really the limit) *"that a so-called critic incapable of grasping the multiple architectonic manipulations of fusion should fail to…"* Fletcher never reached the end of that sentence (his indifference to jazz fusion had long got him in hot water) and regretted that the anonymity of a Joseph Klieg or Barnabas Atwater over in books was not what it used to be. Ultimately there were but three All About Eve cancellations (and two came back because what is the fun if you can't cancel every once in a while) but the incident left him humbled. (Aided to be sure by occasional notes on the newsroom bulletin board such as: Due to the slowness of the mail the Alexandria Public Library - that's Egypt, folks, not Virginia, has terminated its subscription first taken out in 325 B.C. Way to go, Rush, keep up the good work.) It was all a foolish business but he'd been caught being frivolous and who the hell was Barnabas Atwater anyway?

"Wrong with what?"

Steinmetz looked furtive again as if there might be spies. But not for the first time Fletcher understood that the head of circulation was petrified of that man up there. "I had several calls today from subscribers. They were very upset."

"I know, Bernie, me too. It's because of the hotel."

"The one that fell down?"

No, the Carlyle, what hotel did he think they were talking about? He might at least look at the front page sometimes. "It hasn't been our shining hour so far." Fletcher regretted his tone. It was hot and he didn't want to see Agosto but Steinmetz had been unable to come to the boat ride, it was too long and inaccessible a time to be away from his mother. "We have last licks, Bernie, we'll pull it out yet."

Steinmetz nodded without energy. Defrosted as he might be he could recognize hollowness when he heard it. "There's something else," he said. Looking around again, however, he saw Benson, the business manager, emerging from the lobby. He turned away so abruptly he squeezed the lid from his tea container. 'Another time," he said. "Have a good night."

It was Fletcher's turn to nod. He nodded also to Benson, the foremost extent of their communication. They once stood together accidentally on a stalled express between Union Square and Grand Central and it was apparent that after many years in the same building they had nothing to say to each other.

Fletcher idled on University Place, believing he really could go home until a vision of Scanlon demanding to know "how it went" intervened. He went east, taking Eleventh Street. The blocks declined in a seemingly downward spiral, Avenue C more decayed than its predecessor. What he knew of these streets was second hand except for Slug's, the jazz club further south that had closed the year before. Agosto's building was beside an abandoned one with bricked up windows and the cryptic chalk warning that water and gas have been turned off. On its stoop three men, it was *Local* policy not to say wino, were drinking and sleeping. On her stoop there were adolescent boys, playing a radio, making kissing smacks at passing girls. They did not make way, Fletcher stepped around them. He'd been told occasionally he looked like a cop.

Three flights up. The hallways in his own building were washed twice a week, painted once a year. The superintendent, Mrs. Romano, looked after things like a Roman house deity and had slowly convinced him that ricotta and mozzarella (from where she bought it, not the supermarket) were what made life worth living. Agosto's halls were dark, smelly, slippery. Bags of dripping garbage sat on staircase landings. Children cried, televisions prattled on every floor. Personnel had said apartment 8. Most doors were unnumbered. Fletcher working it out tried front left. He knocked, knocked harder. A woman said what, it wasn't Agosto's voice.

"Fletcher from the paper. Rose home?"

Shadow in the peephole. The clicks of three locks, the door opened. A woman in her mid-twenties, real blonde hair, not Spanish, not from New York. "Who?"

"Fletcher. I work with Rose. Can I…"

"She's not here. She went to see her mother."

73

Short but she was taller than Agosto. Fletcher looked over her head at the kitchen. A hole in the ceiling, lath exposed, water stains down the walls. Dishes in the sink, cereal box spilled on the table, overturned jars and bottles. Possibly they were argumentative. What he could see of the next room was sloppy too. Maybe they were just slobs.

"Is she coming back soon? I'd like to talk to her."

"Who'd you say you were again?"

"Rush Fletcher from the paper. I hear Rose quit. I was thinking she'd like to talk to someone about it." Like pumping a bereaved widow, Fletcher disliked the news hawk sound of his words. He'd be tipping a fedora on the back of his head next. Euphemism followed upon lie. "You her roommate?"

"Her lover," the woman said. "Rosie is my lover."

No euphemisms sought or accepted, thank you. Fletcher was detached, uninterested. Scanlon could come over here on roller skates if he wanted to.

"Why'd she quit?" He might have been talking to a campaign manager.

"I don't know. She doesn't like it anymore."

"Must be a reason."

"Just leave her alone, okay? That's all she wants."

Fletcher felt the beer, the crappy day. "She has a responsibility to the paper." That wasn't what he meant to say but was what he believed.

"You're kidding. That's a joke right." Her expression was everything. He wasn't used to that in faces so young. "The way you treat her over there in your fucking clubhouse and she's supposed to owe you something? I mean come on. You fuck with her head, you do everything you can and now you... just forget it."

"Is that what she says?"

"Hey, just get out of here. She just wants to do what you do but that's too much. You can't accept that any of you. It's supposed to be different there but it's not. You kept fucking her over until she quit."

"It's not like that," Fletcher said.

"How the hell would you know?"

As she slammed the door the jamb shivered, a paint chip flew. Fletcher walked to the stairs. He didn't remember Agosto's girlfriend from the boat ride and then remembered Agosto hadn't been there. He meant to ask her if she'd been sick, there couldn't be another reason. He'd meant to ask her but he hadn't.

Jules and Jim

Friday after work Fletcher filled two shopping bags with books and records. They were review copies. He'd been selling books to the Strand for ten
years. There was never much chat. (Only the introductory Books To Go Down
invocation from the buyer, which signaled to someone below there were souls
to be ferried.) It was different at Dayton's where he brought records. That guy
could be gabby.

The man dabbed at damp forearms with an aromatic dish towel. A fan
would help but some New York establishments seemed averse to them.
"Rush," he said, "I want from nows on you should soft pedal the hard rock.
You don't bring me no jazz much."

"I keep the jazz."

"So youse say but no sound effects do I get either. No Jonathan Winters,
that's a seller. I shouldn't have to tell you. And Spike Jones flies out the door. I
mean flies like a rocket. What's the matter, don't you like to laugh?"

"Not especially," Fletcher said.

"My sympathies are all yours. I mean that. Me, I got to have a little humor every day like salt and pepper. This life here is a sandwich and what's a
sandwich without salt and pepper and a piece pickle on the side? I tell you it's
nothing, it's tasteless."

The buyer had trouble breathing due to the weight around his heart and
other places. He sat high on a library stool behind the counter intent on his
clientele. Many were collectors. They went slowly through the record bins,
eyes down, unheeding of their fellows like men silent at pornography. Collecting of all kinds did not strike Fletcher as a communal activity. It perhaps could
not be.

Someone he knew, Heinz, was on the paper until he opted for law school.
This Heinz had an apartment, a large two bedroom apartment, full of albums.
He had specialties, one being soundtracks. He had every Elvis film, rather a

bundle in itself, and nearly every Frank Sinatra. Fletcher had the soundtrack of a French film from the late fifties that Miles Davis scored. It was out of print and reasonably rare. He brought it to an office get together and Heinz was enraptured. He wanted it, right between Viva Las Vegas and Spartacus. Heinz offered money, he offered money and an ounce of grass, he offered money and an ounce of grass and his girlfriend's sister who was a sure thing. The answer was no. Fletcher said it really belonged to his friend Logan, not that Logan would mind if he sold it. A fair excuse but Fletcher did not say what he really felt: that it was distasteful to be so acquisitive. Being a reporter turning lawyer Heinz may have sensed this. If you won't give it up, he said, you're as bad as I am.

Fletcher cleared forty dollars from the two stores. He could get his dry cleaning out, he could pay Becker the ten he owed, he could put ten towards his typewriter fund, he could have a hamburger and some beer and not worry about it. He felt diametrically frugal and spendthrift. The Dayton's buyer was filled with remorse. "I'll never unload these," he said, looking dolefully down through his luscious chins at Hall and Oates and Elton John. He feared the music of the seventies might not provide a lucrative old age. There was a milk crate of unwanted 8 Tracks behind his chair that he studied in reminder of the futility of human endeavour.

"You told me last month business was good," Fletcher said. He had actually said business was so-so, Fletcher taking this to mean better than average, the buyer having the gift of understatement.

"That was last month which is all over and done. A lot can happen yeah in that interim as youse well know as commentator. Look at Nixon. Look at this hotel that falls down out of the blue with no warning. These winds here of commerce is just the same exactly. You can no tell how they blow. Not me, not anybody. As for you I think you should be gregarious sometimes. Think about it, a little gregarious. It won't hurt, believe me."

Fletcher believed him. He left and crossed Broadway up to Thirteenth. Mona lived in a renovated hotel called the Battersea. He remember the ad in the *Local* when it opened. He'd gone to an open house and been given a prospectus and a cup of orange juice. He didn't want either because he couldn't afford it and the model apartment had a view of the Empire State Building. There was a Pullman kitchen and a stacked washer and dryer in a closet and central air conditioning. The prospectus never made it back to Bleecker Street. Walking in now there were ferns in the lobby, recessed lighting, a front desk and switchboard. At the desk a college joe in a starched white shirt, Battersea scripted on the pocket. The place was making a quiet statement. The college joe put his thumb in the Annotated Lolita and rang Mona. He said she would be right down. She was. She came out of the elevator so fast he wondered if he seemed the type that didn't like to be kept waiting.

Even though she hadn't given him time to collect himself in the classic male manner he felt comfortable. He wore deck shoes, no socks, chinos, a blue work shirt from Hudson's. There was no reason to tinker but she was a woman, it was a reflex. He wished Elke lived downtown. He'd caught up with her that morning by calling UNICEF. That was not something he liked to do, call a woman at her job. He'd rather stop by the house, wait on the porch, maybe bring a strawberry rhubarb pie his mother made. When Elke answered she sounded distant, cross. He gave her the lead to be polite, suggesting she'd been busy. She said she was not so busy, just not sociable. They'd talked for hours at a stretch, now the pauses seemed as long. Most painful of all she asked nothing about how he was. They said goodbye. He did not expect to see her again.

Out of the elevator Mona was back in black. No yellow ribbon this evening, her pale skin the only soft tone, her eyes daubed raccoon if raccoons could be said to wear mascara. Dressing for Becker she seemed to be: short black skirt, a tight short black skirt for that matter, commando undershirt, boots that brought her up near his shoulder. Fletcher noticed her breasts this time, her nipples more precisely, he had to crank his eyes back up like a tire jack. On the street she automatically raised her arm for a cab. An extravagance in Fletcher's view, they were only going to SoHo.

"Prince and Mercer," she said.

They rode down Broadway. The cab was a Checker, Fletcher extending his legs in a pose of luxury. He looked sideways. No, she was not decked out for the mother-daughter bake sale. These do not generally begin at midnight. He thought of strawberry rhubarb pie again and the girls in high school in their white socks and mary janes. Even at twilight Mona seemed after-hours. He looked up. This was the first cab he had been in with a grill separating the front seat from the back. They were said to be bulletproof. The hack license was visible but not the driver's face and if he did not want to roll his window down you paid through a mousetrap opening in the grill. Fletcher rolled his window down the permitted third. There was not much breeze at that hour in Manhattan. It hadn't been the warmest day of the week but close. August was proceeding like the drip of a faucet.

A red light stopped them at Third. Fletcher watched a bulldozer pushing out the insides of the Broadway Central. It was a much neater mess than it had been. The sidewalks were clear and a fence had risen at the boundary line. The hotel was absent from the *Times* that morning, rating just a box in the metro section of the News. The item was a week old and showing its age. There'd been death and destruction, front page stuff with real human ache for the shirttail inside. But it wasn't enough, hardly ever was, unless it was war or Watergate. As it stood now the Broadway Central wasn't outrunning a mugging. The bulldozer rounds off the rough edges, the cement mixer covers it over. Coming soon, another downtown revitalization project on this site. The Broadway Central was no longer news, it was real estate.

Mona looked at him. "What happened?"

"Sorry? What happened to what?"

She pointed. "What happened to our coverage?"

Fletcher liked to hear people say "our". The cab began to move. "I don't know," he said, "we let it get away somehow."

"Lousy pictures. Mahaffy must have taken better ones."

"He did." Fletcher flipped the jump seat down and dropped a foot on it. "You don't usually hear much about the news hole from your floor."

"How would you know?"

He lost what she said in the car horns crossing Houston. "What?"

"How would you know what we think? Do you ever talk to anyone in advertising? Editorial acts like we don't exist."

"Is that true? I don't…"

The cab turned west onto Prince Street. "When you spoke to me Wednesday I was surprised. You never did before."

"We talked on the boat ride. I remember."

"That doesn't count. Driver, this corner on the left."

Fletcher reached for his wallet but Mona was putting three dollars in the mousetrap. She didn't wait for change as the cab stopped outside Fanelli's. That was a dollar tip. Fletcher got out streetside and caught up with her at the door to the bar. "Why doesn't it count?"

Mona put a cigarette in her mouth. "Because boat rides aren't real," she said.

Fanelli's had a back room. The bar got an afternoon trade: warehouse men, printers, cutters from the wholesale fabric outlets on Broadway. There was a lunch special but by three o'clock both rooms emptied and you could read a newspaper undisturbed. A good place for an interview. Fletcher first went there at the behest of two movement radicals who were underground. It was a quiet spot to talk. In time he met others though not always at Fanelli's. He believed ideology had rendered the FBI ineffective but he wasn't on the run. It made sense to move around so he went where he was asked: to Prospect Park in Brooklyn, to a safe house on Staten Island, to Hoboken and Elizabeth across the river. He still went to Fanelli's now and then, to meet someone from the Weathermen he called Jake. That was the book he was writing, something of a quest. He was trying to determine why people so much like himself did the things they did.

Mona went swiftly, adroitly to the back room, sat at a corner table, lit her cigarette. Fletcher followed but it was not a table he would have picked. He disliked women smoking though he tended not to notice it in men unless they were sloppy about it.

"Those are different," he said.

"Nat Sherman's… my nighttime smoke. They burn slow and the paper is sweet."

Wanting a beer he looked for Dot, a Friday night waitress he liked. The night bartender was Steve, young and good looking, either a lumberjack or an actor. Steve had a knuckle busting handshake and aura of good health and pep. Dominant in a sense, he set the tone and in a small way, a very small way, was proof of the great man theory of history. Fletcher was puzzled to see otherwise intelligent men seeking the bartender's benediction of approval in front of their dates. Like a god to be propitiated they left him enormous sacrifices. Becker, who knew the Fanelli's night world as Fletcher knew the day, said Steve made mints of money and got laid like a racehorse. Fletcher, willing to believe it, did not often include the bartender in his prayers.

He considered saying I burn slow too but it sounded stupid. And why weren't boat rides real? Mona drank a vodka and tonic and examined in an anticipatory way the back room action as the tables around them filled. Becker was expected to be late so they ate without him. A green salad, hamburgers with cheese (he had American, she had smoked Gouda), a very good baked potato. Mona had two glasses of wine before switching back to vodka. She didn't mind drinking it seemed. Fletcher stuck to the draft Schaefer. From their waiter he found that Dot had decamped for the Spring Street Bar a few blocks away. He was disappointed. He didn't care for the Spring Street Bar. It was full of artists. You could get away with most anything in SoHo by signing your name to it. Too bad about Dot. Mona appeared to find their waiter interesting. He seemed all right but Fletcher preferred a waitress.

"What's he like?" Mona meant Becker.

"Funny, a good guy. A good reporter." One out of these three was true at least, the others could be argued for and against.

"Do you guys ever say some other guy is a crummy reporter?"

Fletcher let this drop by smiling. He was thinking it was pretty easy with Mona because there was nothing between them or going to be but Becker had better get there soon. They were not running short of things to say - she was intelligent, amusing - but they hadn't broken free of the pretense of their evening and it was intensifying. Maybe this was why boat rides don't count.

"Why do you always wear black?" This was an artificial question asked in an artificial way. He knew it.

"I was suckled by wolves. Why do you dress like your father?"

Fletcher thought about this. "I don't think I do. These are the clothes I wear, the ones I feel comfortable in."

"I bet they come when you whistle too."

"Well, you'll like Becker. He wears cowboy boots."

Mona blew smoke from the edge of her mouth. "I didn't say I don't like you, Rush. I was just wondering who you are." He looked away because she was looking right at him. "You're so plain and obvious, you might be someone else underneath. I might be sorry."

He blinked. "Maybe too much personality isn't good for a reporter." Fletcher meant to say it lightly but sounded urgent instead. "I mean I've always been more of a listener than a talker."

"Did you listen to Rose Agosto?"

Where did that come from? "Agosto? Scanlon sent me to see her. She wasn't home. How did you know about that?"

Mona shook her head. "Before that. Before she quit. Did you ever?"

"I talked to her - no, she wasn't on the boat ride. But when she first came on staff, whenever it was. I talked to her then."

"You don't like her much. Why?"

"It's not dislike. I wouldn't say that. She's too dogmatic."

"The Weathermen are dogmatic. You talk to them."

Fletcher wondered how this began. "That goes with the job. I talk to other people I can't defend. It doesn't mean I'm enjoying myself."

Another head shake. "That's defensive, Rush. You'll never make me believe you don't love what you do. Every minute of it. But so does Agosto."

His turn to shake. "I know but loving isn't enough. Her writing is too inconsistent, sometimes it makes no sense. And if you make a suggestion she says it's genocide. That's not the easiest position to take."

"You never complain about how you're edited?"

"Not in public. There are better ways to do it."

Mona dropped her cigarette on the floor and called the waiter. "Everyone should have your self-restraint, Rush. Another beer?"

Fletcher nodded. "You wouldn't want everyone to have my self-restraint. You'd be bored."She made a V sign to the waiter. "In the long run we'll all be bored," Mona said, "but only some of us will be bored silly." This came out in a murmur. The waiter was bending for her lime at his station and she admired his ass. Fletcher looked at her earrings, small black pearls, and the passage in her throat as she swallowed. For a moment, until she turned back again, he thought of Becker not coming at all.

"Did you know that Mona is the Latin name for the Isle of Man?"

He'd almost caught her but she recovered. She was good. "Whenever men say that to me, Rush, I have the feeling they mean something entirely different."

"Why did Agosto quit?"

Mona blew out the smoke of a fresh cigarette. "I'm in advertising, remember? We're on different floors."

"It's not because she wants to hang out after work with the guys."

"Don't be so sure of what a woman wants."

"They don't want vulgarity; I'm pretty sure of that."

The waiter brought their drinks. Mona kept her eyes on Fletcher. 'You're in New York and you're talking about vulgarity. Your heart must still be in the highlands."

"It's pretty flat where I come from. Why did she quit?"

Mona picked up her glass, didn't drink, put it down. "It's not you I don't trust, Rush. It's your good intentions." Now she sipped from her glass. "There's a guy hitting on her. She's afraid of him."

"A guy on the staff? You mean one of us?"

"In case you haven't noticed that's all of you."

"What is he doing, bothering her for a date?"

Mona inhaled, coughed, laughed. "Bothering her is one way of putting it. I wouldn't but you're the writer. He wants to fuck her. She told him no, he wants to fuck her all the more. Get it?"

Fletcher couldn't recall anyone talking about Agosto that way. There were jokes, the kind you hear about women who aren't interested in men, but he never thought they meant anything. And gratefully the Little Latin Lupe Lu bit did not last. "She has a strong personality. I think she'd be able to handle it. I mean women usually do."

"Well I guess this is how she's handling it, Rush."

He heard what she didn't say. "You think I don't take it seriously?"

Mona waited for the noise of a nearby table to subside. "I don't know if you can. Are you five feet tall? Are you lesbian, Puerto Rican, a woman? Do you know how she feels? I'm waiting for you to ask why she didn't tell somebody."

"That was my next question."

"Maybe she's afraid. Have you ever been, Rush?"

Fletcher did not get to think about it. Coming through the side door from Mercer Street was Becker. As he seemed lighter than air this was perhaps not his first stop. He waved, Fletcher waved. Mona sat still.

"For a while I didn't think I'd make it," Becker said.

Oh brother, if you believe that… "We ate," Fletcher said.

"Great; we're all set for some serious drinking then."

In fact Becker was an unserious drinker, a couple of beers being about his limit. And he had a trick, Fletcher had noticed, it was nearly sinister, of leaving bottles and glasses unfinished so it appeared he was drinking more than he was. From the looks of it though he'd have his hands full with Mona who was beckoning the waiter with her thumb. Fletcher excused himself as Becker's arrival saved him from further chivalric watch by Mona's side. He was detached but looked back once to see if Mona was looking. She wasn't.

The toilet was steamy. That it had the interior dimensions of a Volkswagen did not help. Above the urinal on the yellowed tile, not the yellow of marigolds, there was an unfinished tic tac toe game. An odd thing but Fletcher thought of his father who had trouble urinating, who had to get up during the night and could not always return to sleep. He sat in an armchair instead and tried to read but brooded instead on his life and his Republican Party. He hadn't voted in '72. He couldn't vote for McGovern and wouldn't vote for Nixon again so he stayed home. He said that man, meaning Nixon, lies like a circus barker. His father kept busy. Except when he couldn't sleep he was always doing something. Fletcher washed his hands, dried them in his trouser pockets. There was a mirror. Some contemporaries he saw looked wasted, done up. He thought he looked tired, bored. My God, what an unprincipled, selfish thing to be bored.

At their table Fletcher was grimly amused to see Becker with what looked like a glass of whisky.

"Mona's idea; double bourbon."

"I don't like half measures," she said smokily. "Now if you will pardon me I'll go see what the boys in the front room will have."

Rising to let her pass Becker's eyes followed Mona. He sat, as effervescent as shook up seltzer. "She's great. Isn't she great?"

Fletcher nodded. "You drink that, Paul, you'll be sorry."

"Forget the bourbon, I can handle it. Toni called me."

Evidently half measures were good enough for Fletcher. She'd ordered him another Schaefer. "Who?"

"Toni, from Watkins Glen. In the tube top, how could you forget?"

"Oh, don't tell me - she left her Pez dispenser in the car."

"You can laugh but she sounds very mature on the phone. Eighteen at least. Now when I set something up with her I can count on you, right?"

"Count on me for what: bail money? Oh yeah, as to that." Fletcher twisted for his wallet. "Here's the ten I owe you."

"Skip it, Rush. I appreciate... tonight and everything."

Fletcher's arm extended like a punch and stuffed the bill in Becker's shirt pocket. "Let's not have anything on that basis, okay?"

"Okay, okay, forget it. Why are you so uptight?" Becker inspected his pocket. The shirt was Yves St. Laurent and professionally laundered. "But back to Toni. Due to her tender years she won't come in the city without her duenna Laurie along. That's where..."

Mona was back. Being basic she didn't require much touching up. Becker celebrated her return by ringing up half his double bourbon with a debonair twitch. Poor fellow, she hadn't even got him a chaser. Fletcher drifted back in his chair, uninspired, as the prospective lovebirds began to chat. Becker was good at that, chatting, mindlessly if need be. Yet it couldn't be easy having no conscience. She would see that right off; possibly she already had. Mona was not Becker's type, even if she did dress the part. And they couldn't be friends because Becker didn't have any women friends. He was a phony, a philanderer. Well, there probably really weren't philanderers anymore. But there were phonies. And if boat rides don't count why had she come? Come on, why weren't they real? The boat was real, there were lifeboats and life preservers. One year there was even a parrot. Damn, you never thought about a woman much and then she spoke a certain way, laughed a certain way, smoked her abominable cigarettes a certain way and you suddenly needed to know all about her and if she was ever sad or...

"I'm glad Rush suggested we all get together," Becker was saying. "I don't get out very much. My work..."

Fletcher closed his eyes. Becker was like the guy in one of Mary McCarthy's books who signed his love letters C.Y.K. for Consider Yourself Kissed.

Sheesh. Mona used matches, rather neatly. He'd noticed you couldn't strike matches on the front of the matchbook anymore but only on the back. A safety measure; was this government intrusion? He wondered if Mona was very organized, she seemed like she might be. His mother always said a woman needs to be organized. He was never sure what that meant. What if he brought a woman home to meet his mother and she said well, dear, she seems very nice but is she organized? What would he say? He couldn't say she always closed the matchbook cover before striking the match because his mother didn't approve of smoking. That was no good. If his mother didn't think a woman was just right for him what would he do? He didn't want to be bored or bored silly. He didn't want to be bored at all.

"You awake, Rush?" Fletcher opened his eyes, Becker was grinning at him. "Didn't you get enough rest sleeping through the Broadway Central story?"

"We're not done with it yet."

"You could have fooled me. Why didn't you just run the mayor's press release and let it go at that?" Becker turned to Mona. "They squawk if my sheet makes a move north of Houston but what are you supposed to do when they fall down on a big story like this?"

Fletcher leaned forward. "We didn't fall down on it, Paul. Unlike the all singing, all dancing rotogravure responsible for "Hookers of the Holland Tunnel" and "White Slaves of Mott Street" we don't run material we can't substantiate."

But Becker was ready. "Hey, we can substantiate every one of those hookers. I can substantiate some of them personally. And you said yourself "Hookers" was a terrific piece."

"I'll bet he did," Mona said.

"How many times did blow job appear in the first paragraph?" Fletcher did not catch himself in time. He wasn't accustomed to saying blow job in front of women. He wasn't accustomed to saying blow job in general.

"I'll have to check my notes." Becker seemed more boyish than salacious. He got his start at the East Village Other, a defunct weekly known for acid politics, muddy typography and slum goddess pinups. "But why are we discussing blow jobs, albeit a subject dear to my heart, in front of a lady? By the way, Mona, did I tell you on the boat ride how much respect I have for your lipstick?"

"Keep your voice down, Paul."

"Anyway the question is not fellatio no matter what this prurient gentleman says." Becker got louder. Fletcher despaired to see that the rest of the whisky was gone. "No, the question is not the fluctuation, so to speak, of blow jobs in the marketplace of - did you know the German word for pussy is Muschi? My grandmother had a cat named Muschi but never mind that - the question is why did the New York *Local* - Defender of the Meek, Protector of the Innocent, Last Resting Place of the Hippie Ethos and Beatnik Mumbles, yes, the dependable, unreadable little old bombast of University Place..." Becker was off and running. "Why did it cover the collapse of the Broadway Central right under its very own wigwam like it was a Mister Softee truck with a flat tire? Well, I'm glad you asked even if you didn't. I'll tell you why. Why - excuse me, I mean because. Because the *Local* can't do any better anymore, that's why. *The Local* is washed up, kaput, fish sticks. Your readers - where are you? There you are. Your readers get it every week out of sheer nostalgia. Even you, Rush. You've been carrying the goddamn thing on your back for a hundred a week for who knows how long. But what is it now, two years you've been on this Weatherman kick? Fucking prep school, trust fund, anti-war assholes. Poor babies, they took the draft away and nobody cared anymore. I wouldn't buy *The New Yorker* for that and it has cartoons. Face it, Rush, the *Local* is living on its classifieds. Mona agrees. Right, Mona?"

She flicked ash from her cigarette. "I work there too."

"Yeah, but you're in advertising and advertising follows circulation. I guarantee you right now, in a year, less, you'll be in SoHo."

Mona touched a thumb to the middle of her chin. It made her look demure. "I'm not so sure about that," she said. "The paper has problems, true, but I believe in it. I'm even investing in it."

Fletcher looked up. "Investing? You mean you're buying stock?" Fletcher had a few hundred shares he thought little about except at Christmas when he was given more in lieu of a bonus. "Really?"

"Yes, really. Do you find that so strange?"

No, he didn't think he did. But investments, like marriage and children, were part of that still unspoken other world. Here was a vampire with a portfolio. "No, I don't actually."

"Even Rose Agosto has a few shares you know."

Becker was trying to catch the waiter. Impatient, he went to the bar. Fletcher spoke softly. "No wonder the majority stockholder was sorry to see her go. Scanlon likes to keep his eye on anyone with voting power."

He was pleased to say this humorously. Mona lit a cigarette and checked on Becker who was still in the front room. "But he doesn't have 51% now, Rush."

"You mean he's been selling?" Fletcher answered his own question. "Can't be." He shook his head. "The last thing he'd ever do."

Mona shrugged. "That's as good an explanation as any but whatever the reason he is selling. I'm surprised you don't know."

Fletcher was too. "I didn't."

Becker loomed over the top of Mona's head. He gave her a vodka and tonic. "You believe in the sanctity of free love, don't you Mona?"

"That depends on much it costs."

He stepped away behind her, pointing, mouthing to Fletcher. "Lauren Bacall, *To Have and Have Not.*"

"Sit down, Becker", she said, "this isn't volleyball."

Becker did as he was bid, happily so. He had another large bourbon, it looked menacing in his hand. "I didn't get you a beer, Rush, as I know you have to be leaving soon. Oh, those Saturday morning staff meetings, how I envy you. And you'll have so much to talk about this week. Like how we toasted your wieners again on that Union Square business."

"That piece was a little short on direct quotation, wouldn't you say, Paul?"

Ignoring this. "How trying it must be, Rush, to look over your shoulder every week and see as Lefty Gomez used to say the *SoHo News* gaining on you."

"That's Satchel Paige."

"Hell, there's no talking to this guy. But speaking of wieners, my dear, when was the last time you had a really good foot long hot dog?"

"This morning with coffee," Mona said. "I wake up hungry."

Looking as if he'd ascended to the penthouse above the seventh heaven Becker flopped back against his seat. Fletcher tried to bring him down from the empyrean. "Did you come up with anything on the girl they found?"

Becker had to think. "Oh, the one in the bar. No, nothing. She must have stayed behind when the day guy left and got locked in. That's how I see it. Probably seriously stoned, wanted to sleep."

"She lived a long time," Mona said.

"Breathing through a drain pipe believe it or not. Maybe they cut off her air supply getting to her. Nobody knows but what can you do? She wasn't supposed to be there."

Fletcher finished his warm beer. "Why not?"

"What why not? She wasn't supposed to be there, plain and simple. The bar was closed, she didn't live in the hotel. Not like those old people, you know their string was up. Pure bad luck for her, not much else to say."

"Someone must know something about her," Mona said.

"Not so far. No fingerprints on file, no I.D. on her. Just the name Vix is all anybody knows. And that's a boom boom name if I've ever heard one. Here, I got a picture of her." A Polaroid. Clipped inside the cover of Becker's note-book. He flipped it to Fletcher. "Not a bad looking girl. Your type, Rush."

Fletcher stared at it. "Where did you get this?"

"So he wants to know where I got it do he? Should I tell him sugar hips?"

"Why don't you tell me," Mona said, "and Rush will listen in."

Becker squealed his chair closer. "Best offer I've had all week but Rush should recognize the work of Curious George, his Boswell. I mean Rush is the Boswell. I think that's what I mean. Anyway the Curious one took it maybe last winter. It's an unusual approach as she's wearing clothes and no hand-cuffs. Maybe he's got one of you?"

"No, my dear Becker; I've got one of him."

That called for a drink. Becker made a toast in which no one joined him, throwing back the rest of his bourbon. His focus wandered as Fletcher held up the picture. "Shouldn't the cops have this, Paul."

"Ah, the heck with them. I got it off Rocky the day guy. He hates George."

"Any chance I can keep it for a while?"

"No chance at all whatsoever old pal nada." Becker plucked the Polaroid back. "No offense whatsoever either but you know what I mean."

"Just until I can get a copy made?"

"Noop; out of the el question. You tell him, Mona, matter of ethics involved here. Advertising know all about ethics. Don't you, cupcakes? There's a city on the hill and then there's the big rotten apple. That's right. Tell you what though fellow drudge. I won't breathe any of this to you, promise. Cross my heart."

Becker, crossing the wrong part of his chest, dropped the picture. Mona picked it up, looked at it, slipped it back in the notebook. "Is she really Rush's type or are you lying again you terrible man?"

"Sure is his type and I don't mean narcolepsy either sweets. Wait, hold on... do I mean narcolepsy?"

"I think you mean necrophilia," Mona said.

"Oh yes, yes, that is what I mean. Yes, especially the way you say it with such emphasis on... I'd love to have you whisper that in my armpit."

"But tell me, is she his type? Concentrate, Becker, you can do it."

Becker put his finger to his temple like the Scarecrow in *The Wizard of Oz*. "Sure I mean it... whatever it was. Our boy Fletcher here - where are you, Fletcher? Ah, there you are. Our boy Fletcher here likes cheerleaders with applesauce. Always has. Out where he comes from the cheerleaders have little beehive pies and perky little hush puppies that point straight up. It's all that sis-boom-bah that does it. Oh, it's something to see on the Fourth of July when you get them gassed up on root beer and Brylcreem and they beg for it. Lost his cherry behind a billboard you know, that's the real America. The cultural and sexual revolution, he passed that right by in his bumper car. Has a dog named Eisenhower...'

"I don't have a dog," Fletcher said, "and his name's not Eisenhower."

"Sure it is, I've seen it. Brings him Reader's Digest on a plate as soon as he gets home. Nice little Ike; nice little Ike. And his cat - did he ever tell you about his cat, Mona?"

"Nothing so far but you will, won't you?"

"Bet your boots... are you wearing boots?" He looked. "Yes, you are wearing boots. I must be psychic. I could make your boots very happy, Mona."

"Why don't you make Rush happy and give him the picture."

Becker drew a short almost sober breath. "Ganging up on me, huh? Sorry, I don't swing that way kids. But collect me if I am wrong but doesn't the New York Yokel, Defender of the - ah darn, I did that already. Isn't your man Harmon on this story? Let him go find you a nice picture of whoever this chick is.

Ask him."

Fletcher took out his wallet. "Harmon is in Queens fighting about a mortgage. Being black it takes up a lot of his time."

Becker was drifting again. "Whose fault is that... society? Nah, it's Scanlon. Harmon's leaving, the old goat shouldn't have assigned it to him."

"I suppose it hasn't worked out that well."

"Maybe it has," Mona said, "depending on your point of view."

A sharp look each way. "I don't understand."

"You're tired, Rush. Why don't you go home."

"I second that emotion," Becker said. "There's a lot I want to say to Mona and you know

I don't mean any of it."

"I know you don't mean it either," Mona said, "and that's what makes it all worthwhile."

"See, Rush? Made for each other. This might be the real thing for one of us."

Fletcher put ten dollars under the ashtray but Mona pushed the bill back. "It's my party," she said, "from start to finish."

"Thanks, but I'd just as soon chip in. That's how editorial does it."

"Thank you, I'll remember that." She did not smile. "Goodnight."

Becker had his chin in his hand. "Just in time, Rush. Mona's boots are getting cold."

Fletcher left by the side door. He started uptown and his mind did not remain with Fanelli's. It went on ahead. The lights were green but traffic was sluggish, taxis, a limousine, cars crowded with young people from outside Manhattan. He recalled the neighborhood when it was deserted at night, seemingly without danger. Now SoHo had tourists of its own, not simply overflow from the Village. They'd better get used to it. He had. Could he sleep at night above Bleecker and Macdougal without the restless katydid music below. He was not sure he could. On this night he said he would not. Once that meant he wouldn't go to another bar but would go home and sleep well and work in the morning. Often he did go to another bar and did not work well or work at all in the morning. Tonight he said he would not go back to the hotel. As it was he did. He turned out of his way and walked up Broadway. The bulldozers were silent, a security guard with a prop nightstick checking nothing because there was nothing to check. The cops were gone, sightseers too, a week, that's New York. Fletcher looked through the fence to where Spink's, the bar had been. The crash might have come one night when he was there, a harmless reflection as it had not. But there is more than one kind of crash, he thought, more than one kind of collapse. On another night he talked to her by the jukebox. There was a space between songs and out of the jukebox light on her teenage face she said I don't know anyone here. She had a black eye, a fresh one. So he asked her name but the music began again and she moved on to a darker part of the bar. She had a soft voice with an accent and now he knew her name was Vix.

Man Bites Beatnik

I moved to New York City to make it my home in the first week of May of 1960, two days after the musical *The Fantasticks* opened. This show is still running on Sullivan Street I find and so it seems am I. I've never seen *The Fantasticks* and perhaps I never shall but I look for its listing in The New Yorker and am pleased to come upon it each week like a smooth reminiscent stone in a boy's pocket. No, I have never seen that show as I never saw the wand that dropped a spell upon me that first spring. It will close someday I suppose as things do, as youth must fade and enchantment come to an end.

I was twenty-one when I moved here and that is so long ago a woman nightclub singer was still called a thrush in newspaper headlines. I know this because I read newspapers quite often, daily as it were. I wished to be a reporter and report on things. Who wouldn't? Yes, sounds simple I know (lion taming and glass blowing require some training) but appearances can be deceiving. (Save same for hard hitting editorial or memoir.) Take that girl sitting across from me in the Cafe Figaro where I am concocting gripping leads in my notebook. She is reading Atlas Shrugged and though there are three or four newspapers beside her on the radiator (the warmest table at the Figaro) she ignores them. By extension she wasn't the least bit interested in what sort of reporter I should be, rather cruel indifference when you think how important the matter was to myself. She would not raise her eyes my way as I tried to look pensive. If only she'd known how thwarted I was at the time. (Not that women, I've learned, respond much to thwart.) You see the outlook for becoming a war correspondent, my first choice, was not promising. The world, just my luck, was at an uneasy peace for the most part. If only she would look up at least once.

Oh, there was something going on in the Belgian Congo, but in fairness, it seemed kind of gruesome. It might not be for me. My notion of combat was drawn from the more genteel coverage of World War II: following the troops (not too close) in a netting covered helmet, talking idiomatic French, drinking rough red wine in quaint bistros, hobnobbing with the brass and my colleagues, and of course filing copy of a trenchant but highly readable nature. And all this at a favorable exchange rate too. Yes, a flesh wound and a Pulitzer and a worshipful European girl on my arm. The Congo on the other hand didn't seem to have bistros.

Domestically I hoped to be covering the political conventions coming up that summer. Arriving as I had from Warren Harding's home state I knew my way around an election. The insider's view I mean. Considering those credentials it wouldn't be necessary to mention my chairmanship of the prom committee in high school. I ran a tight ship and we had fifty dollars left over. The surplus was intended for new basketballs until it was suggested we give it to the needy. In a stroke of bipartisan genius I brokered buying new basketballs and giving several of the old ones to the needy. Compromise, I could now explain to a sincere but baffled electorate, is the essence of politics.

But the conventions came and went as I sat watching the first snow flurries on Bleecker Street. It was cold my first winter here; you may recall John Kennedy's inaugural breath. Just before commencement of the New Frontier I was camped one night in the Gaslight on MacDougal Street thinking of popping on down to Washington to offer my services to the incoming administration. They'd be pleased to have me I knew but working for the Democrats would not sit too well with my father who still alluded to Franklin Roosevelt as that man in the White House. (My father has admitted though that the Democrats have a knack of passing on their legacy while Republicans simply get out of town.) So it would be a ticklish thing working for JFK. My father might disown me and leave his General Motors stock to my more upright cousins who drilled with their Daisy rifles when China went red. Worse yet my father might learn I'd rung doorbells for Kennedy. (Not many but sufficient to stain my hands pink.) He would die and I would be ranked with the worst of mankind, a parricide. Later when the Vietnam War sat like a ticking bomb on the living room rug my father and I talked only about the Cincinnati Reds. He was wrong and I was right but that does not matter in this reckoning; not as it matters to me that he is dead and I am alive. I could not preach to my father then or he to me so we talked about the Reds instead. I assume baseball was invented for this purpose.

But to return to me entirely. I was in the Gaslight minding my own momentous business when myrmidons of the law appeared, as witty authors say, and reviewed the place as a health hazard. It wasn't really. It was rather a seedy coffee house where I went of an evening in search of women reading Bertolt Brecht. I'd been informed this was a good sign. The police said the premises were overcrowded. Well, they weren't overcrowded with young women, that's for sure. Now this raid had much to do with local politics and bribery. The Gaslight was no more hazardous than sleeping on your fire escape, if not as entertaining, and certainly no worse than other cafes where I spent my time looking sensitive and intense. (I'd decided intense was better than pensive.) The owner believed he was unfairly persecuted for not paying, or not paying enough, protection to the police and I believe he was right. But that is neither here nor there and I mention it only as it bears on my fascinating history. The police asked that we vacate and I, being from Ohio, was about to cheerfully comply when a radical patron leaped on a table top and urged that we sit in. Sit in, I ask you; as if the Gaslight were a Southern lunch counter and we Negroes.

This troublemaker then demanded impressively: what would Thoreau do? That was theoretical in the extreme in my view, Thoreau having been as abstemious fellow of regular hours and not likely to be caught hanging around the Gaslight trying to meet girls. More correct to ask: what would Falstaff do? And to this we could joyfully reply: let us go while the getting is yet warm from the oven. But this firebrand, twisting like Trotsky, answered his own question as his sort invariably do. We shall not be moved, he cried. Great. I could hear the police dogs baying outside, starved for fresh Ohio meat. I casually looked at my watch. My, where has the time gone? I must call home to see if Taffy has had her pups yet. But our madman insists on a human chain. When the tear gas hits, he advised, soak your handkerchief and stuff it in your mouth. Ah, go soak your head I thought. We waited. The tension was unbearable. The cops raised their billy clubs and scratched their heads beneath their caps. They were fed up. They'd taken about all they were going to. They left. I felt it wise to follow but our scout leader, shocked that we all had not been beaten senseless, proposed staying the night as a protest. As I seemed to be wavering - I was, in fact, wavering towards the exit, I was treated to a look that froze the marrow in my jellyfish bones. (Try telling my mother jellyfish don't have bones.) I sat down, too put out to care. He was flocked with admirers, the stinker, and I saw his game clearly. He too was there to meet girls.

The night wore on, innocent and somewhat tedious. Songs were sung and stories told. I amused myself by writing up everything, my own role downplayed in the interest of objectivity. And then a reporter from the *Times* arrived. He was godlike in my eyes. I studied his every movement and gesture. He wore chinos without cuffs, I'd get a pair the very next day. And his shoes, how worn they were, and mine so new looking. I'd bang them on the radiator for an hour when I got home. I knew of course it would take but a moment for his keen newshound eye to single me out as a fellow member of The Tribe. I'd fill him in on the big picture, save him some footwork. I'd show him my rough and fragmentary notes and he would say... why even in this rough and fragmentary state these notes reveal...

At least he would if he ever got the chance but our revolutionary leader is making another speech. And if that weren't bad enough an attractive young woman was gazing at Tom Paine with sympathetic tenderness - gazing down at him actually as he was really quite short, and she was clutching a Bertolt Brecht paperback. I was so mad I wanted to spit. He spoke to the reporter, no doubt engaged in rewriting history and exaggerating his own part therein. Fresh pencil and pocket sharpener at the ready I crept up behind. The man from the *Times* needed me. There are occasions when in the middle of the action you don't realize how important your story is. You must shed your participant status for a more modest Olympian view. But the reporter seemed to be leaving. I politely tugged at his coat. Some story, huh? He looked as if he'd just discovered an oyster in his corn flakes. Yeah, he said, beatniks and folksingers, right up there with the dog show. As the police had before him he left. Must be a three alarmer calling, I mused.

I was released at dawn after promising to return with blankets and a copy of the Constitution. Good riddance, I said. Back at my hotel room, that charming inkwell, I could not sleep. It was too early to begin banging my shoes on the radiator so I assembled my notes. I wrote out the story and wrote it out again and later when I went to the Figaro I took it with me. An acquaintance there told me of some trifling personal distress he hoped I could solve. I interrupted and gave him my story and clearly impressed he suggested I take it to the *Local*. They go for neighborhood stuff like that, said my tablemate. He was one of those irritating people who try to do you a good turn but don't know when to stop. Neighborhood, I said, this is of national importance. I waved my typescript in his face and stalked out.

As I happened to pass the *Local* office on my way to buy the right chinos I stopped to call on the editor. He was delighted to see me. Well, I began, I suppose you heard of all the excitement at the Gaslight last night. Why no, he coyly rejoined, did someone sing on key? We enjoyed a good laugh over that. Both of us knew the game and I had what he wanted. As he read his excitement was ill concealed. Is this true? Do you, I said, take me for a writer of fiction? He apologized but still wanted to play. Why bring it to me? Why do anything, I shot back, brutally. That brought him round. All right, he said, I think I can use this but you have to follow it up. He went on: what does the average beatnik on the street think of this? Got it, I said. No one cares of course, he said, but it's cheaper than a photograph. I'm on my way, I said. And I really thought I was.

My investigation into what did not come to be called Gaslightgate continued throughout the spring and summer of the first Kennedy year. Other espresso houses, nightclubs too, were beset by city officials attempting to close them down. It was a mayoral election year with the customary crackdowns on vice. The allegations of riot and mayhem around Bleecker and MacDougal were strained even by Ohio standards but it was true that local residents wished the noise and clutter reduced. Beatniks sat at little marble topped tables and wondered where they would go if the purges were successful. They did not know and the hip priest and jazz rabbi could not tell them. As the municipal wind harried them perhaps understood that something more inexorable than civic improvement was in the works. They saw that the blush of the beatnik time itself was nearly faded and they soon would go the way of the cast iron lampposts with only a few remaining on the streets as stark reminders of another era.

Yes, I was a muckraker to an extent and proud to be so. But as far as muck goes the Gaslight issue did not quite stink to high heaven. It had, for corruption, a not unpleasant smell like sphagnum moss. Still I thought it pretty putrid as I tried to explain to a girl at the Bigelow Pharmacy over grilled cheese and lime rickeys. I was positive we were headed for the kind of romance that leaves the rest of the world sick with envy. We were not it seems, especially after I went on at some length about the importance of my work. That stuff gives me a pain, she said. Another time, get this, I had a critical date with a girl who was a dancer and majoring in psychology so I don't have to tell you. I spent the day making myself look rumpled and after a nap with my clothes on I was perfect. We went to Folk City and for some godforsaken reason Bob Dylan was the opening act. It was his first billed performance and he did four or five songs. I thought he was awful, just terrible, really bad. I was about to be extremely amusing at his expense when I caught my date's expression. She was staring at Dylan like he was an orphan and she was Boys Town. As for me I might have been something put out by management to keep the chairs warm. But I tried to be generous. There must be fifty guys in Washington Square Park who can sing better than that, I said, and you can hear them for nothing. Well, maybe I should have put it another way. He looks so hungry, she said, and so rumpled. That hurt. Dylan looked like a bum and she wanted to take care of him. I was in a suit and tie and she wouldn't hold my hand. Listen, she said, why don't you write about him instead of that muck you're always going on about? But you don't understand, I said. I sure do, she said, and I'm getting his autograph.

The following morning found me in my editor's office. (He was called Chief to distinguish him from the rest of humanity, with which he had little in common. He was assisted by a man I shall call Duffy as that was his name.) You see I had a number of suggestions to make the paper more contemporary and international in scope. Chief, I said, I want to write about music. The chief seemed to develop a sudden twitch. What's that, music? You know, Duffy said, like when you got married each time, there was a band. There wasn't a band in West Virginia, the chief said; there was a fifth of Scotch but there wasn't a band. I forgot about that one, Duffy said. Her lawyers haven't, the chief said.

I attempted to bring the conversation back to me. But chief, I said, I have a… Listen kid, the chief said, I know you worked on your college paper but try as I might I've never held that against you. If we (the editorial we) ever have to cover a soapbox derby, a broken gravy boat or a defrocked homecoming queen you're the man I want. Yes, chief, but… Just don't tell me, he continued, don't ever tell me, tell me anything else, but don't ever tell me you have… Don't worry, chief, I said, I have a fresh perspective. With these fatal words the chief's twitch increased but then his eyes sawed me in two. He

ripped off his tie and tore open his shirt and there on his chest was the most resplendent tattoo I have ever seen. It was The Great Seal of the United States of America. The chief beckoned me closer. Written on the unfurled banner clutched in the eagle's terrible beak were words I have never forgotten...
Fresh Perspectives Don't Sell Newspapers!

Sadly, I still had not learned my lesson for the day. You bet chief, I said, and don't worry, you won't be disappointed. I soon knew I'd said the wrong thing. The chief stood up, I'd never seen his legs before. Grabbing me by the lapels I was raised aloft until my head was even with the transom. He spoke as follows:

One day, kid, I knew I would never run the Herald Tribune. But now I have a paper, don't ask me how or why. My readership won't fill Yankee Stadium. And what readers they are. I've got college professors, parlor pinks, beatniks, ham radio nuts, witches and warlocks, broken down hoofers and out of work mezzo-sopranos, a burlesque queen, Swedenborgians, my ex-wives and a flea circus on Cornelia Street. I've got every headshrinker, failed novelist, sourdough crackpot, ban the bomber, actor from Sheboygan, saxophone player, reformed con artist, flagpole sitter, rooming house philosopher and cafeteria egghead in the whole damn Village. What I don't have is a sports page, stock quotations, a sob sister, crossword puzzle, laugh of the day, horoscopes, household hints, Weegee photographs of dead gangsters or a reactionary, red baiting gossip columnist who can't spell. In other words I don't have anything that makes a New York newspaper real. But I have you and you tell me I won't be disappointed.

The chief released me and I fell to the floor. Duffy, he said, how come we never have any cheesecake? Just one little picture of Betty Grable is all I ask. We have integrity, Duffy said. I don't want integrity, the chief howled, I want Ava Gardner on cantaloupe. Listen to me, Duffy, this is what I ask before I go to that great newsroom in the sky. I want a train wreck, Duff, with all the trimmings. I wanted twisted steel, a sleepy engineer, a courageous colored porter whose name we won't print and gore, buckets of it, Duff. I want Gasoline Alley and Barney Google. I want elephants in the Lincoln Tunnel, a gypsy caravan in the Polo Grounds, a rich widow and the shoeshine boy, a lost wedding ring from Sheepshead Bay that turns up in a rump roast on Fordham Road. Do I have to spell it out for you, Duffy? I want vice, scandal and monkey business I can kick off my shoes and run barefoot through. God help me, when was the last time we had a headline with Sloe-Eyed Call Girl in it?

As the chief collapsed weeping on his desk I felt this had happened before. I'll get the medicine, Duffy said. It was kept in the bottom drawer of a file cabinet. A touch of fever, the chief said, it comes and goes. He asked me to leave but as I turned I thought I heard him speak. Yes, chief, I said, did you say something? Nothing, he said, nothing. But when he believed I was gone I heard him whisper again words that will stay with me forever.

BARE GOP HAVANA LOVE JUNKET

Yet they kept me on and to this day I'm not sure why. I began to write a weekly column in a condition of happy mischief. It is a small authority a column, like being the high priest of hell week who adds to the scavenger list of quaking freshmen a passenger pigeon and the last words of Calvin Coolidge. I failed to realize it was I who was the most junior member of the fraternity, that it was I who was hazed and made ridiculous. My colleagues understood they had a live one. I did not. But like a Klondike uncle this man Duffy bequeathed his estate to me and if I have squandered the substance with pretentiousness and easy living the fault is mine. When he read my copy over my shoulder he sometimes said: maybe it ain't you, maybe it's the ribbon. And then he would walk off, comforted by the sound of paper torn from the carriage. Duffy, may he rest in peace, was harder to please than my father.

I called my column *Straight No Chaser* after a Thelonious Monk composition I used to hear in the cool rathskeller of my college. I found it too hip for words but no one else ever has and I still get complaints about it. You can't, they say, write about Lou Reed or The Dead Kennedys in a column with a hokey name like that. I'm pleased to recall though that Duffy liked it. Straight No Chaser, he said over my shoulder, that's pretty good; reminds me of a tip sheet they had years ago called The Horse's Mouth. For his part the chief referred to my column as the Shirley Temple or the raspberry frappe. He mentioned it sideways about once a year when he asked: I see by the masthead that you still work here, why is that?

I was never sure. The trouble is you get so attached to that which will not remain. These people, this place, a job. This city, New York, has a failing memory all its own with unforgettable encounters of recall. The remodeling is continuous but uneven and as these small or large bites of the apple are taken you may still see, as in Madison Square, a fire alarm box or stately clock that a horse drawn omnibus once passed. The century here turns around each corner. My first Christmas in the city, to be a New Yorker, I went to Herald Square for my shopping. As I left Macy's through the eternally revolving doors I came upon cobblestones and trolley tracks. They were still there then and I felt for a moment in the chestnut smoke that I could buy an Evening Sun with a dime and ride the streetcar home with the change. The streets were asphalted not long after, a change I regret to say I did not notice until it was pointed out to me.

Do you see what I mean? Perhaps not. I meant to say that for people like me this runaway timepiece of a city was pleasant to behold because of a security we secretly harbored, the stationary calm of our hometowns that we paid into and borrowed on like a life insurance policy. And yet on my last Ohio visit my Saturday afternoon Main Street wore a different face. It was quiet as a Sunday morning. Stores were boarded up and others seemed lifeless. When I asked I was told well, it's either go under or go out to the Mall. You ought to see the Mall, I heard, it's something all right. But it was something I didn't want to see. My town was always close behind me but there is distance now like those friends from whom we part because one or both of us was unwilling to work at it. Because we could not hack it downtown we've gone out to the Mall in search of something newer or better or more deluxe. It may be there but we don't hear it in the easy listening music or see it in the fluorescent pools or find it on the map declaring you are here and J. C. Penney's is there. Personally I don't find a map that says you are here and Penney's is there to be much of a guide. A voice from nowhere compels you to follow the camel to the holiday display and like a fool you do though it saddens you to see a manger and wise men between the Swiss Shack and the Belgian waffles. You know this relationship you're having out at the Mall is sterile and unrewarding but it's so tough downtown with all those hard hearts and broken windows.

So I come back to New York because it is my home now and I am no longer indifferent to change. I feel protective of the city's older design and look with pleasure for the ornaments of the past still hanging from its boughs, long past their season. My mother read a magazine article once while her hair was drying about a young man from a good family who became a gigolo in New York and drank champagne from a lady's slipper. She worried about me. And my father asked if I intended to join the ranks of The Wall Street Journal by writing about degenerate poets, musicians and saloon keepers in the "Village". When my father said "Village" you could hear the quotations marks rattle like loaded dice in a cup. So he worried too. But I had by then a widening sense of limitations and could say there was never any need for concern. I assured them it was not at all what my life had been. I was as small town as ever. Indeed I can prove it. I sat down one day on the front porch of Manhattan with a fair piece of lumber and my pocket knife and whittled away to such a point I do not know where the time has gone.

The Local... Making All The Stops

At Saturday's staff meeting Scanlon removed Ellis Harmon from the Broadway Central story and gave what was left of it to Lindquist. Harmon wasn't there, the gracious Scanlon having told him to tend to his wife and mortgage in Queens with all blessings. It inclined one to say gee, chief, damn white of you. Whenever you got Scanlon's blessing, delivered with his choicest big top bluster (he might even stand up) it was not out of order to check your wallet and count your fingers. Didn't matter in this case. Harmon was now on the other side of that forbidding geographic divide, the East River, beyond the grasping reach of his editor. *The Local* was seldom seen in Queens and as a result Scanlon did not much care what went on there. (Kitty Genovese and the airports excepted. *The Local* had hammered for years for direct rail links to JFK and Laguardia and the Genovese murder still hurt nine years later.) If anyone tried to sell him on Queens they received the penetrating death ray usually reserved for clergymen and academics. Bestowed once it was not a dismissal you risked again. (When Duffy married late in life and moved to his wife's apartment in Sunnyside Scanlon mildly asked if many inoculations were required.) No, Harmon could not be safer on a slow boat to Philadelphia.

Fletcher wished to remark from the comfort of his orange scoop that giving Lindquist the hotel would not sharpen the focus. Scanlon, however, forestalled comment by an extended grouse, touching on favored topics like company loyalty and well, company loyalty. He was sorry to say Rose Agosto had resigned, very sorry indeed. Head bowed 45 degrees, he looked agreeably stricken as the semi-circle facing him murmured surprise. Yet from his scoop of vantage Fletcher noted the murmurers did not include Paige Phillips or her assistant, Jackie, or Gayle Romanov, the Washington reporter. (Romanov was an infrequent Saturday disciple. Given a choice, she said, between the heat and hot air in D.C. and the heat and Scanlon in New York the judges were unanimous, it was Congress with a perfect ten.) Nor did the copyreader Judy Frisch raise her head at the announcement. (She was new. Rothberg was trying to call her Judy Blue Eyes but it wasn't catching on as her eyes were brown.) Fletcher concluded that in some circles at least the news about Agosto was not news at all. Perhaps Mona told them or they knew the same way she did. He hadn't said anything and certainly the old man would not. Walking out on the paper was walking out on Scanlon. He wouldn't let it be known if he could help it until the departure could be placed in its proper historical setting. This would include tastefully arranged mirrors and the indecent implication that Agosto quit because she was about to be fired.

Fletcher tried twice to tell Scanlon about his conversation with Agosto's roommate. He'd even said lover, causing an editorial eyebrow leap (the All High had perhaps the most acrobatic eyebrows on the planet) but that was all the reaction he got. But roommate or lover, Scanlon wasn't listening. Don't bring me hearsay, he squawked, you were supposed to speak to the little lady yourself. That was Friday morning and Fletcher was not inclined to pursue. But following Mona's information Friday night he tried again with his boss before Saturday's meeting. This was no better but Fletcher, indecisive, was to blame. He was uncertain how much Scanlon, a well known hothead, should know. You could never be sure with him. On the one hand he might declare it all malarkey, Agosto was imagining things, no man on "our staff" would pull that kind of stuff. Alternatively, he'd believe it, hit the ceiling, and set about finding the guy in a typically clumsy, gumshoe way. The scenario grew grimmer. Scanlon might try to rattle it out of Agosto's friends; he might haul everyone into his office and bellow until the guilty party confessed. Fletcher could just hear him. "All right, if whoever made this mess doesn't own up right now like a man there'll be no turkeys this Thanksgiving and no boat ride next June." As ham handed potentates everywhere like to threaten they'd all suffer for the actions of one. So it could go either way. The most erratic of geysers, there was no telling when Old Steam Kettle would blow.

As it was Fletcher did not have to decide what to say or how to say it because Scanlon waved him off with an "after Labor Day" grimace. Two strikes and you're out, Fletcher conceded, revising the rules. If Scanlon wanted Agosto back then the big gringo would have to go get her on his own. And if all he really wanted was her press pass and the admission she was leaving for personal reasons, something like "female trouble" comes to mind, that was all right too. They could both go to hell. Fletcher had an eye ache, his admission to having drunk too much beer, and he'd awoken with Becker's mockery of the *Local* on his mind. No doubt Becker had awoken with Mona. Thinking about Mona ruined the flavor, not that there was much, of his two weak cups of Maxwell House. She probably despised him because he did not drink espresso. (And he did not dress like his father. His father almost always wore a tie.) With nothing to contribute Fletcher didn't want to sit through the meeting; he didn't want to watch Scanlon pencil poking his half eaten roll and butter into the debris on his desk; he didn't want to… He wanted to go home. The temperature had fallen to the 80's, he might get some work done. As soon as Scanlon commenced to drone Fletcher felt he was slipping back to immortal algebra. He might be fourteen again and staring out at the trees beyond the schoolyard. There are some who insist algebra never ends and maybe they are right.

And the staff meeting was not quite scooting along. They generally proceeded from Scanlon's mood and his mood for once was deliberate. He looked disappointed with his Agosto bombshell, seemingly a dud. The men it appeared were unconcerned and the women kept their own counsel. Scanlon paused, ear cocked, awaiting a response, any at all. Like an actor in possession of all the good lines Scanlon was distressed by the flubs of his fellow players when it ruined his own timing. The stage was where he belonged. You could picture him striding across the boards in purple tights to wring a soliloquy by the neck until there wasn't a drop of dramatic ooze remaining. Clearly there was something more to say about Agosto but he was professionally waiting for his cue. It did not come and the groaning pause grew so wide it might swallow them all. Scanlon told Baines to take up the front page.

Fletcher yawned, excused himself. At his desk he pretended to look through his files. He'd never walked out on a meeting before but it wouldn't be walking out if he went right back. But another hour or two of that, unbearable, he couldn't breathe in there. Giving the Broadway Central to Lindquist was not only stupid, it was insulting. Somebody said it's a pancake but I didn't get what they meant. What was the good of arguing? You either got blasted and told to mind your own business or you got the comforting arm around the back and the "yes, yes, lad, I understand, but he has to learn too". Duffy would never have stood for it. They weren't a newspaper anymore, they were a house organ, a pennysaver, the yearbook of Greenwich Village High. No, it hadn't worked out that well. But maybe it has, Mona said, depending on your point of view. Fletcher finished his charade of searching his files and sat with his hands on his knees. Rothberg's mission was not long in coming.

"Uncle Scrooge wants to know where you're at."

There was no good excuse. "Tell him you heard I went home."

"He won't like that, Rush."

No, he would not. Monday morning the intra-office envelope on Fletcher's desk read Open Me First. He didn't. He drank his coffee from the Zeus Brothers and thought about Maria Schneider. She was the actress in *Last Tango in Paris* and all things being equal he would as soon sleep with her as win a Pulitzer for distinguished commentary or the Cy Young for distinguished right handed pitching. Having worked well Saturday after ditching the meeting and most of Sunday afternoon Fletcher went uptown to what New Yorkers were not calling Dry Dock Country to see Last Tango at the Trans-Lux East. Dry Dock Savings Bank had a campaign pushing themselves as the heart and soul of the neighborhood around 59th Street and Lexington Avenue and if the hoi polloi began calling it Dry Dock Country that would suit them just fine. Admittedly the area didn't have a name other than "around Bloomingdale's" but Dry Dock Country wasn't going to fly any better than the city designating Sixth Avenue the Avenue of the Americas. Calling Sixth Avenue the Avenue of the Americas was like wearing plaid Bermuda shorts in Times Square. It tended towards the conspicuous.

Last Tango was five dollars, a lot for a movie, about the same as a balcony seat on Broadway. After some debate he borrowed the money from his typewriter fund because he liked Bertolucci films and Brando was in it and Brando wasn't in much anymore and Fletcher thought Brando was all right. He knew this at fifteen watching On the Waterfront and never changed his mind. Tango was an exclusive showcase or premiere engagement or some such thing and that's why it was five bucks as opposed to two-fifty around the corner for *Serpico* or the latest James Bond. It also had notoriety being about sex and depressing sex at that.

Fletcher was disappointed with it. Paris seemed bleak and uninspiring and Brando old and tired though maybe Paris was intended to be so and Brando the same. The story was tough to follow. Brando is a painter named Paul getting over or not getting over the death of his wife. Maybe she killed herself, maybe not. The painter establishes a sexual gambol with Rosa, a young woman played by Maria Schneider. She is perhaps everything middle age slump can ask. She visits and then goes way again. On the plump side, the actress appeared to live on bouillabaisse, whipped cream and chocolate. It had been a long summer. Fletcher was excited right down to the bottom of his buttered popcorn. The film slipped away otherwise and by the end he was twining his hair around an index finger, an indication of boredom. Only Brando's mystifying death scene where the former Wild One delicately disposes of a piece of gum before expiring brought Fletcher back to attention. It was a great actor's grace note, like a horn player signing off with a dweet doo dah all his own.

When he exited, deflated, into the eventide of Dry Dock Country a woman handed him a leaflet. The bold print condemned Last Tango as pornography. Fletcher accepted it out of politeness and did not read the rest until he was waiting for the traffic light to change. He went back to the woman and stood until the rest of the audience came out. She was not aggressive at leafleting. The real pros, seasoned by years of anti-war activity, blocked your path until you took what they were shoving. She stepped back too much and the crowd went past her.

Fletcher didn't think Last Tango was pornagraphic. For one thing he'd watched it, intrigued at times, and he had no interest in pornography. That was peep shows, or Variety Photoplays on Second Avenue, or *Times* Square. It was a grainy home movie passed around in college of a girl on a bed with her legs apart masturbating with a Clan MacGregor bottle. He saw this at a stag party senior year, it was not very erotic. (But memorable in a sense, he thought of it when he saw that brand of Scotch.) The home movie was followed by a Donald Duck cartoon. As it flickered past, Fletcher's roommate turned to him and whispered: I think I'm getting hard.

The woman with the leaflets was about fifty. I don't think this movie is pornographic, Fletcher said. As she turned towards him he saw a Women Against Rape button on her blouse. How, she said, did it make you feel? Fletcher was confused. I don't understand, he said, what do you mean? About me, she said, how did it make you feel about me? But I don't know you, he told her, I've never seen you before. Not combative, he did not want to argue. He wanted to say that *Last Tango in Paris* was not pornography on any level of his experience. Obviously a film costing millions of dollars and made by conscientious artists was not the same as something in a brown paper wrapper. She might want to take that into consideration. About me, the woman said again, how did it make you feel about me? A line was forming for the next show. There were couples holding hands, women together. Look, he wished to say, look at these people here, they aren't... Instead he said he was late for an appointment and he took the train home.

Nursing his Zeus Brothers coffee at his desk Fletcher wondered if Maria Schneider had made other movies. He flipped the intra-office envelope over and back, there was something stiff inside. Was she French or German? German was too reminiscent of Elke, maybe the actress was French. Schneider meant tailor in German he was sure. There were Taylors in Monacacy Court House. His father told him they changed their name from Schneider during World War I. Schneider was a Duffy expression. They schneindered them good, he'd say when one team beat another. It was from a card game, gin maybe. Fletcher looked at his calendar. From the day Duffy told him he'd "come down with cancer" he said he wouldn't stay after the older man died. Now he'd let the months go by and Harmon had beaten him to the punch. And now with Agosto gone it was harder still. Scanlon would string him along with promises but never send him on assignment. He'd have to quit. He hated the word. He'd never quit anything in his life except his paper route and that he still regretted. (The boy who succeeded him, his mother said, was doing very nicely with a Cincinnati law firm.) But there was a choke collar around his neck, he had to quit.

Fletcher swiveled, stared at Scanlon's door. He should bust in and have it out with the old man once and for all. What they would have it out about he wasn't sure but they'd have it out about something. And then he would walk, or run, a free man and not come back. Too bad Scanlon was busy at the moment. He was hunkered down with his son-in-law, Chuck, the not blatantly successful ad man. Chuck was married to Scanlon's favorite child, youngest daughter Angie; a girl most likely to succeed who proved them wrong by her choice of husband. Chuck (short for Chapman and not for Chucklehead as Scanlon insisted) worked for Bascomb & Bascomb, a Park Avenue South advertising agency whose clients included a pet cemetery on Long Island and

Paraguay. (The exquisite full beat that Scanlon inserted between Park Avenue and South when mentioning the agency was all one could ask of Manhattan snobbery.) Chuck might have improved his position at Bascomb by marrying the boss's daughter (he was like that) but unfortunately he was already married to the daughter of the only account he'd ever brought to the firm. As his father-in-law liked to say Chuckles had one foot in Paraguay and the other on a banana peel.

The Local… We Make All The Stops. Fletcher hated that slogan. They'd been using it for six years and it seemed in no danger of being replaced. It was Chuck's idea, one of his few. Engaged to Angie at the time and feeling his oats he pestered Scanlon about his attitude towards advertising. This attitude simply put was: I don't need it and neither does my paper. A well written, well edited newspaper will sell, a poorly written, poorly edited one will not; that is all ye know on earth and all ye need to know. Better dogmatism than this a millionaire's money can't buy but it did not appease an on the make advertising man-child. Chuck asked his bride-to-be to interfere and she respectfully approached her father. Daddy, she said, you are a crumb, first class. Scanlon was sorry to hear it. Besides being waist deep in the regret and shattered crockery of the third and least illustrious of his marriages, Angie alone of the three children he shared with his first wife treated him with any affection. He didn't want to be in her doghouse too. So he relented to a degree and dipped a toe, a very small one, in the whirlpool of publicity. Chuck was thrilled but if he was expecting largesse he got something rather less. Remember, Scanlon instructed, anything worth doing is worth doing cheaply just to show them how good you are. Good natured Chuck didn't believe him and that was only his first mistake.

Fletcher went through his mail. In keeping with his contrary mood he ignored Open Me First and ignored the usual press releases and music industry puffs. Not much of interest. A half-dozen letters reminded him that he didn't know what he was talking about, one or two above the norm. His sour comments on Watkins Glen (and in retrospect he agreed they were pretty sour) would be a lively source of self-doubt in the coming weeks as participants sobered up and told him where to get off. No matter what Scanlon said the *Local* was often read long after publication. Back issues floated around coffee shops, bars and barber shops and Fletcher received communications beginning: "While waiting to have my hair cut yesterday…". Columns a year old came back to haunt him. It was like hearing about something you said when drunk.

The Local… We Make All The Stops. Not as pretentious maybe as Dry Dock Country but for sheer repetitiveness it was up there with *I Got My Job Through The New York Times.* Presented with Scanlon's notion of an ample advertising budget, hardly enough to hire sandwich board men, Chuck fulfilled himself like a poet liberated by the confines of the sonnet form. His plan, it was genius really, was to present the *Local* as a kind of spicy information guide: where to go in New York for a legal good time, *La Dolce Vita* style.

(Scanlon: What's this la dolce vita stuff that nitwit is going on about? Fletcher: It's an Italian movie, chief, about social decay. Scanlon: Oh sweet Jesus, this is just what I was afraid of.)

Chuck began crashing staff meetings to "get a feel for the place" so he could better understand "what was needed". Scanlon so much enjoyed hearing what his paper "needed" it gave him a facial tic not pleasant to behold. Fletcher likened Chuck's dogged determination to that of an Arctic explorer, an enterprise the adman might soon find himself pursuing. Scanlon chewed pencils in half and positioned his daughter's photograph so her eyes would not be upon him as he contemplated the awful things he wanted to do to Chuck. The articulation of these awful things made the editor's face light up like a whiff of airplane glue.

Scanlon cursed the day his daughter went to work for Cosmopolitan. A magazine of all things, and worse, a woman's magazine. (If Scanlon kept a dartboard he might have put Helen Gurley Brown on it.) Yet he admitted he had no one to blame but himself. He'd let Angie go to Sarah Lawrence instead of locking her in the root cellar and that's what you got. Sarah Lawrence was full of vipers who would introduce you to a ten watt bulb like Chapman. (Angie: He likes to be called Chuck, daddy. Scanlon: I imagine he would, dear.) Short of having the errand boy of Bascomb & Bascomb shanghaied, a scheme greatly appealing to the Long John Silver of the HMS *Local*, Scanlon could think of nothing to waylay the engagement. Angela was in love with the chowderhead, that's all there was to it. Why she couldn't marry money for her father's sake (if not for her own) was a mystery. There were so many rich and useful families with sons just as dopey and useless as Chapman, his little girl could have had her pick of them. His oldest Veronica had married in this way but it did the old man no good, they hadn't spoken for years.

It was Scanlon's fond hope that Angie would join the *Local*. A few decades under his protective wing and she'd be ready for real responsibility. Early retirement at one hundred, make that one hundred and ten, had always been Scanlon's dream. Angie could assume the reins then, she wouldn't be a day over sixty, and all would be as dynastic as one could wish. (The summer she actually did intern, before Sarah Lawrence turned her to stone, Fletcher saw her put her hand to Scanlon's forehead when she thought he was running a fever. Never before had Fletcher realized his boss might be subject to illness like other people or that he could be touched without electric shock.) Luridly, the fiendish editor held a desire that his daughter and Fletcher might take a shine to each other. Arranged marriages were his cup of tea; an arranged marriage over which he would exercise control, as his son-in-law's boss, was his cup of tea with a shot of Canadian in it. But there was no attraction between them. Angie was an Upper East Side girl, she found it grubby downtown (the *Local* was in its Fourteenth Street digs then) and Rush Fletcher struck her as a rube. She didn't say rube, she said he was a darling. But she meant he was a rube. Her father, foiled, lamented the willfulness of children.

Losing his daughter to Chuck was one thing but Scanlon loathed having him near his newspaper. All those cardboard advertising dummies could be ignored (and were) but having the flesh and blood advertising dummy uninvited at staff meetings was intolerable. Chuck sealed his doom one Saturday by innocently asking: why don't we have restaurant reviews? Bringing up restaurants was bad enough, Scanlon believed writing about food to be on a moral par with arson and looting, but the plural usage galled him. The owner of the *Local* wanted his writers to say "we"; he wanted his readers to say "we"; but Chuckles was neither. He was instead that irritating bonehead his overeducated, spiteful daughter was marrying and he had no right to say "we". Scanlon no longer cared if Angie called him a crumb. He'd gnaw a solitary bone in any doghouse she chose but that wedding cake imbecile was not getting a foothold on the New York *Local*. Chuck was banished from editorial and everywhere else. As recompense Scanlon increased the ad budget until it rivaled what the paper spent on rubber bands and Duffy's daily carnation. Chuck was charged to create a subway campaign that would be the talk of the town. And he did. It was *The Local*... We Make All The Stops - and there it had been for six years.

So it was out of the ordinary to find Scanlon holed up with his son-in-law. They'd been in there for an hour with the door closed. Fletcher wondered if Scanlon had greeted Chuck in the customary jesting manner, the jest being to ask after the health of the General. The General was General Alfredo Stroessner, the President For Life of Paraguay. It was Scanlon's delight (he had few and this was one of his dearest) to tell anyone that Paraguay's dictator never made a move without consulting his right hand man in New York, Chuck. The fact that Chuck had nothing to do with Bascomb & Bascomb's Paraguay account made the joke, if that's what it was, all the more fun. Fletcher once attended a dinner party at Scanlon's featuring not a few guests unfamiliar with their host's sense of family high jinks. Tell me, the old man said to Chuck, what is the General really like? Scanlon lengthily described a repressive fascist regime transformed into Disneyland through the magic of American advertising. It was arch and made everyone uncomfortable. It was beyond Chuck to respond in like manner. Scanlon ate him up and lingered over the scraps. All Chuck desired was to sell toothpaste and play tennis and for this he was held in contempt. You might deserve it after all but if you didn't spit in his eye now and then Scanlon only thought the less of you.

The raveled string of the intra-office envelope snapped as Fletcher tugged at it. They were as old as the paper itself, the remaining 11 x 14 manilas, smeared with a generation of ink: creased, frayed, and coffee stained. The good luck gift of a stationer in 1956 the envelopes were embossed with the *Local*'s first address, 99 Fourth Avenue, near the Cooper Station post office. At the time the building belonged to the family of Scanlon's second wife, a small time pharmaceutical bunch who enjoyed backing odd causes. Scanlon presented himself as a cause, which of course he was not. He was a man whose aspiration in life was to own a newspaper and if he had to make himself out a ban the bomb, bleeding heart, anti-establishment gadfly then so be it. Some of that was in him anyway but mostly he believed in a good story and getting it across. That marriage ended shortly after and some suggested that was no coincidence.

Fletcher never worked at 99 Fourth, the *Local* had moved to Union Square by his arrival, but he recalled the manila envelopes when they were relatively new. Not pristine certainly but far from the faded limp survivors of 1973. They were still firm back then, cleanly buff colored, with bakery strings that wrapped around secure paper buttons. Now the buttons were mostly gone and the strings unraveling. Fletcher was beginning to hoard them. He had three good samples in his bottom drawer and this one marked Open Me First wasn't bad. The buttons were okay and he could fix the string with a staple. He was perhaps as fond of them as Scanlon was. Martinis at lunch and the sight of 99 Fourth Avenue atop an out box upon his return could reduce the editor-in-chief to creamed corn. He'd loved it at 99 Fourth when everyone did as they were told. Those were the days.

Shaking the envelope as he opened the flap a photograph fell out. It was the Polaroid of Vix. An index card followed. "Would you do as much for me? Kisses, Mona." He picked them up, shuffled them, dropped them back on the desk. The newsroom coffee was not as good as the Zeus Brothers but he went to the machine and refilled his blue cardboard cup with the Greek vase on one side. It was he always assumed a generic Greek vase. He sat down and looked at Vix. Nothing on the back. It was hard to write on Polaroids. They were very American, the other America. Immediate, they felt like plastic, like an office party hug. Warhol and Ansel Adams worked with it, Mahaffy would not. He said using a Polaroid was like fucking a mannequin. And he spoke, he said, from experience. Fletcher turned Vix face down. A few afternoons in the sun spot on his desk and she would vanish forever.

Scanlon's door opened, the editor sounding mirthful. It was insincerity piercing like ammonia, evidently Chuck was getting the treatment. The happy couple (Chuck was clucking too) glided down the aisle like a used car salesman and his mark in a lot full of clinkers. Fletcher wanted to pick up his phone with a quick "yes, Mr. Mayor" but didn't get the chance.

"Say, Rush boy, look who's here a-visiting."

There was nothing worse, literally nothing worse, than Scanlon's occasional affectation of what he considered country bumpkin talk. Fletcher extended his hand. "Haven't seen you for a while, Chuck."

Chuck had a Mark Cross briefcase, a light Brooks Brothers suit with the precise amount of shirtsleeve showing, opal cufflinks with a pinkish tinge. He didn't wear a wedding ring. "Angela was just asking about you the other day."

Why do people say those things? "Give her my best." Why do they say that?

"Old Chuck here has some great ideas for that new ad campaign you and I have been kicking around, Rush. We'll all be working together on this."

Fletcher didn't recall "kicking around" any such thing with the exalted one. And old Chuck never had a great idea in his life. And what was this "working together" business? Was Scanlon really trying to drive him insane?

"The chief is a natural at communication," Chuck gushed.

Scanlon glowed like a red lollipop. If they'd been smooching like this for an hour in his office it's a wonder they still had clothes on. "Yeah," Fletcher said, "he's always talked a good game."

The smile of the benevolent master of communication turned to parchment. He re-cocked his elbow to lead Chuck away.

"Still single, Rush? You guys have got it made these days."

Chuck winked as Scanlon led him off, a victim of the forceful glad hand. The comradely wink did not leave Fletcher feeling warm inside. It made him uneasy like locker room towel snapping. Chuck had a way of making the most timeless expressions of male kitchy-koo awkward both for himself and their object. It was if they were written down on that perfect shirtsleeve to be delivered when the demographic was right. He did not have the spontaneous knack of carrying them off. Still that only reflected on his sales approach, which stank, his soul for all they knew might be as pure as Ivory Snow. And maybe he meant what he said about being single. Scanlon was not above implying, he was not above anything, that his daughter's marriage was not a happy one. This state of affairs did not displease him. The master of communication was also a master of the veiled, one might even say hooded, innuendo. Some sort of inadequacy involved, he'd hint; it left you ashamed of yourself and, just like a newspaper, wanting more.

Scanlon was not gone long. He might be cuddling up to his son-in-law for some reason but the welcome relief of an inviting elevator was impossible to resist. Scanlon did not try. Prodding Chuck through the closing doors he turned swiftly on his Johnston & Murphy heel without saying goodbye. Fletcher saw him coming.

"What was all that about?"

"What was all what about?"

"You and Chuck and that beautiful music you were making…"

"Rush, I've misjudged that boy."

"No you haven't. He's still Chapman, the toast of Paraguay."

Scanlon looked aggrieved. "Do you ever stop to think, Rush, that our Chuck might be a little tired of those Paraguay jokes by now?"

There was no arguing with Scanlon but you had to try. "They're your Paraguay jokes, John, you invented them."

"What happened to you on Saturday?"

Adroit, you don't hear the gears. "I went home."

"I know that. Why?"

What could you tell him? "Because I was sitting there, John, and I knew I had nothing to say. Nothing at all."

Scanlon was ready. "It's a staff meeting, lad. You don't have to chip in. All you have to do is listen to me."

"Lindquist, John. How could you put Lindquist on the story?"

Scanlon looked as if he were trying to recall something distant from the days of boola boola and bathtub gin. "That's the hotel you mean?"

"You know damn well it's the hotel I mean."

"What the hell is wrong with you? You're acting like a sissy, walking out on me like that. You would never have done that to Tom."

He meant Duffy. "Duffy would never have let you give the job to Lindquist."

"Lindquist, Lindquist; what is this? Do I have to take you to St. Vincent's to have Lindquist removed from your brain? I'm surprised at you, lad. Is this personal? Have you something against him... something I should know?"

"It has nothing to do with Lindquist, John."

"Then why do I keep hearing his name? Now is it you feel threatened by him? How could you even think such a thing? I couldn't get along without you. I was calling you all weekend, worried. Where were you for God's sake?"

Fletcher couldn't lie. It would be the same as lying to his father. "I disconnected the phone because I didn't want to talk to you."

"Now why wouldn't you want to talk to your old boss who only wants..."

"Don't play me, John, don't play me like that. Tell me the truth - why are we falling down on the Broadway Central? They're getting away with it, you know that. You used to be on fire with a story like this. If we can't do anything, all right, but we can try. They're happy it fell down. It's like an old man who tells you he's worth more dead than alive."

Scanlon grinned. "I trust that's not a reference to me."

"They'll walk on this, John, you know they will. The owners will collect the insurance and sell the land and thank their lucky stars."

"It won't be the first time, lad."

"The first time, is that what you say now? The first time I walked around the Village with you we were on Greene Street and you said this is the Asch Building and Triangle Shirtwaist was on the ninth floor. And you told me what happened. I'd never heard any of it before. And you told me they walked. The men who ran the place walked. And you said that's why we're here so it won't happen in our time. That's why we're here, John. You said it yourself. But we're here and we're not doing anything."

Late morning and the newsroom was filling. Scanlon turned left and right, nodding hello, spruce in his pinstripe and blue grounded paisley tie. Turning back to Fletcher's desk something caught his eye. He reached out so sharply he knocked over the empty Zeus Brothers coffee cup. It was the manila envelope he wanted.

"99 Fourth Avenue," he said, "now those were the days."

"They're falling apart too," Fletcher said.

"What? These?" Scanlon did not agree. "Some things do but these were well made. You can't get envelopes like this now." He continued to poke about the desk with a finger, looking his seventy years, looking more. He lighted on the photo of Vix. "Someone I don't know about?"

Fletcher shook his head. "The girl they dug out of the Broadway Central bar."

Scanlon turned the Polaroid over, flipped it back on the desk. "A chippy probably. There's no story in that."

He straightened up, stiffly, and walked to his office. The manila envelope was folded under his arm.

Funky Broadway

Cops in quantity did not agree with Fletcher. In and out of uniform, plain clothes to the retired, they were as hermetically sealed as aluminum cans. Outside the Ninth Precinct on Fifth Street their cars were perpendicular parked like the main drag of a cowboy town. It set them apart, as so many things did, in a parallel parking city. For the most part family cars, Ford and Chevy sedans, driven in from Queens and Staten Island, and more and more from the suburbs. The owners completed an eight hour turn and then escaped like leisurely bats out of hell. Fletcher did not know a policeman who walked to work. He assumed he never would.

Pete's was next to the precinct house, half cop, half neighborhood. When the shifts changed it was all cop, a companionable bar short on nuance and long on sports memorabilia. The New York Mets were much in favor, their team colors predominant. Their mascot, Mr. Met, emblematic of all that was wrong with modern baseball, had his own shrine. Friday afternoon, two weeks after the hotel fell down, one week after the story got a toe tag, Fletcher was in Pete's hearing Okie from Muskogee on the jukebox. A hot day, the third in a row near one hundred, the bar's air conditioning was dissipated in smoke and shouting. They drank their beer standing up in Pete's, watching the clock. When Merle Haggard stopped singing Fletcher asked the bartender for the man he wanted. It was not a passport to the magic kingdom. The bartender scowled as if he'd been asked for Fruit Loops, milk on the side. "Who wants him?"

"He's expecting me. Fletcher from the *Local.*"

"There's a reporter here, Fleck something."

The bartender's voice would have carried in an airplane hangar. It was a wonder the photograph of Babe Ruth didn't look around. Twice in his career Fletcher had been struck in the head because he was wearing his press card. The first time a cop hit him from behind. The second time he saw it coming.

That was worse and that was a cop too. The two incidents left him with a hesitation for which he over-compensated. He'd give his profession automatically, stridently. He was used to the sound of it but this bartender was like the town crier.

A loud two finger whistle. Fletcher went to it through a tangle of cops. A young guy, younger than Fletcher, was at a table balancing his checkbook. It seemed a prosaic activity for a narcotics detective. Fletcher sat, thinking for the thousandth time no one ever looks the way you expect them to. His street name was Stash (not inventive but perhaps believable) but now shaved and short haired he was back to Bill. Except for the shoulder holster Bill the cop looked much like Fletcher.

"That was good work you did the day of the hotel."

Bill nodded. "A real shame about those old people. There's no justice."

"No justice?"

"I don't want to die watching TV. That's all they were doing and the roof falls in on them. Some guy sticks a knife in somebody and enjoys it and he's alive. Does that seem fair to you?"

Fletcher could not answer that. Instead he put the Polaroid of Vix on the table. "What can you tell me about her?"

Bill looked over his bank statement. "Not much."

"How about where she lived? How she lived?"

"No mystery there. Whoever wanted her I guess."

"You mean she was a prostitute?"

"I mean you could pick her up in a minute. Maybe she took money, I don't know. What difference does it make?"

"Some." Fletcher felt the talk turn crisp, sawed off. "Ever speak to her? Notice anything unusual about her?"

"No, nothing. Trampy, not much to look at."

"Was she from somewhere. Maybe a runaway?"

"She wasn't fresh from Port Authority, I can tell you that." The cop was adding and subtracting on a napkin. "She knew what she was doing."

"But she might've run away, once."

The pencil stub broke. "She wasn't underage, she could do what she wanted. What's all this about?"

"She spoke to me one night in the Broadway bar. I thought she had a kind of accent but I didn't catch it. Not American."

"I wouldn't know. To me she sounded…"

"Exactly… how did she sound to you?" A mistake, too eager.

The bank envelope was flipped on the table. "She sounded like somebody in a bar. That's all. Listen, I'm kind of…"

"Ever hear her called anything but Vix?"

"No; don't think so." Bill looked over Fletcher's head. "Wait, maybe. I saw her one day waiting in line at the check cashing down by… maybe she had a job someplace. And you should talk to the bartender. She was washing her pantyhose or something in the bathroom one night and he yelled at her. Called her something like... I don't know. Maybe her last name. Talk to him."

Fletcher nodded. "She was waiting in line?" He wiped damp fingers on his pants. "Bartenders are famous for keeping their mouths closed. You're from New York aren't you?"

"I don't get this."

"Not much to get, Bill. Just a girl sitting in a bar that was closed, locked up. I wonder why. You think she was waiting for somebody? It's a possibility."

The cop pulled his chair back. "Sorry I couldn't tell you more. Good luck with it..."

"What about..."

"I can't talk anymore... I'm waiting on reassignment."

"You say somebody could pick her up in a minute. Anybody in particular? Somebody she went around with even for a..."

"No, nobody special. Talk to the..."

"Was she ever your girl?" Fletcher did not wait for the cop's change of expression. "That's not so out of the question, is it?"

"It's none of your fucking business but I tell you I don't screw around on the job. I got a girlfriend, I don't need it."

"I want to know why she'd dead. You said yourself it wasn't fair."

Bill stood up, rammed his bookkeeping under an armpit. "I wasn't talking about her. I was talking about those old people watching TV. Nobody asked her to lock herself in the bar. She wasn't supposed to be there sleeping or washing her underwear. It's tough luck."

"It's a lot to pay for being tired."

"You don't see what I see. Now I suggest you don't ask me any more questions. I suggest I can't help you."

Suggestions that he ask no more questions would be considered at a future, indefinite point. "One last thing..."

The cop stared very carefully "No, there is no last thing. Get lost."

He walked off. Near the front of the bar he stopped and talked to another man. Their faces turned back to the table. Fletcher wasn't happy with his method. Forestalled, he had not got much. *You don't see what I see.* Sooner or later they all told you that. Ever willing to learn, Fletcher was willing to believe it was so but still.... At the bar the two men continued to speak. Fletcher headed out, passing them. Bill moved aside.

"Thanks," Fletcher said. "And by the way, I did talk to the bartender."

It was very hot when he opened the door to street. As it closed behind him he heard *Okie from Muskogee* come on again.

Curious George the bartender was out of work and drinking too much. The juicy mouth full of spittle was the giveaway. When the hotel collapsed that was the end of his job and he missed it. The Broadway bar was his dukedom, he was like fat greasy royalty there, but he knew better than most you can't put a place like that back together somewhere else. It would never be the same. It was like those ancient civilizations like Babylon where the sex was so incredible but it's all ruins now. George's dream was to have his own bar called Babylon and tell everybody jones and not much else.

He got his name from the Swedish erotica movies *I Am Curious Blue* and *I Am Curious Yellow*. Early in his tenure at the Broadway when those films were current George greeted women by leering "I am curious too" at them. His leers were not run of the mill like what you get from your minister or the guy in the delicatessen but all encompassing like a mud bath. They were not to every taste but George with a bartender's memory for preferences would customize. Big and bearded, peering out of slovenly but oddly fetching eyes, he found every woman exotic no matter how many winter coats she wore. With George it was always ladies night at the Broadway. Two for one; three for one; if you were really good looking it cost more to drink at home. That brought in a lot of women that brought in a lot of men and everyone was happy and Curious George was sitting pretty.

Now all that was over and George was quite morose. Other bartenders with their own dukedoms were sympathetic but you know what they really felt… better you than me, buddy. That would have been George's reaction at least. He was floating from place to place getting a snootful free but not much else. A bartender without a bar was like an old friend with a noisy but not necessarily fatal disease. Before long you were a nuisance, hanging around too much and not long on yuks. In the space of two weeks George had traded his big Havanas, he got them by the box from a guy in Montreal, for a good long suck on the exhaust pipe.

George knew what it was, they were jealous. He always got more than his share of big shots at the Broadway, musicians and actors and real high fashion models and people with a name and a face and little beyond that. Some of this had to do with cocaine. You scored in the hotel lobby or on the corner outside and did it up in the bar under George's watchful eye. He didn't have to be asked for water to dunk your sore nose in. George accepted a toot now and then but it was to keep him up and drinking. It was no place to be wired and out of control. A dukedom like that was no small responsibility. Cocaine gave his place cachet and attracted the famous but you still had to be careful. Might be he talked it up in an oversized way to other bartenders. Some of them ruled ancient holdings where alcohol remained the legal tender. They considered Spink's, now the Broadway bar, an outlaw state.

Fletcher knew him before he was Curious George when he was just plain George, a mostly lumpy, sweaty guy who was the day bartender at McCormick's, a saloon on Cortlandt Street at the upper edge of Radio Row. Fletcher went there occasional Fridays (walking downtown beside the West Side Highway where good sized chunks of iron were known to come loose upon saints and sinners alike) for the fried fish special. For under two dollars you enjoyed a mound of flounder and potatoes and a schooner of beer, refills a dime. They threw in clam chowder along with bread and oyster crackers on the communal, knife scarred tables. The house mustard, inflamed with stale beer, made the mice stand up straight. As Fletcher sat at the bar working remnants of his meal out of his teeth with toothpicks, he'd speculate why the haystacked, unbuttoned bartender put up with being bossed around by the loudmouth Irish owner. That was George, the Hungarian beast of burden, twenty going on forty in front of you. But you had to be careful. He looked like the kind of bartender who might tell you the story of his life.

McCormick's went under when Radio Row was bulldozed to make way for the World Trade Center. Fletcher missed them both. The Row was the place to browse for vacuum tubes and other electronic parts and to mingle with men known to both Ohio and New York, tinkerers. Edison and Ford were tinkerers and they had changed the world utterly. Pennsylvania Station went around the same time. It was a thing of great beauty while Radio Row was nuts and bolts and Fletcher thought cities need them equally. So he did not see George for a long while and did not think about him. The next time they met was 1967 and George was at the Surfmaid not far from Fletcher's apartment. George was different. Whatever finishing school he'd gone to he'd come out summa cum laude. Later when George was holding court at the Broadway he seemed to Fletcher someone who had been truly enhanced and liberated by the sixties. It didn't matter that he'd never attended a political rally or tramped to Tibet; he was lifted with the tide and transformed. At the Surfmaid his hair was long and he'd grown a beard so majestic it might have been thatched by elves. The droopy work clothes of the ethnic schlub were replaced by motorcycle boots, Levi's, dashikis and a bush hat. His bulk was disguised. Soft and inclined to slump previously, he was now impressive, a presence. An earring and a touch of superb artifice completed the picture. Ordering a drink one night George seemed unusually tall to Fletcher who sneaked a look behind the bar. George was using five drainage racks on the floor. He loomed, a star in his way.

But the Surfmaid was established, a bit stodgy and predictable. The evolving George required a stage of his own, an arena he could fashion from scratch. The Broadway Central hotel changed hands and the new owners hoped to do something about the genuinely low life bar in their lobby, that discarded peanut shell called Spink's. It was, in the gentle parlance of another time, a bucket of blood. Fights were common, robberies too. The too obviously drunk were followed and rolled for their wallets. Pimps talked shop in the booths and addicts shot up in the toilets. You might say Spink's had atmosphere to spare. Duffy said to Fletcher then: If this was wartime the MP's would close that joint. But it was wartime, 1969, it just wasn't supposed to feel that way. A pair of sailors were roughed up there one night, boys who had walked uptown from the Statue of Liberty. It made the dailies, got on television. The owners had the influence to hold onto their liquor license but the publicity was not good. That's when George, coming from the West Side like Wild Bill Hickok, presented himself.

They laughed at him at first sight. He proposed they fire the rotation of punchdrunk clowns who worked nights at Spink's, most of them lived in the hotel, and put him on Mondays through Sundays. He said he'd take care of everything. The owners laughed somewhat less. Words like "take care of everything" are to certain ears as inviting as raindrops on roses to a parched fawn. George kept talking. He said he'd take care of things, there'd be no more trouble, guaranteed. The owners were no longer laughing. "No more trouble, guaranteed" had a sweetness they could not resist. Everyone puckered and they gave him the job. George quit the Surfmaid without notice and decamped to Broadway. He didn't bring much but he brought his sap with him.

When McCormick's closed George did not get a gold watch for his years of service but he did steal the old Irishman's sap. It was a club about fourteen inches long, an inch in diameter, with a bar of lead inside. Tapered at one end with a rubber grip it was a fierce weapon in almost any hand. It was something more when George wielded it. His first days at Spink's were calm enough. He smiled a lot, umpired arguments, gave out drinks. He was a big marshmallow in a bush hat. His second Saturday night there was a fight and knives came out. George did not say break it up boys, have a drink and we'll all be friends. He did not care what the fight was about or if one man was right and the other wrong. He jumped over the bar, something you would not think he could do, and swung once at the head of each man with the sap. The full weight of his body was behind each blow. The eye of one man was crushed in the socket. George told the cops they'd beat each other up and the cops were pleased to believe it. George might save them some trouble. It was his Broadway bar after that.

In 1970 Fletcher wrote about the Broadway bar and about George. He looked upon it as downtown stuff. He'd been going through back issues of the *Local* from the fifties, a time when the paper devoted more coverage to the neighborhood. Aside from news there were short memory laden pieces about butcher shops, boarding houses, elementary schools and the cafeteria intelligentsia of the Depression. There were profiles of Village residents, notable and not so notable but mostly forgotten. Little of it set the page on fire but Fletcher felt they were like your own inner memoir, like a pattern of clouds, and exempt from classification. They appeared under the collective heading *Old Sapokanikan*, a name taken from a lower island Indian tribe extant in the days of the Dutch. It was their oyster shells and arrowheads beneath the concrete and their stream, Minetta Brook, flowing under the fountain in Washington Square Park.

Scanlon hated *Old Sapokanikan* and said it was written by a retired washerwoman in whose veins ran the purest gin and honeysuckle. In truth the column was reader submissions and Scanlon put up with it as it cost, he gleefully admitted, "not one red cent". The Village then was full of the variously literate happy to have something in print and the editor was pleased to oblige, up to a point. By the early sixties the *Local* was making money and Scanlon did not need them any more. He gave *Old Sapokanikan* the boot, sniggering as he did so like a vicious juvenile delinquent strangling a grandmother, his own. ("I've wanted to do that for years.") For months the paper received letters, some quite heartfelt, lamenting its disappearance. Imagine that, Scanlon said, they actually miss Old Sarsaparilla. His better nature aroused he heaved a sigh for times gone by and threw the letters away.

Fletcher was taken with the column and asked one day what happened to it. The same that will happen to you, Scanlon told him, if you don't stop poking around in the files. Scanlon took a dim view of reading back numbers. But if not encouraged Fletcher was reminded that the *Local* began as a neighborhood sheet. (It was all the funding the paper had.) Scanlon subsequently retreated from this in his effort to create a national weekly and indeed their library sales and out of state subscriptions grew far more than expected. Fletcher was part of this evolution. Except for select nightclub reviews everything he'd written in the later years might have fit comfortably in a coast to coast publication. It was a gradual change, one he didn't much like. Even as he battled with Scanlon over other postings he knew New York was the world he was ignoring.

So in the spring of 1970, around the time he was booking Oscar Peterson for the boat ride, Fletcher published what came to be a celebrated series on the Broadway Central bar. It was work he was in the mood to do. He said it was only downtown stuff, nothing special, but he believed it was Manhattan on the cusp of a new house and he wanted to track it. And this time he had the qualifications. He was looking at the Village and what was passing through as he had in the past. This time though he was on the outside, he wasn't part of it any longer. Every newsroom has an old guard and he like Red Rover had gone over to it.

It was never Fletcher's intention to make more out of George than George was. That the bartender was a self-promoting blowhard (in local terms combining William F. Buckley with Murray the K) was undeniable but it was on a rather small scale just the same. Even the least pompous disc jockey reached a larger audience in an hour than George did all year. Yet the blue and yellow emcee had his own discount charisma because an era of eclecticism suited him. He was ignorant but overcame it by talking loudest. He prospered with those evanescent modern success stories who tolerate abuse and intimidation from their inferiors. And he prospered with others, the less well known and the not known at all, who enjoyed seeing him do this. There may well be no second acts in American lives as Fitzgerald said but there is nonetheless always a chorus.

Fletcher was backstage at a Crosby, Stills and Nash show at the Fillmore East that spring when Graham Nash asked if he knew the Broadway Central. Fletcher was puzzled but dutifully accompanied the singer, some entourage and roadies, the six blocks to the bar. About midnight, the drinkers were many and not at all the usual inhabitants of Spink's. The crowd appeared to have been bussed in a from a gallery opening or photo shoot. Fletcher had not been by for months and the change startled him. He felt out of step on his own turf. He didn't stay. Nash was an affable sort, standing drinks, but Fletcher avoided if possible the personal largess of pop stars and the corporate seduction of their record labels. He went home but was back at the Broadway a few nights later.

George had a rooting section. They laughed at his jokes, some delivered with a bullhorn, and inspired others to do likewise. The uninitiated were fair game and they walked in from everywhere to be tormented. Fletcher had long ceased to understand what made a nightspot popular; what the special mix was that attracted the faithful and kept them for a season or two and sometimes longer. Many of the required meeting places of his first years in New York were gone and those remaining were dead letter offices, undisturbed by fashion. Manhattan, where times passes more quickly than other zones, was a Janus faced arbiter of cafe society. You were often halfway out before you were fully in.

Newcomers to the Broadway were greeted with water balloons and rubber darts. George seemed to have a latex mania as it was considered a sign of true favor if he included a condom along with a woman's drink. Rubber pig noses were another of his toys. There were many supplicants but only so many noses and that was how George wanted it. He had a genius for exclusion. The gift of a pig nose meant you were numbered among the select and if you didn't get a pig nose it was quite obvious you hadn't. It was these noses that led Fletcher to call his first piece on the Broadway "Curious George's Novelty Shop". It looked reasonable when he wrote it down but it was an approach he regretted.

It was a mistake as it shifted the focus too much to George. Having known the bartender at his luckless drudgery at McCormick's Fletcher felt immune to his fascination. George was like a hometown soda jerk making good in the movies, the metamorphosis was too transparent from an aisle seat. Fletcher led with George but dropped him after the second paragraph in pursuit of something more elusive. He didn't catch it but thought it didn't matter, buried as he expected to be in the middle of the issue. But Scanlon, his editorial antennae twitching, plumped "Novelty Shop" on the front page along with a first class Mahaffy of George in full pig regalia. (As head "Oink" George got to wear ears too.) Two additional photos inside were intended to display the crowd but George was hoggishly prominent in those as well. It was not what Fletcher intended.

George was off to the races down on Broadway and nothing much Fletcher wrote afterward called him back again. If not larger than life George was momentarily astride it. His insults, his props and his bottomless tastelessness, dropped him center stage and the celebrated who came to participate kept him there. Yet Fletcher had to give George his due. The bartender had no hints of folk wisdom or working class wit, the sort of sociological pretense that might land you in the Sunday *Times* Magazine. He was a circus clown for the circus pitched on the edge of your id. Pie throwing, itching powder, whoopee cushions: George's realm was a whizbang of gassy practical jokes. His collection of compromising Polaroids was inaugurated as he trumped his curiosity to women and proclaimed himself a talent scout of the libido. (He took the expression from Fletcher's first article and said Fletcher had got it from him. He loved to read about himself but as Fletcher had first learned on his high school newspaper everyone does.) The Broadway began to resemble the bedroom of an indecent pussyhound. (Pussyhound somehow got by Scanlon and to a degree opened the gates, the *Local*'s stylebook subsequently began to loosen.) Some of the old customers lingered in the daytime, to be swept out by night. Fletcher wrote that the dilapidated vinyl booths (they stuck to your skin all seasons of the year) holding their fleshless skulls resembled catacomb vaults. George wanted to know if that was good writing. Hey Fletcher, he said, who's the fucker and who's the fuckee in this? Fletcher didn't know. And he realized, his face reddening, he had never seen a catacomb.

It made no sense but Fletcher's Broadway series, six parts in all, brought him a measure of fame. He was not used to it. *The Local* did not encourage self-promotion and Fletcher was no exception. If Scanlon suspected you were getting too much play he'd yank you back for a spell of anonymity until you cooled off. He had a gift for hiring staff who were not outraged by this as long as their copy was left relatively untouched. Scanlon purchased acres of good will (subdivided rather quickly) with the freedom he offered but he desired no prima donnas, no op-ed darlings. (Scanlon was moved to tears by the plight of syndicated columnists. Requiring reporters to think three times a week, he said, was inhuman.) Fletcher never questioned his editor about space allocation. It was his paper, or most of it was, and he shouted from the mountaintop that the first time a reader bought the *Local* only to read this or that writer they were doing something wrong. It happened of course but Fletcher did not necessarily disagree with his boss.

So it was unsettling experience to have agents and a publisher calling with proposals to expand the series into a book. Fletcher did not think the six parts could have expanded to seven. Four was sufficient but Scanlon insisted on two encores because the articles were getting good press on their own. Fletcher obliged but reluctantly because the Broadway had been a good hook but not the kind of thing you should repeat. (If Fletcher admired one thing about the Beatles it was the distinctiveness of their singles.) By the fourth week there was the unmistakable impression of commenting on what was much your own creation. Fletcher's objectivity was gone and he was haunting the Broadway like Walter Winchell at the Stork Club. It was not a comparison he craved. (But Duffy said to him once: Winchell was the ugliest man alive because he was all ears.)

The bar was more popular than ever and half the customers seemed to be there because they'd read about it in the *Local*. As the cumbersome master of the revels presided there was snake dancing and a conga line and choreography of George's own devising called the Caterpillar. Space was cleared and women undulated around the circular bar to Wilson Pickett's *Funky Broadway* (a song with lyrics as mystifying as Marianne Moore). The invitation if not the compulsion was to do the Caterpillar on your belly, not the most inviting activity on a floor full of spillage. The mood was self-fulfilling for whatever happened added to the legend and much that never did was tacked on too. George could not lose. One night Fletcher was there and he was very sober. Someone rather drunk asked if he was the writer who wrote about it and Fletcher said he was not. He got up and left.

Fletcher was lying to Bill the cop. He hadn't talked to the bartender but he'd been looking for him. He left Pete's and returned in steamy discomfort to the office. On a late Friday afternoon the newsroom was quiet as he carried two bound volumes of the Last Judgment variety from the files, heaving them on his desk. Each held three months of the paper, January through June, 1970. There were other things he'd rather do. Reading back issues from the fifties was recreational; reading his own copy was hanging by your thumbs. Newspaper writers like romantic poets do not experience organic growth. In any given year you hit the ball out one week and went down swinging the next. (Scanlon: Is that a baseball reference? Fletcher: No, chief, Wordsworth.)

He read for an hour until Mahaffy called. "Good, I got you. A large, disgusting fat guy of your acquaintance is in the Shipwreck. Should I…"

"No, leave him. I'll run over. Thanks, Joe."

"Yeah, he's on his beam ends; he ain't going nowhere."

Fletcher left the files on his desk, an infraction of *Local* by-laws, and hurried down to Bleecker Street through Washington Square. He needn't have rushed; not so much on his beam ends, Curious George appeared to have been hauled out to have his bottom scraped. Shipwreck Kelly's was a broadminded establishment as a rule and unemployed bartenders could get therapeutically soused there without interference. Fletcher was damp from his double-time walk but once through the saloon doors he felt bathed in restful coolness. George was at a round corner table in the back, head on his chest, a fly in his beard.

He seemed inanimate. There were shot glasses on the table but these were ornamentation. George was drinking from a bottle on the floor. Fletcher sat without invitation. He hadn't seen George since the night he took cousin Amanda to the Broadway when she sweetly gushed at the unsullied depravity of it all. But the Broadway by that date was twice removed from the raunch of its peculiar heyday. Fletcher would not have allowed her a peep at it otherwise. When George made the cover of New York Magazine in 1971 - Bartender of the Year or some such blather - his satyricon was showing wrinkles. He was busy but the shine was scuffed and the crowd younger, not a good sign. By 1972 he was still lasciviously telling women he was curious but they didn't know what he meant or didn't care. The Swedish movies were gone with the Strawberry Alarm Clock and love beads. Before the hotel collapse he was holding his own but more than ever it was cocaine and heroin, their discreet availability, keeping him afloat. George looked poorly, like a sideshow wooly mammoth. Fletcher felt remorse. When the hotel fell down on top of the bar he had not given the bartender a thought. Like that lawman Hickock of old, fate had dealt George aces and eights.

"You look awful, George," Fletcher said, paternally, "really lousy." George raised his head. "Tell me about it."

"No, seriously, I mean it. I hope your Blue Cross is paid up."

George grunted obscenely. He was robed in the djellaba an admirer had brought him from North Africa. The hooded gown suited his bulk but Fletcher had the unsettling sensation he was naked underneath.

"Too bad about the bar, George; a real shame."

The bottle came up. "You're telling me. Of all the fucking dumps falling down it's got to be the one falling on my fucking place. And let me tell you... you want a drink?" Fletcher thought not; something to do with the worm in the mescal and George's blubbery lips. "Let me tell you I was coming back. The Broadway was hot again."

Unequivocally false. "I think you're right, George."

"You bet your titty I'm right. You saw what happened: they stole all my best ideas. Now you got these glitter clubs and everybody dressed like fags. You can't tell the girls from the boys. I started that."

"I was wondering who it was."

"I was the one who scoped it out, the first. You know, you wrote about it. Before me you went to a place and there was jazz and there was folk and all this crap and the nice waitress brought you a Pink Lady and you knew you'd never get your finger up her ass because the vibes weren't right. But my bar was wild man like all these chicks were in heat. Anybody can get you laid but I got you fucked man, really reamed."

George's mescal bottle seemed medicinal. At the Broadway he had insisted on the tradition of lemon and salt but there was no time for that now. He seethed it instead through his teeth. Fletcher put the Polaroid on the table. "What about her, George?"

He didn't look at it. "Don't know her. Listen you got to write about me again like the other time. You got to say how Curious George is still on top. I got a lot of offers but can't think which one to take. Maybe go uptown. It's dead down here."

"You took this picture, George. It's one of yours."

"So I took a picture and you're busting my chops." George grabbed the photograph, held it up. "What can I tell you? She could be anybody, I don't know."

"She's the dead one in the bar. The one they dug out."

George blinked. "Oh yeah, sure. Tough luck. That was tough, yeah.

What's that you call that, fate?"

"I talked to Rocky, George. When he closed Friday afternoon he went over the place good. Checked the toilets, everywhere. The cleaning lady's been afraid there might be somebody in the bar waiting on her. Rocky said the bar was empty when he left. The girl let herself in, she had a key. How come she had a key, George?"

"She didn't have a key. I don't give keys out to nobody."

"Sure you do, George, sure you do. If there's a good reason."

"Maybe she took it from the register some night. We're not Fort Knox. What do you want from me?"

Fletcher plucked the photo back. "What's her name?"

"How do I know her name? What's with names with you? I know important faces, that's all…" All purpose nature had given George those winning eyes. He blinked. "What are you doing with it if it's supposed to be my picture? Tell me that."

"It got blown right off your bulletin board."

George took a mouthful, nearly choking. "You got it from that fucking cop."

"What cop, George?"

"Don't horse me around, you know what I mean. That undercover piece of shit, Stash. He's like the mob this guy the dirty bastard. Tried to move in on me, know what I mean? Tried to tell me how he's my friend, how I need him. Fuck you, I told him, Curious George don't need no fucking friends."

"They say he's a hero; saved a lot of lives."

A derisive snort. "If he's a hero you can have my balls for baby shoes. I'll tell you who's the hero: me. I'm the hero for not leaving him face down in the gutter some night. Ten different ways I could twist his neck for him. Ask him about this chick. Go ahead."

Fletcher pushed shot glasses aside to lean forward. "George, George, why bring cops into it? I don't care about your business with him. I want to know who she was."

"I'm telling you, she's nobody."

A shot glass rolled over. "Everybody is somebody."

"That's what you think and you're wrong. Nobodies stay that way, that's how it is. She's nobody, nothing, Kotex…"

"What happened the day she pissed you off? You didn't call her Vix. It was something else, like… what was it, George, another name?"

"Yeah, sure, that's her. Vix, like the cough drops. But I don't know nothing else. And I don't get pissed off at chicks. That's not my scene."

"But you did, George, you did. She was washing her clothes in the bathroom. Something like… it was her pantyhose, right? She was washing out her pantyhose in the sink, maybe hanging them up on the mirror or the door. And you caught her and you hit her and you called her… what did you call her, George?"

"I called her a fucking whore, a fucking pig. That's two names, Fletcher. She treats my place like a laundromat what am I supposed to do? She does that to me after I..." George wiped his mouth with the djellaba sleeve. He clawed at his beard. "What is it with you? You're coming in here asking me about pantyhose. You're a twisto, Fletcher."

"I'm asking you about a young dead girl, George."

The same snort as before, louder. "Don't give me that. I know you. I know what you're like. All that time you were watching me I was watching you right back. You got high on me. You sat over there in the Broadway with your hand in your pants. That's like you, you like to watch. You ever make it with anybody in my place? You ever go home with anybody and get it off? What's the matter, Fletcher, you afraid of pussy? Yeah, this is a good chick for you. She's a stiff."

George got up clumsily, the neck of the mescal bottle in his hand. It was like watching a tent unfold. As he buckled against the table shot glasses fell to the floor. "Take yourself over to the Anvil, Fletcher. Take it up the ass until you like it. Be good for you. Fuck you and fuck the dead bitch and fuck everything else. Fuck it."

His bearings were not quite there but George righted himself. He had a pigeon-toed walk. Swaying, he headed for the saloon doors, whacking them each way as he left. Fletcher bent down for the shot glasses. It was the oak table that always stood near the coal burning fireplace. His initials were there somewhere with Logan's and with Maggie's. They were harder to find every year. He didn't try, getting up instead. He'd mostly wasted his time with George but in such an agreeable, uplifting fashion it would be selfish to complain.

He went to the bar. "Sorry about the ruckus, Barney."

"I called the Salvation Army for a pick up but they don't want him." Barney waved a postcard. "Maggie is expecting."

"I know, I heard. Maybe they'll come home now." Fletcher turned to go, came back. "How many checks do you write per month?"

Barney shook his head. "Strictly cash, don't leave a paper trail. The nuns taught me that." "I wish I'd gone to that school."

"Too late now, Rush," Barney said.

Fletcher gave the bar a tap and went out through the saloon doors.

A Clean, Well Lighted Place

Boiled Onions smell bad, of moist armpit and burger grease. It atomized off him with every asthmatic breath. He was the window guy at Dave's Luncheonette, southeast corner of Canal and Broadway. Bald and sweaty, nose like a toad, taller than most fire hydrants, he had veins in several autumnal colors. He bubbled in the heat like stovetop alchemy, a Merlin of heartburn and pocket gas. Wafting his full bodied aroma over the hot dog fry Boiled Onions smeared his soft oval fat man's mouth with his Dave's paper cap and slicked it back on his head. He was tired, he'd been standing since 1946.

Broadway and Canal by Chinatown was not a bosky dell. Traffic off the Manhattan Bridge flogged to the Holland Tunnel. Horns erupting, garbage trucks fuming, pushcarts challenging buses and sidewalk vendors caroling in a rush hour all day long. Boiled Onions did not notice it. He did not notice he'd been shouting all his working life. He said most things twice to save the bother of repeating them.

"The press, the stinking press. Come in here, in here."

Fletcher was at the Broadway window as the Onions sliced a knish swaddled in a paper napkin. It received a squirt of mustard in its midriff and was handed to a man at the inside counter whose jaws began to snap before the knish was free of the cook's fingers.

"It's a zoo here, a zoo. Feeding time at the zoo. Hey, you want a story? I got a story, I got a story for you."

Fletcher walked around to the Canal side entrance. He paused at the open door, bracing himself. Dave's was cooled by two standing fans the size of cargo plane propellers. Either one alone could knock a St. Bernard off a pork chop, the two together could blow you back on the street. The noise they made was unutterable. Fletcher vaulted for the counter where you were partially out of the violence of the winds. The Onions coughed on his hands, wiped them on his apron. It left them no cleaner.

"This guy here, this guy, he wants a story, always wants a story. I got one for you no charge. Free I give you this story. Here's the story. The story here is you get born, you get hard, you squat large. That's the whole story no kidding. You hungry? You want a hot dog?"

Fletcher didn't want a hot dog and he'd heard the story. None daunted the Onions gargled in self-appreciation. He had four or five men at the stand up counter shoveling hot dogs and hamburgers.

"A hamburger sandwich on me. Say the word for a hamburger sandwich."

The word remained unspoken. Squeezing between two chomping customers Fletcher asked for a lime rickey. The knish eater was gone, replaced by a truck driver demanding three franks, heavy on everything. It was an order that brought out the acrobat in the Onions. Saturday was no exception to the brisk trade. Dave's was the last greasy spoon before the noodle houses began. The Onions said you did not have a Chinaman's chance in those chink parlors though he had nothing personal to say against the oriental inclination who kept their noses very tidy. Only in the city of downtown New York, Fletcher once wrote about him, could a Boiled Onions become a hot dog philosopher king.

"Tripe, laundry, east side, west side, all smells the same."

Two Chinese boys wanted egg creams. Dave's was known for its egg creams, said to be the best in town though this estimate was not universal. The Gem Spa on St. Mark's had its partisans too. Fletcher could not tell the difference but he was from Ohio, as was pointed out, and incapable of judging. A Dave's egg cream was prepared in a paper cup inserted in an aluminum goblet while the Gem Spa used Coca-Cola glasses. This was the nub of the debate, paper versus glass. As a matter of principle Fletcher liked Coca-Cola glasses but remained above the fray by ordering lime rickeys. Boiled Onions admitted he did not make the best egg creams but all agreed they were the loudest.

"Who wants 'em. You got 'em. Two egg creams coming up. Look at these hands, like a surgeon they are. A surgeon's hands I got I'm not kidding you. I could take your lug nuts out for you where you'd never miss them. No charge, on me. Two egg creams right here, two."

The Onions banged a swollen knuckly paw on the cash register ringing up No Sale. "So what's with you? You want something? I got no time for nosy reporters. See this guy? Don't tell him nothing. He'll put it in the paper and send it to your wife. No kidding, in a minute he does that. He'll kill you in the newspaper this guy I mean it. You'd better have a punch in the nose someplace than have this guy know where you was last night. Me, I got no worries. I was here, where else would I be? What? What?"

"I'm looking for someone," Fletcher said.

"So big deal. I'm looking to get rich. I won't. What? What?"

"It's a guy named Stutz I heard about."

Eggish eyes retreated within folds of dewlap. The Onions looked sideways and clawed at Fletcher's wrist. "Over here. Over here."

Boiled Onions bumped along down the aisle past the Italian ice freezer. Fletcher followed on his side. Once out of the lee of the hot dog counter the fans shifted the part in his hair.

"Who's that? Who we talking about here?"

Fletcher had to shout. "Stutz; a guy named Stutz. Where can I find him?"

"What are you shouting? I'm not so deaf you got to shout." Onions was shouting. "That's nobody I know, nobody. Forget about him, forget it."

"This Stutz is something to do with the bars?"

"Yeah, maybe he does. So what?"

"Something to do with the girls in the bars?"

"Yeah, maybe that too. So what? Forget him."

"I want to ask him…"

A short pudgy arm bolted at Fletcher's shoulder. The swollen knuckly paw could grip hard. "That's what you don't want to do, ask nothing. You don't do that."

Fletcher was patient. "It's nothing private. I won't…"

"You don't know this guy."

"Onions, that's why I come to you."

"You don't get me. You don't know this guy as in you don't want to know this guy. Get me? You don't know this guy I tell you."

"It sounds like you do. Where is he?"

The Onions released his grip. "They hurt people this guy. Honest, no hippy dippy stuff. They got no use for questions and guys like you. I got no use for you." He scrambled back to his grill, stabbing with his trident fork, muttering at the smell of seared hot dog flesh.

"Gimmie that one," a mouth at the window said, "burnt."

There were more arms reaching in from the sidewalk. It was like this until they rolled the windows down and locked the doors. Back at the stand up counter, out of the typhoon, Fletcher took a pretzel from the pretzel tree and chewed it. A teenage boy wanted a hot dog with ketchup, causing a long yellow Onions tooth to curl in disgust. The boy's face was hormonal fire, as if the Chinese had no antibodies for American acne. Fletcher would not wish adolescence on a dog. He took out the Polaroid. "Maybe she worked for him. I want to find out."

"That's too much," the Onions said, "believe me."

Fletcher did not want to be dissuaded. That morning he ran into a former Fillmore bouncer who was waltzing a Hollywood actor around town for room and board. I'm reduced to it, the bouncer said. His name was Skilly and he was with a modeling agency whose sidelines included bodyguards who did not look especially like bodyguards for clients who did not want to look like they needed one. It was not cheap. The agency rented out women on the same basis. Skilly was not overly big or combative and had a mild unscarred profile. Otherwise he was ferocious and quite effective. As a bodyguard he might be taken for a friend and he had interests like stock car racing and soul music.

You could talk to him while he was keeping people from touching you.

Skilly was on Fifth Avenue in front of the Brevoort apartment house when Fletcher saw him. His actor was upstairs with a woman they met at Max's the night before. At four A.M. the actor said he would be down in ten minutes. It was nine-thirty, Skilly did not expect to see him before noon. What the hell, he said, he got paid for it. But he was hungry and Fletcher went around to the Zeus Brothers and got him coffee and a ham and egg on a roll. They drank coffee and talked about the Fillmore. Skilly was unsentimental. It was just a job, he said. Most any time he'd rather go up to the Apollo and hear singers who really knew how. Skilly was from northern Florida. He didn't like black people so much but he bought all their records. Fletcher asked what the actor was like. Not bad for an asshole, Skilly said.

Fletcher showed him the Polaroid but the bouncer shook his head. It was not likely he would know her. When you worked the stage door there were so many girls they looked the same after a while. Some were pretty and some were not and that was it. Skilly lived a bit monastically down on Ludlow or Chrystie, Fletcher could not remember which. They were rough streets but Skilly was not bothered by it nor was he bothered by anyone there. Fletcher was there once and remarked on the Scientology books on the floor. I can't do this forever was all Skilly said about that. Fletcher liked him without understanding him.

She died in the Broadway Central, Fletcher said. I hate that place, Skilly said. He meant the bar. His thumb gestured at the Brevoort. The kind of place this guy would like, he said, I'm glad it got squashed. Skilly looked at the picture again. Did she dance? Fletcher didn't get that. Topless, Skilly said, go go stuff. Fletcher said he didn't know, he hadn't thought of that. It's a package, Skilly said, you get the girls, the protection, the stage set-ups. He said he worked a few of those bars after the Fillmore closed, didn't like it. Too slimeball for me, he said, but if she was hanging around at the Broadway you never know. Fletcher had nothing else, asked who he should see. Skilly munched the last bite of ham and egg, swallowed his coffee. Try Stutz, he said, that's mister topless. The trouble was finding him home. Look south of Canal, Skilly said, he likes the cops better down there. Fletcher said thanks, said he would. But Rush, the bouncer said, be polite, say she's your sister.

"So believe me," Boiled Onions said again, "whatever you want is too much."

Fletcher believed him but not fervently. He waved the Polaroid. "A friend of my sister's. I got a message for her."

"Your sister? This is a working girl." The eggish eyes rotated in their pouches. "You really got a sister?"

"No," Fletcher said, "but this isn't a working girl."

Onions jabbed a hot dog through the window at a cab driver. "Then what's she up to with Stutz? It's the same difference practically." The cab driver got the wrong change. Onions smacked another quarter down. "Go away, you're bad for business."

Fletcher put the picture in his pocket. "Where do I find him?'

"Look in this place called Dream Lucky and leave me alone. Dream Lucky, that's on Desbrosses."

Not so familiar. "Over by the river?"

"Down from the tunnel, the tunnel. You want it on Park Avenue? So do me do you a favor and go to Park Avenue for the weekend. Who's eating? Who's hungry? I got red hots here. I got…"

Fletcher passed around the counter through the fan storm. He could hear Boiled Onions on the street. "Your mother never fed you like this. Your own mother I guarantee. A hot dog like you never had, no charge for the bun. Who's hungry? Who's eating?" Fletcher was on Broadway, the bald head goggled out the window. "A working girl will get you trouble every time. Remember me that, nothing but trouble." He began to bleat. "Act stupid. You hear me? Act stupid like you don't know. Easy for you. Act stupid."

A block down Fletcher crossed to Lispenard Street. He assumed he'd stumble on Desbrosses before long. The only topless bar he'd been to was on Nassau Street near the stock market. It got a mix of construction workers and men in suits. Mahaffy took him there when they were scouting playground murals. The girls did not dance. They stood behind the bar, five or six where one bartender would have sufficed. They wore cowboy hats and flimsy fringed vests that covered their nipples. When they turned sideways you saw their breasts. Drinks cost twice what they did at the Blarney Stone next door. Mahaffy said you were paying for the ambience. According to Mahaffy all the girls were college students though perhaps they were not recent graduates. One man was reading the Post, two others were talking about the Eastern Airlines shuttle. Two televisions were on, both tuned to The Dating Game. The girls watched with interest and Fletcher too, absorbed and hoping the contestant made the right choice. It was all about the choices you made. I come here all the time, Mahaffy told him.

Beach Street, where the mounted police kept their horses. He'd gone wrong. He backtracked to Hudson and looked north. The next block up was Hubert, that was no help. He was giving no sign of knowing this part of town. There were factories, parked trucks, a roasted metal smell of manufacturing. A cab coming slowly south stopped on the deserted street, honked its horn. Out of a doorway a woman tossed a cigarette. She trotted to the cab and put her head in the back window. Tube top, short black skirt, fishnet stockings, white Nancy Sinatra boots. Her ass rode up high like a cat scratching. Fletcher dragged his feet. The cab lurched away, nearly taking the woman's head along. She swore, violently, but as she turned she said hi hon-ee to Fletcher. Looking beyond her he asked if she knew Desbrosses Street. 'Brosses? She didn't need the first syllable. You must be going to Dream Lucky, she said. Fletcher said he wasn't. That's just for watching, she said, I got the real thing. She poked at his zipper. Come on hon-ee, she said, you know I'm cute. He thought she was but went around her. She pointed. Dream Lucky that way, she said, if it makes you hot hon-ee come back to me.

Desbrosses Street was nineteenth century shipping and receiving. Red brick warehouses with noble arched bays lorded over the cobblestones for two blocks. A third block descended to the highway and river. It had the broken sidewalks and clogged catch basins of municipal abandonment, There were gutted automobiles and a discarded spool of Con Edison cable. Next to a loading platform with arabesques of graffiti there was music. It wasn't loud and nothing said bar but propped in a curtained storefront window was a cardboard cut-out, a naked bosomy woman sitting in a champagne glass. Fletcher went in.

The guy inside the door was no bigger than a moose. That was probably big enough.He bugled a short sentence that did not sound welcoming and shut the door firmly behind Fletcher. The air conditioning was jacked up, almost polar. Fletcher went to a bar, small enough to be portable, and took a stool. There were only three, one other was occupied, a smallish man face down near his drink. Fletcher heard his breathing. The decor was mirrors, your reflection all around. The music was easy listening, at the moment Some Enchanted Evening. Across the room on a spotlighted runway two women in peach and pink baby doll outfits pretended to struggle. One tugged at the panties of the other and they broke apart. They were early twenties, white, dyed blonde hair. One had large breasts that would not stay in her chemise. The other was the aggressor. Her chest was smaller, hair under her arms. She stalked her opponent, spitting and rubbing her crotch. There were ten, twelve tables arranged around the runway. Two were empty, the rest had one or two men each. There were briefcases on the floor, gym bags, flowers wrapped in florist paper on a folded New York *Times*.

"You drinking or just looking?" Startled, Fletcher swung his knees around.

"Yeah, okay. What have you got?"

"This is a bar," she said, "what do you think we've got?" That she wore only a bikini bottom did not help matters. "It's all five dollars."

"Everything is five dollars?"

She was succinct. "Everything. And asking for water won't do you any good. Chivas, beer, club soda, orange juice; if it goes in a glass it costs five bucks. Not including tip. So?"

"A beer is fine," Fletcher said, "whatever you have." If there was a right foot here he was not getting off on it. He interviewed a girl at Woodstock who was naked when he was clothed. That was in the country. This was not like that. This girl had goosebumps, he wondered if she had health insurance. He didn't and he thought about it more since Rothberg's pneumonia the previous winter. Scanlon quietly paid for Rothberg's hospital stay but the issue remained, the staff was unprotected. Scanlon insisted the paper could not afford a plan but he personally would look out for everyone.

The barmaid was older than the girls on the runway. She had stretch marks, sort of a belly. It was not unattractive. She opened a can of Old Milwaukee and poured it in a spotted glass. Fletcher pushed five dollars her way.

"Don't forget me," she said.

Under the circumstances that would be difficult. "This air conditioning is freezing. Don't you get cold?"

"I'm a cold type. You get used to it."

A peach and pink waitress put a tray on the bar between Fletcher and the man sleeping. She had a lump of fives and tens in her underwear elastic. "Hi," she said, "I'm Melody."

In a pig's eye. "I'm Jerry," Fletcher said.

Some Enchanted Evening had become *Moon River*. "Isn't this a pretty song?" Melody hummed. "It's from *Breakfast at Tiffany's*. It won the Academy Award. Did you know that?" Fletcher shook his head. "I know all the Academy Award songs. Ask me one."

"How about *Born Free*?"

Melody was dejected. "That's too easy," she said.

"What about this year. Know that one?"

Melody brightened. "Oh sure, it's *The Morning After* from The Poseidon Adventure. I saw the whole thing. Did you like it?"

"I missed it," Fletcher said.

"You didn't see it? It won the Academy Award."

So did *All About Eve*. The door moose was grunting. Melody put four fresh drinks on her tray. They were all Scotch, indifferently poured by the barmaid from the same bottle of Teacher's. They were not generous drinks by any means. "You can stay pretty sober here for five dollars," Fletcher said.

"Those were doubles," the barmaid said.

"Good thing I came in during happy hour."

The look on her face was not a smile but it was better. Fletcher sipped his beer, it was warm, and leaned forward until he realized he was leaning at her bare breasts. He settled back. "The music here is kind of…"

"It changes later," she said, "they play rock music."

"This is like drinking in an elevator."

The indifferent shoulder. "How come you don't like it? You look like the guy who owns Mr. Ed."

"Thanks. Are there more girls later?"

"There's more everybody, everything. We get real exciting people after midnight." She looked at the tables. "Not like now. I hate it like this."

"Yeah, I know what you mean. I thought I'd check it out before I brought the guys down."

"I can't wait." She lit a cigarette. "What guys?"

"The guys in my band. J. Geils."

"Yeah right, you're in the J. Geils band. Come on."

Fletcher savored his Old Milwaukee. "Road manager, plain clothes. You ever try to book rooms at the Plaza in a motorcycle jacket?" He swept his head around the room. "But it's kind of white bread in here. Vix told me you had more action than this."

"You can have anybody you want, black, Spanish, Chinese. It's like I said, there's more of everything later." The barmaid looked sideways and spoke softly. "You said Vix told you something. You know her? You know Vix?"

He did now. Fletcher dripped the rest of his beer into the glass. "What, Vix? Yeah, I know her. From that place that fell down whenever it was."

"What fell down? Did some fat slob work there?"

"Sounds right, yeah. She was hanging out there and I went in a few times. Five five maybe, skinny, short black hair."

The barmaid nodded. "How's she doing? I haven't seen her."

"Well, me too. We've been on the road but I used to see her there. Talked to her a few times. You know…"

"She told you to come here? Did she mention Cheryl? That's me." Cheryl looked sideways again. "You got to buy another drink. I can't stand talking here for nothing. That's not how it works." Fletcher bought another Old Milwaukee. It was like the installments on his Christmas Club. Cheryl made herself busy by the sleeping man rinsing spotty glasses. She poured the sleeping man an eyedropper of Scotch and took a bill from the fives under his ashtray. Fletcher closed his eyes. The naked girl at Woodstock had shivered, it was early morning and cool, and the fine pale hair on her legs rippled like wheat. Four years ago.

"That's a good idea," Cheryl called to him. "Bring your friends down. We do private parties all the time."

Melody returned with her tray. "Hi, Jerry. You're cute. Don't you think he's cute, Cheryl?"

"He's adorable. Here, bring Marvin a drink." She meant the door moose. Some other men had come in. They were not like the men already there. Three of them, they joked with Marvin and whistled at the girls on the runway. The girls gyrated and wrestled. The song was Love is Blue. Two new girls, pink and lavender, stood by the steps to the runway. They waited, sharing a cigarette.

"I was thinking she got sent back because I haven't seen her."

Cheryl offered a cigarette, thin and rose patterned. She put one in her mouth and Fletcher lit it with her lighter. "Sent back?"

"Do me a favor. If you see her tell her Cheryl has the money. I was sure she'd come around by now. Three hundred. I got all of it."

"I guess Vix used to work here."

The barmaid blew smoke over Fletcher's head. "No way." She laughed, she was missing two back teeth. "Vix didn't have enough on top for this place."

"Enough on top?"

"Her tits weren't big enough. What road do you go on?"

Fletcher tried grinning out of that. "I figured she was a dancer."

"Here and there, nothing heavy. Clover was a good place but it got closed up. Just last month. No touching there and you didn't have to take your clothes off. She couldn't…" Cheryl looked sideways. "But the tips weren't so great. Listen… just tell her what I said about the money. I was worried about her."

"If I see her," Fletcher said.

More men arrived, Cheryl was busier. Marvin the door moose rousted a table of early birds, they were drinking too slow. They arose, docile and uncomplaining. Fletcher did not have another five dollars. "Vix talks kind of funny," he said, "where does she come from?"

Cheryl poked out her half-smoked cigarette. It was long and snapped and flipped ashes on the bar. "Me? I couldn't tell you."

"Where's she afraid of being sent back to?"

"You got a lot of questions about somebody you don't even know."

Fletcher paused. "I liked her I guess. Don't you?"

"It's different if I like her."

He was losing her, had lost her probably. It had gone too fast and he could not climb out. It was too late to change. The sleeping man on the bar exhaled short and long like a factory whistle. Fletcher stood up. "Do I see Mr. Stutz about a private party?"

"Are you crazy?" Cheryl turned away. "You don't see anybody."

"That's who Vix told me to see about her."

"She would never tell you that. What is this?" She looked sharply left and right. "A cop. You're a cop."

"I'm not a cop," Fletcher said.

"Some kind of cop. Why can't you leave her alone? She never did anything to you. Leave her the fuck alone."

He couldn't tell her now. "It's not what you think. I want…"

"Don't touch me." This was a scream. You get used to everything. He'd forgotten how it was, how she was. He leaned too close with his open hand at her. He didn't have too see Marvin to know he was coming.

"You bothering this lady?" It seemed a rather winsome question for Dream Lucky. Fletcher had no answer. A door slammed and he saw Cheryl holding a bar towel in front of her breasts. Eden perhaps had gone down like this. Unable to satisfactorily explain how it started or where it would end he gave up.

"Just get him out of here."

Fletcher preferred to leave on his own but Marvin did not agree. Someone else, from the slamming door maybe, gripped his arms from behind and a knee went in his spine. Fletcher had the thought this was unnecessary. Marvin's hand locked under his jaw and like an odd mythical animal they hobbled and butted to the door. Marvin's practiced other hand opened it and they threw

Fletcher out on the sidewalk. He hit hard, it hurt, and he felt very warm. He'd forgotten how hot, how humid it was. Marvin resumed his other function, there were customers going in. They laughed. Don't handle the merchandise, one said. There was a New York Telephone step van down the block. They were working late. The things you notice when you are flat on your ass for dubious reasons. Fletcher did not get up until he heard the door to the bar close.

He went home. He walked uptown on Varick Street to Downing, then crossed Sixth Avenue to Bleecker. He walked slowly, a scrape on the heel of his palm stinging when sweat got into it. Coming along to the Cafe Figaro opposite his windows the Village seemed riotous. He'd left it somnolent in the afternoon. At his apartment entrance he found the remnant of a watermelon feast, rind and seeds strewn about. He dropped a few of the more prominent wedges in a galvanized can stenciled 185 but stopped when he saw the girl in his vestibule. She was a teenager, camped by the mailboxes. She waved to him, not a confident wave. He didn't know her.

"You're Rush... aren't you?"

Still nothing. "Yeah, I'm Rush."

"I'm Laurie," she said. "You gave us a ride, remember? From Watkins Glen."

Now he did, he went in. "You looking for Paul?"

Neither her face nor the oversized New York Rangers shirt were clear in his mind but the name was right. Laurie and somebody else, the current gymnasts in Becker's personal Fantasia. She looked fifteen, neighborhood of.

"He said I should wait for you."

"Becker said I should wait for you?" Fletcher hadn't spoken to him for days. "How long have you been here?"

She backed up. "A couple of hours I guess."

Fletcher hit the brass bank of mailboxes with his closed fist. The sound seemed explosive in the small vestibule. "Goddammit."

If she had a shell she might have pulled herself inside it. "I'm sorry," she said. "I rang your bell and walked around but when it got dark I came back and stayed here. He said you'd be home soon. He said you... I'm really sorry. I don't know where they went."

Fletcher slumped against the mailboxes. Now he had two hands that hurt. And he had dented Mrs. Riccardi's mailbox. Next time he should pick on his own. He flexed the newly wounded hand on his knee and looked at the girl. She wasn't adept at putting on makeup if that's what it was. Maybe it was crayons. "I'm a jerk," he said. She pulled at the sleeves of the stretched out Rangers shirt, twisting them. She retreated another half-step until the wall stopped her. "Well, let me think now. You hungry, Laurie?"

She looked down, looked up. "Yeah, maybe. I mean I kinda am. I mean I really am."

"Me too. Come on, let's go eat."

Fletcher had two places he could get credit. He didn't know if they liked falafels in Queens but in any case Ishmael's was packed. So they took a walk to University Place. She said she walked around the block a few times and stood in a head shop listening to music but they told her to leave because she wasn't buying anything. Then she was afraid this guy was following her so she went in a drugstore and got in a phone booth and pretended she was calling and when she came out of the store the guy was gone but she wasn't sure maybe he wasn't really following her. When she started to talk there was a lot of it. She said he was lucky to live on a street with so many people going by. It never got boring. She never got bored, she said, the whole time she was standing there. Luckily Mrs. Romano went to her son's apartment on Saturday nights to watch color television and criticise her daughter-in-law so she hadn't been there to give Laurie the third degree.

At the Zeus Brothers the youngest, Michael, the one who did not have a Cadillac yet and got the weekend night shifts, was at the register. As he wanted the next hand me down Cadillac he showed his trustworthiness to Harry, the eldest, by counting the toothpicks and mints. Sometimes he picked up the March of Dimes box and shook it. He had the same lacklustre moustache as his three brothers but was more American and Fletcher knew through the grapevine that Michael went to Cheetah on his nights off and danced with Dominican girls until the sun came up. I'm a little short, Fletcher said to him. Go eat, Michael said, I'll tell Harry. Laurie was already in a booth, flipping the cards on the tabletop jukebox.

"I suggest the cheeseburger deluxe," Fletcher said. "It comes recommended by no less a hamburger authority than Jughead Jones."

"I like this place," Laurie said. "It's nice."

Fletcher smiled broadly upward at the fluorescent fixtures. "Hemingway has a story called *A Clean Well Lighted Place*. It's about an old man in a cafe and the waiters and everything else..."

The waitress brought their Cokes. Fletcher had the impression you could no longer blow the paper off soda straws. It was, he assumed, more government intrusion into the simple lives of everyday citizens. Laurie had abandoned the jukebox. "Who's the most famous person you ever met?"

"Easy: John Lennon."

"You're kidding. You really met him? When?"

"I think... two years ago. When *Imagine* came out. He's fun. You interview him and he interviews you right back."

"That's unbelievable. Who else?"

"Robert Oppenheimer a long time ago," Laurie didn't respond. "He was a physicist. Worked on the atom bomb. He came to my college and was the first person I ever wrote about." Fletcher sipped his Coke. "Who's the most famous person you ever met?"

"You are, absolutely. I never met anybody else I know of."

"What about you and... I'm sorry, I forget her name. You good friends?"

Laurie peeled the damp paper from her straw. She was using two. "Toni.

Yeah, I guess. Maybe not as good as last year but we still hang out. She's kind of a slut."

Lucky Becker. "What's that mean exactly these days?"

"You know. She'll spread her legs for just about anybody."

Maybe not so lucky Becker. "Got a boyfriend?"

"Me? Not really." She got the straw unwrapped. "No, I don't mean not really. I don't have a boyfriend. Some kids do. It's not important. Not for me anyway." Her eyes went back to the jukebox. "I'm really hungry."

Their cheeseburgers came. The deluxe included French fries and onion rings, lettuce and tomato, portions of coleslaw and potato salad, pickles. Fletcher couldn't wait to start. In the roomy booth, beneath the acoustic tiled ceiling, he raised his fork. It rattled against his plate, he couldn't hold it.

"Are you still sick? Your hand is shaking."

He hadn't noticed it. He waited, it stopped. "I'm not as hungry as I thought," he said.

They ate. Laurie had his coleslaw and potato salad and most of the French fries. "Can I call you Rush?"

"What else would you call me, Laurie?"

She didn't know. "I read your column about Watkins Glen. I guess you didn't have a good time. Because you were sick, huh?"

Forced to remember. "No, not that so much. I'm not sure why I didn't like it. Maybe it was the air conditioned trailers. The audience was out in the sun all day and backstage they had the buffet tables and air conditioned trailers for the bands and all their friends and so forth."

"But they're the reason anyone goes. I mean that's what they get, isn't it?"

Fletcher pulled the batter from an onion ring. "I guess so, Laurie, I guess that's what they get." He felt tired.

"I had a great time." She finished her cheeseburger. "Really did. It was supposed to be the biggest festival ever. But I got slammed when I got home. My mother and father are separated and I go back and forth and I tried to work it you know so they each thought I was with the other one but I got caught. They picked a great time to actually talk to each other. I'm not supposed to leave the house until school starts but I couldn't stand it today. My father works at Kennedy and doesn't get home until early in the morning so I... I mean I was really bored and Toni said Paul called her and she wanted me to go. You know..."

Fletcher did not have to consider it. "Yeah, I know. Try not to get slammed again though."

"It sucks not being able to do what I want. I wish I could be like you. Really, I mean it. Maybe not this minute but when I'm eighteen and can move out. Be a writer or something and be independent."

"Did you ever write anything?"

Laurie noisily finished her Coke. "Not yet, but I figure it can't be that hard."

"It isn't really. The trick is finding someone who will pay you to do it."

"Did you always want to do this?"

It was a question that went to the heart of things. "I probably did. I wanted to work for a paper called the Herald Tribune but it went out of business."

Laurie went to the bathroom. Fletcher had a dollar and some change and he left it for the waitress. He held the ice water glass against the bruise on his palm. His mind went back through the day though he preferred it would not. When he looked up Laurie was twisting the sleeves of her Rangers shirt. She'd missed a spot of ketchup on her face. Standing up he wiped it away with a napkin and she punched him lightly on the arm. They went outside. He put his arm around her because the sidewalk was brimming and he was not so steady himself.

"Rush," she said, "I should go home, you know, before my father gets back. Is that all right?"

"Yeah, that's all right. That's very all right."

She needed the F train. She didn't know where it was but he did reflexively. At the entrance on Sixth Avenue he took a business card from his wallet. "After school starts give me a call. You can come down to the shop some Saturday and I'll give you the nickel tour."

She took the card. "What's the shop?"

"That's what newspaper people call their office. It's a rotten life but maybe you'll like it."

"Maybe I will." She punched his arm again. "Thanks."

"You okay on the subway?"

After some struggle she got a token out of her jeans. "I just stay in the car with the conductor."

She ran down the steps and out of sight. Fletcher went home. When he thought about it he was almost sorry but he didn't think about it much.

Horsemeat in the Hamburger

Mona was taking boxing lessons at Swoboda's Gym above the movie theatre at Twelfth and Greenwich. She called Fletcher Sunday morning and said she got through at ten, they could have coffee. He said all right. He wrote his column, answered mail, listened to most of *Sketches of Spain*, took another shower and was still ten minutes early. One day he would have to learn to walk slower. Hitching himself to a car fender below the Day of the Jackal marquee he waited. The door leading up to the gym opened and beefy sounds of pugilism descended. It was like the far off melee of a schoolyard. A man like a Dick Tracy character came out, looked huskily left and right, spat, went back in again. Fletcher did not get boxing though Joe Liebling, one of his dreamboats, wrote a fine book about it.

She emerged at five after with a Nordic pin-up type, enormous shoulders and a waist no thicker than a Lord & Taylor mannequin.. He wore track shorts and a heavily stained Yale sweatshirt. As far as Fletcher was concerned this proved the Ivy League was not what it used to be. The guy was like the dump truck without the dump. Watching him talk about himself (could he have any other subject?) you were inclined to ask if men like that were good lovers or did they just show up and look the part? Yet their equivalent on the other side of the dance floor, self-absorbed women with great bodies, did you dismiss them so readily? The Nord was ten years younger than Fletcher, making him five years younger than Mona, making her too old for him. He, Sven or Hans or Max, could not value what Fletcher thought of as her fey sense of humor. Fletcher valued it all too well. It made him rather nervous.

"There you are," she said. "Why didn't you come up…"

A wan but perhaps not fey smile was his reply. He did not want to be introduced to the wasp waisted Rhodes scholar (speculative but possible) but feared he was about to be. Maybe they were all going for coffee together, an insight turning Fletcher's wan smile to robust frown. He hadn't left his cozy

Dutch oven on Bleecker Street for that. Wise men say when in doubt give off bad vibes and in this case it appeared to work. The combustion of male competitiveness hung in the air like burnt toast. They all understood it wasn't meant to be a party. Yale man smudged Mona with an athletic kiss and took off like Jesse Owens in the direction of Eighth Avenue. Fletcher was not displeased and looked it.

Flushed like pink grapefruit Mona was dressed for church in gray sweats, her stark black hair pulled back with a tightly wound bandana. The bandana was the faded blue of a chambray sky. "I hope I don't smell," she said, "they don't have a girl's shower up there."

Fletcher didn't think she did, would not have minded. "Where did you find Eric the Red?" That came out wrong.

"Someone is in a good mood." Mona's boxing gloves were tied together by their drawstrings. She looped them around Fletcher's neck and squeezed. "These are some knockers you've got, Rush, real bathing beauties."

Fletcher was embarrassed, tried to take them off. "Just let me touch them once," Mona said, "please."

He forced a laugh. "It always surprises me how much these things weigh."

"If you only knew how often I've heard that." Mona walked off and he followed, carrying the gloves. "Hold onto them for me," she said. "they make you look so butch."

"Is this for self-protection?"

She stopped. "No, it's for fun. I've wanted to learn to box for years. Then I can teach others less fortunate. Like you. Put up your dukes, Fletcher…" She reached for his wrist. "What happened to your hand?"

He thought it over, told the truth. "I got thrown out of a bar last night."

"You got thrown out of a bar? Really?"

"The first time it ever happened to me."

"I can't begin to tell you how this arouses me. And after exercise too." She gripped him by the boxing gloves. "Tell me everything."

How did one put it into words? He'd tried not to think about it all morning. "They thought I was trying to grab a topless waitress."

"They thought?" Disappointment. "You weren't?"

"Of course I wasn't. It was a misunderstanding."

She released him. "My ardor passes. What were you trying to do… sell her a subscription?"

"It's not important… I was looking into something."

"So it appears. But at least you were in a topless place. That shows promise."

"Okay, well… I'm sorry I'm not like Becker but I'm not."

She turned away, turned back. There was something in her face as if he had called her a name. "Did I say that? Did I say I want you to be like Becker? Please don't presume to know what I want, ever."

He could not tell if she meant it. "I wasn't presuming. I…"

"Why can't I kid you? Why can't I? What's wrong with that?"

"There's nothing wrong with it." They would have been better off with the Viking there. "I… I thought we were going for coffee?"

"Yes; let's" Stiffness remained. They walked along Greenwich until she stopped abruptly at Bank Street. "I suppose breakfast is out of the question. You're probably broke and you won't let me treat."

"I'm not very hungry." It was true. "You buy the coffee."

At Abingdon Square they got coffee at a Korean's. Mona had a ten dollar bill wedged in her sneaker. "Buttered bagel, bialy, Danish? How about a French cruller, Fletcher?"

He declined though he knew she was hungry. This was discourteous but he could not help it. "Not right now, thanks."

They crossed the street and took a bench by the World War I memorial. The square was shabby and untended, an overnight drunk asleep on the patchy grass. The water fountain was broken, cans and bottles underfoot. Looking down through the bench slats he saw a syringe. It had never been his end of the Village.

"I'm sorry. Maybe boxing makes me confrontational."

You could say that again. "You look good in sweats. Like an athlete."

"If I could find a pair in black I'd wear them to the shop." Mona opened her coffee. "You don't mind if I say shop, do you? I don't want to offend your editorial sensibility." He shook his head. "Thank you. Advertising doesn't always feel like we belong. But maybe I'll wear this tomorrow. If anyone says something about the dress code I'll tell them Mister Rush upstairs said it was all right."

The coffee burned his tongue and styrofoam was an abomination. "We don't have a dress code."

"Oh, don't we? Maybe not for the writers who can run around like Salvador Dali if they want but it's conservative attire for the underclass."

"I'm always hoping someone will point out my resemblance to Dali. But you never struck me as inhibited by any dress code, Mona."

"I've been pushing it but don't think I don't hear about it."

"I don't… hear about it from who?"

"From whom, dear." Mona produced cigarettes and matches from inside a sweat sock. "My first of the day, I swear. So… you hear about it from the dowager empress herself, Mrs. Bailey. You don't have to do with the advertising director but others are not so lucky. By the way, she's having an affair with Benson."

Fletcher waved at cigarette smoke. "She is? They are?"

"You know… I wish I had a little Rush doll on my pillow at home. It would be so cute. Did you really lose your virginity behind a billboard?"

"Becker made that up…"

"Hmmm, Ohio isn't it? Was it in a car by any chance?"

He sought another direction to look in but couldn't find one.

"Mostly…" "Mostly for you or mostly for her?"

"Could we…"

"Just tell me what kind of car it was. For my scrapbook."

He took a bite of coffee. "It was a Hudson if…"

"Oh, a Hudson… and you were exploring, weren't you? That's so sweet. I bet Hudsons are roomy, aren't they? I wish I had a memory like that. A phone booth just isn't the same."

"About the dress code, Mona."

"Front or back… the seat I mean." As Fletcher looked like he was about to get up she stopped. "Okay, Mrs. Bailey isn't really the problem. She's just a conduit, you should pardon the expression."

"You mean she…"

"You really don't believe me, do you?" A sip of coffee, a cigarette puff. "Haven't you ever noticed that the girls in classified all look like they're waiting for the headmistress to show up? Sue Katz, her desk is next to mine? She brought in Balducci's, that's a terrific account. She got married in jeans but has to wear a dress to work because that's what Scanlon expects."

"I don't think that comes from Scanlon."

"Everything comes from him, Rush. He's like God the Father in Michelangelo."

Fletcher thought about Michelangelo and the ceiling of the Sistine Chapel. He thought about Scanlon. "I think of him as more like Yosemite Sam in *Looney Tunes*."

She threw her cigarette away and rubbed her fingers in Fletcher's hair. "There are men you want to hurt and men whose hair you want to brush. Which are you?"

He pushed her hand away. "There shouldn't be dress codes. And there definitely shouldn't be dress codes for some and not for others."

"Good. I'm glad you feel that way, even if you won't let me scratch your head in a purely friendly fashion. But dress codes aren't a big issue."

"Then why…"

'Don't look exasperated at me. They're important but they're not a big issue because they can be changed easily. By executive order you might say. It's those nagging institutional problems we have to deal with."

"You're sloganeering, Mona. It doesn't suit you."

"I may be sloganeering but it's not politics. It's economics. And economic slogans are something we can all gather around and enjoy like a bonfire on the beach. We'll tell ghost stories. You can even bring your ukulele, Rush."

He drank his coffee. "I don't have a ukulele."

"I wouldn't try telling the girl in the Hudson that. Seriously, how long have you been with the paper?"

There are additions and subtractions that come precisely to mind. "Twelve years last April," he said.

"Do you make a hundred dollars a week yet?"

"I make one fifteen and I'm due for a raise." He crunched his coffee cup and a dot of cold coffee spilled on his arm. He wiped at it. "I like my job. I enjoy it. I'd like to make more money so I could save something but… It's hard. The best offer, the only offer, I've had the last year was from *High Times*. They should only know. What do I do there, write about peyote safaris in Mexico? I've smoked two joints in my life and didn't like either one of them." He laughed, she didn't. "I don't know what it is. You work for a paper and it really gets inside you. I know some older guys who worked for papers that folded and it's like their orphans. You never go home again in the newspaper business. You have a press pass. You go most places but you don't go home." Fletcher started to rise, stopped. The coffee cup dropped between his feet. "Maybe I'll leave."

"Maybe you won't."

"Yeah, maybe I won't."

She reached her hand behind his head. "I really do want to brush your hair." The hand came back. "I don't know why I like you so much."

"I don't either… do you?"

She nodded. "Yes, very much. I liked you when I didn't know you and thought you were weird. I'd see you coming in the building and think, my God, who is this guy? Look at him. Look at the way he dresses."

"What's wrong with the way I dress?"

"Not much. If it's 1958 and you're waiting for American Bandstand to come on. I was sure you couldn't be for real and now I'm afraid you are. How could you be, Rush. Where have you been all this time? I don't want you…" She fumbled with her cigarettes, didn't light one. "I don't want you to get hurt."

He was bending down for the fallen coffee cup. "What's that?"

"There's going to be a strike, Rush."

She'd brought it out so quickly he only took in the last two words. "A strike? Where?" He was sitting up. "At the paper?" The smile he expected did not appear. 'But I haven't heard anything about it."

"You're not supposed to," she said. There were other ways of putting it but she could not think of one. "You're too close."

"Too close? I…" He knew he was stammering. "Who's running it, Mona? What's it about?"

"There's a lot involved." She was reaching, not finding what she wanted. "I can't…"

"You mean I'm not being consulted; I'm being warned."

He was right but it was no easier. "I wouldn't call it a warning. It was something I wanted to do. Just so you'd know. It's…" She gave in on the cigarette. "You don't have to," she said, holding the match, "but I'd like it if you didn't say I told you. I don't…" She waved her hand. "It's up to you."

Fletcher stood up so suddenly she hit him with her extinguished match. He looked down. "I guess you don't think I'm much of a reporter. Well, don't

139

worry, I don't give up sources. But you must be right. If I was any kind of reporter I'd know about this myself." He considered laughing. "I should stick to writing record reviews."

She reached up for his arm but he backed away from her. "It's not about you, Rush."

He considered that too. "If it's not maybe it should be." He looked for a trash can. "Have to go, I have an appointment. Thanks, Mona, I'll see you."

She called after him, twice, but he didn't stop. A block away he still had the crunched coffee cup. Saying he had an appointment was true if inarticulate. He could have said he was going to the cemetery (why does cemetery always receive the definite article?) but he did not like to talk about Duffy to anyone who did not know him. If Mona remembered Duffy at all it was as a portly, red-faced man smelling strongly of cigars and inexpensive whisky in the elevator. She wasn't a reporter so Duffy was of no use to her. And she had never seen him dance. His last boat ride Duffy hadn't danced because he was dying and it didn't seem like the thing to do.

At Fourteenth Street Fletcher bought two tokens and took the A train to Forty-Second. He caught the minatory Times Square shuttle to Grand Central and went down deep staircases to the Flushing line. He looked at signs because these midtown movements did not come naturally to him. The Flushing line cars were newish, a kind of Mets blue, installed for the last World's Fair. It was the train you rode to Shea Stadium. In 1964, for a joke, Scanlon and Duffy sent Fletcher who was being a pest about one thing or another out to the Fair. He was severely instructed not to return without something juicy. Fletcher spent a long day there, got sore feet and a sunburn, came back with nothing. The next morning found him trying to be invisible and Lord Shiva and his sidekick allowed him to sweat a while before they pounced. Ashamed, Fletcher admitted he hadn't found anything at the World's Fair. Good, Scanlon said, I'd fire any writer of mine who brought me a story from that goddamn corporate circle jerk. That evening the oracular Duffy put it his own way over beers at the Shipwreck. This World's Fair, he said, is as crooked as a snake's hind leg but it ain't no horse meat in the hamburger. Fletcher was relieved but not enlightened. He'd enjoyed his day at the Fair, especially riding in a Mustang convertible at the Ford Pavilion, but professionally it was a dud. After another beer he asked again why the Fair was no story. Because nobody lives there, Duffy told him.

On the other side of the East River the Flushing line breaks free of the tunnel and becomes an El. It rides on a roller coaster trestle through a factory zone, great industrial palazzi of Silvercup and Dentyne and Eagle Electric. Fletcher got off at Woodside and walked across Queens Boulevard to Calvary Cemetery. It's Catholic and as large as a small town. The cemetery he knew at home was not much bigger than his high school gymnasium and he knew all the names in it.

At the cemetery office they gave Fletcher a map with an X marks the spot on it. The day of the funeral he and others followed the hearse in a cab. They were all jittery with hangovers from the wake and later they all began drinking again. So he didn't clearly recall the geography of Duffy's grave. It was easy to get lost. The mimeographed map dampened with perspiration as he climbed a fair hill, the Chrysler and Empire State spires piercing the August haze behind him. You were that near to Manhattan but it was pretty far for the most part. At the top of the hill he rested beside a tall white cross overlooking the boulevard. As his breath returned a shrill whistle blew, a noontime whistle from a firehouse he could not see. It was beyond the traffic on the other side of the cemetery wall. The whistle was a commonwealth sound that was like Ohio.

According to the map Fletcher was lost but he saw May Duffy as he came down the hill. The gravesite looked familiar because it was astride a grassless, undeveloped patch like a field turned up for plowing. May Duffy was saying the rosary. She was a small, gray woman without a hat sitting on a stone bench. The bench was about what her late husband would have called a sacrifice bunt from his final resting place. Fletcher knew what the rosary was but didn't know how long it took. Waiting near a tree he had more shade than she did.

They were a late childless marriage. Duffy lived in Manhattan and worked for newspapers. In other words he spent considerable time with other men drinking and talking about race horses. May Moran lived in Sunnyside in Queens with her parents who when they died did it very close together. She taught English at a junior high and moderated the debating society. For his part Duffy only thought about marriage when he was at a ballgame and saw a man with a son. Otherwise he did not and when mid-life was gone he thought about it only in the past tense if at all. It was May's conjecture that she had no time for marriage and her colleagues agreed because they felt sorry for her. She knew it was true but what is truth. When she was fifty she wrote a lonelyhearts ad and Duffy who was a little older answered it. He saw the ad because she placed it in the Daily Racing Form that she bought regularly at her newsstand. They meant to go to Niagara Falls for their honeymoon but got no further than the track at Saratoga.

Scanlon found it passing strange that Duffy should take up marriage in his fifties. It was no more suitable to that time of life, he said, than hot rods or stamp collecting. (On other occasions he recommended stamp collecting, the hobby seemed to haunt him somehow.) According to Scanlon matrimony was a bad habit contracted when young, beyond a certain point you were certainly immune. Even if you broke out in spots now and then there was always talcum powder. The editor insisted Duffy would not last out there. ("How in the name of God can someone live in a hellhole called Sunnyside?") Give it six months, Scanlon guaranteed, and he'll be sleeping on my sofa. But Duffy's romance began in the spring when the Triple Crown is in the air. (Their first winner together was Dalliance, a three year old. She paid $7.60 on a two dollar bet and they went to Schrafft's.) When he walked into the *Local*'s newsroom with the *Star-Journal*, the Queens daily, under his arm Scanlon clawed his own cheek with his fingernails. Idolatry in the Old Testament causes the same reaction. So Duffy never required the editor-in-chief's living room sofa. And it was precisely his embrace of regular hours that convinced Duffy to stay with the *Local*. A weekly let him go home early and stay there and when she had corrected her homework and and he had filed his City Hall column they were free in a manner Scanlon could not understand.

"Hello, May." Fletcher walked up to her after the rosary was shut in her purse. She had a papery, powdery cheek that he kissed near its spot of rouge.

"You look very well, Rush," she said, "just like a shining knight."

"Can I quote you on that?" She seemed older than in the spring when they went to lunch in the city. "It's been a long summer, hasn't it?"

"Oh, there's no end to it. Just when you think we've had the worst it gets hotter. And when I think of you in that awful apartment."

'You've never seen it. How do you know it's awful?"

"I can use my God given imagination. How is your book?"

A harsh topic. "I wouldn't say it was writing itself."

"Well that's your own fault then. You should get away from the *Local* and finish it." He knew what she really meant, that he should get away from Scanlon. "You know what I always say, Rush."

"I hear it in my sleep. 'A newspaper is no place for a writer'."

"You may laugh but it's true. And Tom would say the same."

"But he wouldn't mean it…"

"Yes he would. The rest was all bluff." Mrs. Duffy dabbed at her wrist with tissue. "Did I wear too much perfume?"

She had. "No, it's fine, May," Fletcher said.

"You remember how he used to talk. What was it he used to say… I can't remember now. He called something the best writing he ever saw."

The jewel robbery at the Pierre."

"Yes, that's it. Of all things, a hotel jewel heist." The word heist was not alien to Mrs. Duffy. "Can you imagine that? Of everything he ever read he said that was the best. And it wasn't in a good paper either."

"It was the *World-Telegram* I think."

"Well you see what I mean don't you? You don't think that was the best writing… including Shakespeare and everyone, how could it be? You don't think the best writing anyone has ever written could be about a hotel jewel robbery?"

Fletcher thought it over. "Maybe…"

She smacked him softly on the hand. "You're as bad as he is, Rush. No wonder the two of you got along so well. But you'll never convince me. I've read…" The impression left her. "I haven't heard from John."

"He's been busy I know." This bordered on mush. The editor-in-chief was occupied in the day but spent many evenings in riotous Upper East Side excess. The dead could be very dead to Scanlon.

"I had a lovely letter from Jim Logan," Mrs. Duffy said. "You know, his mother and Tom were very close. He told me shocking things from when he was a boy and stayed with Tom."

"The Poet's Corner they called that apartment."

"I have a picture I know he would want. His mother and Tom. And there are some baseball things. I want to give you something but I haven't gone through it all. I can't. I start I... I can't."

Fletcher took her hand. "You're not alone in how you feel, May."

"Yes, I know. I'm not alone in that." There were no tears. "He had so many friends, Rush. And some of them with day jobs."

They smiled at a Duffy remembrance. "It's not the same at the paper."

She didn't hear that. "We weren't married so long, Rush. Only a few years... I don't see why I can't go back. How can you love someone like that? He drank, he was profane. And those terrible cigars. It's in the curtains, the slipcovers. Everywhere. It always seems like he's just come home."

"We missed you at the boat ride, May."

She fussed at the scrap of black lace pinned to her hair. "It was Tom you missed, not me. I won't pretend..."

"I was sorry you didn't come. I didn't have a date."

"It's time you got married yourself instead of this dating." The smile did not last. "I hope I wasn't rude. I meant to call and tell them... I can't bring myself to dial the number. The switchboard will answer and I'm afraid I'll ask for Tom."

Fletcher folded the cemetery map in quarters, in eighths. Duffy had said when I'm gone kid her along but he could not. At home they talk about grandchildren or the weather or next year's garden but he and May had only one subject and it brought only pain. Fletcher felt faint on the white slab in the sun.

"I know," he said. But he did not know what he knew. "Tom's desk is the same as it was." That was true. Even Scanlon appeared to avoid it like a taboo.

Mrs. Duffy almost whispered though there was no one near them. "Rush... is there anything wrong at the paper?'

"Wrong? No, May, everything is..."

She was not quite calm. "A man called last week asking to buy my stock. The stock Tom left. He seemed to know more about it than I do but wouldn't give me his name. Well I told him no of course but I've called John three times and can't get through to him. Have you..."

"Somebody speculating, May. That happens."

"This man whoever he was said I'd want to sell while it was still worth something. He was not very pleasant. Rush, I've promised that money to my sister's son for law school."

"I'll talk to John... don't worry." It was a useless thing to say.

"I didn't want to bother you with this but..."

Fletcher nodded. It was easier than speaking for again he did not know what he knew. It was Duffy's birthday. He was the kind of man who probably did not know his astrological sign but knew an alibi when he heard one and what falsity sounded like. He buttered you up when you needed it and gave you hell when you needed that. Walking away with Mrs. Duffy Fletcher understood he needed some of each.

The Ratio of the Circumference of a Circle to its Diameter

From Tudor City Fletcher walked down the Isaiah staircase past the inscription about beating swords into plowshares to the United Nations. He presumed the religion of many delegates to that institution did not require reading the Old Testament. This was Forty-Third and First Avenue. It was not six yet. He was early again though he dawdled in Grand Central reading a day old *Boston Globe* left in the waiting room. It was not a bad paper on a given day. It was not a bad town for that matter. It wasn't New York but it was all right. If he looked around he might find a *Hartford Courant* or a *Providence Record*. There might even be a *Buffalo News* or a *Utica Observer-Dispatch*. How about a *Rochester Democrat* or a *Plattsburgh Press Republican*? They were all newspapers and he didn't work for any of them.

Crossing the avenue Fletcher held his breath against a whoosh of bus exhaust. What do they burn in those engines? It was enough to turn to you blue like arsenic, or was that strychnine? A police beat man would know. Breathless he turned to look at the sky. The east side of First Avenue allowed a fine prospect of the back wall of the Tudor City apartments. It was tenements and slaughterhouses below when those regal buildings went up so in keeping with Tudor tradition they raised only a drawbridge of windowless brick on that side. That was fine as long as the slaughterhouses and dives and brothels were out there festering on the mud flats of what was once Turtle Bay but the Rockefeller land was cleared and handed over as the UN site. Now if you had windows that way you'd be gazing at the Secretariat building and paying a lot more. If there was irony in the real estate business this was it.

Moral: don't take much for granted in New York; don't bet much will remain the way it is or where it is. Fletcher had his handkerchief out. Just south you had a Con Ed power plant with three steel town smokestacks. It was genuine industrial grit and grime but you never saw anyone with an easel and paintbox knocking off pastels for the tourist trade. There were too many impressionists in the world and not enough naturalists. Those smokestacks must have complemented the slaughterhouse like beer and pig's knuckles. They did not suit the procession of international flagpoles so well but that was the lay of the land in cheek by jowl Manhattan. The flags were limp in the haze, sunk in another bowl of August porridge. Fletcher went north to the totalitarian looking and totalitarian sounding Secretariat to the plaza beside the General Assembly building. General Assembly had an equally Orwellian or maybe just junior high ring to it. The last tour of the day was breaking out of the world's foremost bomb shelter. Fletcher went once, his first year in the city, more than enough for most. The United Nations was a backroom pool hall with Cold War tough guys out to take your money. It never gave you a story unless a Mercedes with diplomatic plates ran over a dog and kept going. They usually kept going.

Elke had said six, not sixish. He assumed she meant it. She'd been punctual the other times they'd met. Fletcher gave high marks for this in a woman. When his parents went to the movies on Saturday night his mother kept his father waiting just for practice. His father retaliated by not putting his shoes on until she was ready. They did this their son understood because they had never doubted their love for one another. Elke called his apartment the night before, Thursday night, said it would be convenient to meet after her work the next day. If he wished... he so wished. She was not in any degree apologetic or yielding. Another man, perhaps, would have put her off a week or declined entirely in a pointed way. Presumably there were courses you could take at the New School for this. There were after all other fish in the sea, some not so cold and bottomless. He'd said yes without hesitation. He did so, he believed, because he was responsive to women and inclined to be gracious. It was a lot of words. Easier to say he wanted to see her again soon. He knew it, so did she no doubt. So he was home all day Friday and to demonstrate an indifference he did not feel he refused to take a shower before he left.

Standing in the plaza, a white granite griddle, Fletcher was sorry he hadn't taken a shower. Heat all around, he walked the esplanade. There was no breeze but traffic on the FDR was moving and the river too. The illusion of coolness that like other illusions had its plus and minuses. Not much action on the esplanade. A photographer with a tripod, post-war sculpture, a man and a woman on the grass. He looked American, she didn't. Fletcher looked back at the security kiosk. No Elke... he would not wait more than ten minutes. An illusion, he would wait an hour or more. He walked past the photographer who was sighting towards romantic, myth shrouded Long Island City. Perhaps he was making a picture postcard of the electric Pepsi-Cola sign on the other side of the river. Nice work if you can get it. At night representatives from the Cameroons, from Ecuador and everywhere else, got a good gander at star spangled Pepsi-Cola whether they wanted to or not. Maybe they liked it, said they didn't. You can never tell about that.

The money wasn't bad, she traveled, worked alone. Fletcher was thinking of a girl Rothberg knew, a film scout. She went here and there making storyboard sketches of movie locations, expenses paid. A sweet job you could say but Fletcher was not envious because the work was out of his league. He couldn't draw and as much as he liked films he was not visual. That's when the shapes and patterns you see arrange themselves into something else, spontaneously. If Fletcher looked from his apartment window at the Figaro cafe his eye settled on the corner mailbox. He could look at it until someone, a woman say, stopped and put a letter into it. The camera follows the woman along Bleecker and shows what she sees or how she is seen in relation to the street. That was film making maybe. From his window Fletcher continues to look at the mailbox on the corner outside the Figaro. It was static but sometimes you get lucky and the mailbox explodes. Maybe that was writing. Then you must describe the woman down to her heels and if you were any good you could. The trouble is you are forever working backward from the event and it gives you a stiff neck after a while.

Fletcher was too far from the kiosk, their rendezvous, and returned the way he'd come. To his disappointment the photographer and the couple on the grass seemed no more suspicious from a different angle. They were not an assassination team awaiting the secretary general's evening stroll and nothing would make them so. U Thant probably didn't take an evening stroll anyway, he was probably at the beach. He was probably at the beach in Burma at his family jamboree. That is if Burma had beaches, Fletcher couldn't remember. If you had any brains you were at the beach. Reporters stayed in the city and hoped for the best. Shooting U Thant along the peaceful banks of the East River might just push the heat wave off the front page and he'd have an exclusive. He might get a bullet hole too but what a story.

They were not in love the couple on the grass, too much space between them. And when they stood the man did not help her up, Fletcher's idea of vivid romance. He drew even with them as the man looked at his watch. The man shook his head and then checked his watch again. If this was a first date it was not going well. The man hurried ahead as the woman called after him. "Then I shall see you here," she said. The man did not respond, she didn't expect him to it seemed. She had a handbag and a superfluous raincoat. Fletcher was caught in mid-step. *I don't know anyone here*, he still heard Vix say. Here... anyone here. He looked at the face of the woman with the raincoat. Then I'll see you here... *here*.

"Miss," he said.

She gripped her handbag. "Yes?"

"Would you mind telling me where you're from?"

"No, I suppose not... why do you ask?"

"Your accent. It reminds me of someone I knew."

The handbag tighter. "Oh yes." The oppressive weather, the questioning. "I'm from Rhodesia. I'm emigrating you see."

Empathy, so had Fletcher in a way. "It's not quite an English accent, is it?"

"Yes, it is different. Not everyone notices."

"Could I…"

"I'm sorry, I don't mean to be rude… I have an appointment."

Fletcher knew the sound of that. She made a second apology with her eyes and moved awkwardly away through the sculpture garden. Her shoes were flats and she had thickish ankles but he didn't think he would need to recall her. He dug for a dime and jogged to a phone booth on First Avenue. It was occupied and he stood with impatient arms folded. Looking uptown he saw the woman come out of the north entrance of the sculpture garden. She crossed the avenue and Fletcher lost her in the traffic. She'd ditched him easily. The urine scented booth was free. He dialed the *Daily News*.

"City desk. Bob Hickman please."

The *News* phone circuits sounded like mice in a barn. "Hickman."

"It's Fletcher."

"Been calling you. What's up?"

"I'm over at the UN."

"Great. Meet me in Costello's."

"Can't. I got a date."

"Bring her along. She won't mind once she meets me."

Possibly so. Hickman was good looking like a movie reporter in a movie where the reporters are good guys. Some country must have made one. "Listen: do you know of an honest immigration attorney?"

Hickman laughed. "Of course not. I do know a leprechaun and Francis the talking mule but I don't expect to meet an honest immigration attorney in this life."

"How bad are they?"

"Depends on how much you need them. They tie you up in knots and charge you for the rope. Why the interest?"

"You know, just a hunch."

"Man, those words are like *Hey Jude* with a bottle of beer in your hand. I'll get you a name. Anything else?"

Fletcher hesitated, felt regret. "Yeah, okay. How about a guy named Stutz. He rents dancing girls."

"Stutz… Stutz. There's a bell ringing on that but it's not loud. Is he from Jersey? I heard about a guy consolidating that stuff last year but it went off the radar."

"I'm looking for his clubhouse."

"You got it. I'll see what I can find." Business done. "So, what's on tonight?"

Fletcher dropped in a nickel. "Oh, just some drinks. "She's not…"

"Need a few bucks?"

Now Fletcher laughed. "No, I don't need a few bucks and I don't need you to deliver them either."

"I'd be discreet. You'd never know I was there."

"Isn't that what the press always says?"

Having got that in Fletcher hung up. Out of the booth he saw Elke by the security kiosk. He knew her in spite of the changes. Her snapped back hair had grown out, she was a touch Jane Fonda in *Klute*. She'd lost weight and was in distinctly American clothes plus a formidable pair of Frye boots. There were blue jeans and a fringed vest. (What Levi's must cost on the black market in Eastern Europe, now there was a piece waiting to be written.) Previously she'd worn skirts and peasant blouses, he did not care for the cowgirl look. He missed the ankh, the loose silver bracelet, the open sandals. He liked women's feet. And there was makeup now. But it was wrong to be reviewing her and he stopped. She would not do that to him. They, the others, didn't he was pretty sure. And if they did what was the point. He didn't change, he was always the same.

"I am one, two minutes late," she said, "and you are calling the other girl."

This was different too. "That was my agent. I just had a great idea for a thrilling chase scene right here at the UN. Sell it to the movies. Make a million bucks. Go to Rio. Want to go to Rio?" Fletcher felt pumped up because she was the part of humanity that wore earrings and she had called him and it was so obviously Manhattan on a Friday night.

"Like *North by Northwest*."

"What's like *North by Northwest*?"

Elke passed her arm over the plaza. "Thrilling chase scene."

"Oh yeah." He'd forgotten about Hitchcock. Their conversation had precluded them from kissing at first and Fletcher feared the moment had passed. But Elke took his hand and kissed him on both cheeks. There was perfume on her skin.

"It is not important," she said.

What wasn't? Rio? *North by Northwest*? That he hadn't run home and showered and shaved again? That he didn't have a job at the moment? "It's good to see you," he said. "Does Burma have a coastline?"

Elke was hungry and wanted to eat. They went to a place she knew on Second Avenue, Le Petit Veau. It looked like an abandoned oyster bar on the outside. That was a good sign though there was no menu in the window and that might be a bad sign. Fletcher had not got paid. Elke knew the owner, she and UNICEF friends went there. Annette was the owner and she poked a long loaf of French bread at Fletcher as if she thought he was not half bad for an American. She laughed in at least three languages. Le Petit Veau reminded Fletcher of Connie's Barbecue Pit on Main Street in Monacacy Court House except Annette brought them snails as an appetizer and there was wine in dark bottles instead of root beer in mason jars. If Connie saw a snail in her kitchen, not likely, she would step on it.

"There's this great place in my home town like this," he said. He pierced a snail with what he presumed was a snail fork. "Well, not exactly like this."

"I would like to see Ohio."

That could not be true. "I always go home for Labor Day. There's a kind of family get-together and…"

"And you have another girl there like the one in your apartment?"

"I told you she is my cousin."

Elke poured their wine. "I have a young cousin too but I don't keep him in my apartment. It is… is it fishy?"

"Yes, fishy. I mean fishy in general, not in this particular." This was entertaining. "She ran away from home. Well, she ran away from camp." Fletcher re-phrased that. "I mean she was on her way home from camp to start college and decided to come to New York first. She's impulsive… sometimes. Not always."

"And you love this sometimes not always impulsive cousin."

A wide, wine purple grin. "Well yes, I do. She's my favorite cousin. I've got about eight hundred of them."

"You truly have eight hundred cousins?"

"The results of the last census aren't in yet but yes, I'd say eight hundred is in the ballpark."

Elke frowned expertly. "In which ballpark is this?"

"It's not any one ballpark. A ballpark figure means an estimate."

"You have promised before not to talk about baseball."

"I'm not talking about baseball. It's an expression, an idiom."

"But why is it in the ballpark?"

"Because out of the ballpark means something else." Fletcher had never enjoyed snails so much. He'd never had them before. "You're being intentionally difficult."

"I am not difficult but I don't believe you have eight hundred cousins. Maybe you have five hundred and you are saying eight hundred to impress me. But I am not impressed." She held her hands about a foot apart. "American exaggeration. *C'est ca les hommes.*"

There was no waiter. Annette herself brought a chicken casserole Fletcher didn't know they'd ordered. Annette liked Elke. They talked rather fast, Fletcher not catching any of it. Elke's father was German, the mother Alsatian. It was as much of her personal history as he knew. They shared the casserole and a second bottle of wine. Fletcher was willing to cast his typewriter fund to the four winds. He didn't need a typewriter or even pencils with erasers if he didn't have a paper to write for.

"Burma does have a coast," Elke said, "on the Indian Ocean."

"I was wondering where U Thant goes to bury himself in the sand."

She looked puzzled. "Yes, but he is retired now."

Fletcher felt stupid, with good reason. "Right, sorry, the new guy is Waldheim."

As his face was red she spared him. "Why is Amanda running away to you?"

Fletcher thought about it. "She's nursing a broken heart." He thought about it further. "She had sex for the first time this summer I think. That's a guess."

"I am sorry for her. She is sad?"

He peered into the chicken he didn't like. He wasn't used to wine and it had fuddled him. "Right now she's kind of hyper. She's been cleaning my apartment, a characteristic Ohio activity."

"And what will happen?"

"She'll go back home I guess. My mother..." He wiped his eyes with the table napkin; he supposed it was a serviette. "My mother is negotiating her return. It's my fault you see. I'm a bad influence. I'm Heathcliff, semi-Byronic, a bounder, a cad. Maybe I'll rent a garret and grow etchings. Even her broken heart is my fault."

Elke poured him wine. "You have nothing to do with it. Maybe you want to think you do but you don't."

"I don't want to think I do. I'm not flattering myself."

"Her heart will get better. She was not in love."

"She wasn't?"

"You are not in love with the first one. They are only a corkscrew."

Now that was flattering. "Is that true?" Fletcher was struck by this. He'd been in love he believed but said he knew nothing about it. Conversely he assumed women knew all about it in an occupational way. If Elke was right he was sorry to think the first girl he slept with had not been in love with him. At the time he thought so, unquestionably. He hadn't been in love with her but with another girl who did not sleep with him. He never thought of her much, his first girl, except to think she was thinking of him. He changed the subject. "It's college and all that. Doing what's expected of her. She'd like to move here and be... I don't know what."

"Like you," Elke said. "You came here from there."

"But I went to college first like a good boy."

She laughed without smiling. "So I have seen. Too bad. You can't help Amanda, that is why she came to you. If she truly wants to run away she would go to..."

"Tibet?"

"Yes, Tibet, why not? Or Paris or even Mexico. Somewhere there is no cousin Rush, a good boy. And she would change her beautiful American name to... who can say? Coming to you is a suicide note lacking the suicide."

If Fletcher looked into that statement deeply enough he might be discouraged. He didn't. "Mandy is intelligent, she'll work it out. I almost joined the army when I got out of high school and look where I am today. She'll make up her own mind but it has to be in Ohio and not in my apartment. I can't afford to feed her."

"You should have brought her too."

Fletcher regarded the brick warm bistro walls. "I should have. She'd like this, she really would." He drank wine and rationalized. "But when she's not being hyper she's eating carrots and sleeping. She's probably in bed now reading *Crime and Punishment*."

"You are so sure? Did you lock her in?"

"No, I didn't lock her in."

"So, she might be… anywhere."

He begged to disagree and said so. "She isn't anywhere; she's right where I left her. She wouldn't go out without… well for one thing she doesn't have any money."

"Money is never necessary. Is she pretty? I thought you were keeping her for yourself but now you talk like her father."

"Her father is a prize winning Maytag dealer. He's known for his impasto technique and a kind of right wing meadowlark quality." He didn't know what he was saying.

Elke skipped this. "What is it she called you?"

"What Mandy called me? When?"

"When I asked for you on the phone. She called you…"

Fletcher felt red again, it was the wine. "She called me Pie. That's my nickname where I come from. Like apple pie."

"Yes, I see. Like violence is as American as cherry pie." Her serious face went very well with wine. "Not… the ratio of the circumference of a circle to the diameter?"

"No, not at all like that. I was not good at math."

"But I was and I will call you Pi without the 'e'. So it will be like you are in Ohio with me but different."

When they finished eating Elke lit a cigarette. She was a frugal smoker. Fletcher considered suggesting a movie but he didn't want to go to a movie. He didn't suggest it, he desired real life. They paid the check, splitting it. Madame Annette did not charge them for the house wine. Elke spoke to her again as they left. There was laughter between them. Fletcher feared the joke was on him but didn't care. He felt too good. Sometimes beer gave him a headache as he was drinking it. The wine had fuddled him, true, but he was left lushly pink as well. And Elke had never been so… the word would not come. Outside it was twilight and they walked up to P. J. Clarke's on Third Avenue. They'd been there twice so it was a place they knew but it was crowded and hot this time and they didn't stay long. Movie alley was just uptown but Fletcher still didn't want to see a movie and have their intimacy chilled by a long line and air conditioning. You could be alone in a bar but waiting for a movie to begin you were thrust like a helpless newborn into the lap of other lives.

And they might argue about the film. Because of *North by Northwest* they were talking about movies at P. J.'s and Elke said she'd been to a revival of *Z* from 1968. Fletcher was disturbed because *Z* had played at the Bleecker Street

Cinema, three blocks from his apartment. That was over a weekend earlier in the month and there were lines. One night perhaps a woman's sturdy European laughter had washed over him in a wave of humidity. This was rather abstract jealousy and a foolish proprietorship. The Village was not his private reserve. She could go there without him if she chose and yet... he let the thought be and concluded with saying that Z was clumsy and overrated, too much appreciated because it had a leftist point of view. *The Local*'s film critic, he said (exaggerating), carried it on her all time ten best list. In fact, Fletcher exclaimed (exaggerating wildly), it was the only film anyone had ever heard of on her all time ten best list. Elke wasn't listening. She liked Z but did not feel the need to defend it. She said it was more fun to go to the Village with him.

Leaving the bar Fletcher said he should call Amanda and Elke said he could call from her apartment. He knew where she lived but hadn't been there. They went back to Second Avenue and halfway to First on 49th Street. There were high rises on the block but her building was a four story tenement with a Chinese laundry on the ground floor. She was two flights up in the rear, the rooms would not get much light. Fletcher thought of his apartment as old, it did not always strike him as cheerless. Elke's place was bleak and had an itinerant look. There was a roommate, a girl from Bolivia who was back home for a month. Elke and she took turns sleeping on the sofa. Fletcher sat on the sofa, called Amanda. She had switched to *A Farewell to Arms*. She wondered if it made sense that Hemingway's characters speak the way he writes when everybody really speaks differently. Good point, he said, and he told her not to wait up. Amanda said she wouldn't.

It was plain. Fletcher wanted to make love to Elke because of who she was. There are other reasons but in this case that was primary. He wanted to tell her he loved her because of the apartment. It was such an untender place he wanted to take her away from it though where that would be he could not imagine. To his own apartment, to Paris, to Monacacy Court House. But where he saw her he could not see himself and where he was she was not. It was a pity they were not much alike. It was a pity no one is much alike but that's why there is a UN of which Kurt Waldheim and not U Thant is currently the big cheese. She took off her awkward boots and gunslinger vest and brought an opened bottle of wine. He was glad of the wine because his heart was pounding. He felt eighteen again in the speechlessness of desire. The sofa was uncomfortable but Elke out of her boots and vest was closer with her legs curled beside him. Why had she called if not for this? That broad back and moderately plump face, she might have been from a farm state with 4-H ribbons. He knew she wasn't.

"I wish you liked me more," he said.

She looked at him. 'I like you as much as necessary. How much is that? You don't know. I don't."

It was not a kissable response. "I didn't hear from you when you came back. I was sorry. I wanted to see you."

"No, well… it was not a good time. You understand I hope? I was not picking you out to be unfriendly."

"You're different tonight. Why?" The wine was sour. He put his glass on the floor. "From before I mean, you seem so…"

"I'm trying," she said.

He reached for her. "Why do you have to try?"

"There are some things… I thought tonight perhaps but no, I can't."

"I want to kiss you. You might…"

She moved away. "Don't…"

"I don't understand, Elke… what happened?"

"There is nothing happened. Tonight isn't good. I will tell you sometime. I thought… you should go home."

"I don't want to go home. I want to stay."

"Please, I don't want to argue. You won't stay if I say no and I say no. All right?"

Yes, that was all right. He understood, thick as he was. It was fine, just fine. But the annoyance Fletcher felt was an undressed demon and did not remain. If he thought about it he might laugh. She had made him laugh a half dozen times and you can't buy that. He took his wine glass to the sink. He did it slowly so she might speak but when he looked back from the front door her head was down on the sofa. Even simple words are sometimes an indecency so he left without speaking. He had not been there fifteen minutes. At Lexington Avenue he rode the local down to Astor Place and walked home. On his corner outside the Borgia teenagers were passing Boone's Farm around and shaving hash into a pipe. He'd been thinking of a piece for the fall, that a new generation was distinct after ten years. God help us all if it comes down to five. It was speeding up and he was slowing down. Upstairs Amanda was asleep in his bed. She'd been reading Hemingway and Susan Sontag. What kind of dreams that would give you was anyone's guess. He put the books on the nightstand and clicked off the light. If it was winter he could tuck her in and cover her broken heart with another blanket. Her broken heart and the hair on her arms she thought was too dark occupied her mind. She told him she loved watching the world go by from his window. He did too. It was an addiction without a cure except aging out.

On the living room coffee table Amanda had written: Call Mr. Hickman! Important!! Can I be your secretary? I'm a really good speller!! Fletcher looked at the clock. He felt like talking to someone and Hickman was a night owl.

"How was your date?"

"Fun while it lasted," Fletcher said. "Where do all those people in P. J. Clarke's come from?"

"Probably out-of-towners. No offense, Rush."

"Pat Moynihan was in there gassing. Isn't he the ambassador to India now?"

"The hamburgers are better at P. J.'s." The sound of a beer can opening. "So, having nothing better to do tonight I made a few calls on your behalf. Re immigration..."

"Let's talk about that a second." Fletcher took off his shoes and settled back. "Say you get off a plane at Kennedy without papers. What happens?"

"Airline is supposed to bounce you back. They don't always."

"And when they don't?"

"Depends." A sip of beer. "I'm no expert but if you're white and English speaking you might get loose on your own leash pending a hearing. You could also ask for asylum but that's a different category and tough to prove."

"So if you look like Che Guevara?"

"Most likely then your new address would be the immigration lockup on Church Street. Not bad. Better than alimony jail."

"So otherwise Customs, passport control, whoever it is, they release you, give you a hearing thirty days hence and you..."

"Skip. It happens, Rush, no doubt about it."

"I'm not talking about somebody overextending their vacation. I mean somebody who couldn't get a visa in the first place."

"Need I point out to the soul of the New York *Local* that this, may it always be thus, is an open society."

"No, but at what level does this decision to let you walk get made? And can they be influenced by the usual means?"

"I would say yeah, you could buy someone somehow, but why?"

"I don't know. Let's hold that. Back to you."

Hickman was trying to stop smoking; it wasn't working out. Fletcher heard a match and his breath. "Julie called me tonight. I've got the kids the whole Labor Day weekend."

"Is it the same guy?"

"Yeah, the biology teacher from Mater Christi. Getting serious I think. He sounds all right. I mean he sounds fine. I just don't know if I can handle a step-father in the picture. This custody arrangement is one thing but a step-father? I wish I paid attention to biology in high school. I wouldn't be in this fix."

"Yeah, but you've got half an infield and you're their father."

"True and as to that I've got my itinerary here: Central Park, ballgame, the Circle Line. If there's a mob hit this weekend I'm never speaking to a gangster again."

"Don't forget F. A. O. Schwarz."

"Stop spending my paycheck. Okay. After running down several immigration attorneys no better than they should be I give a call down to the police shack. Finley is there. Know him? Duffy did. An old Brooklyn Eagle guy still drinks his coffee down at the shack. I mention Stutz and Finley says yeah, a very dirty guy. But he's nothing new, Rush. Under one name or another he'd been in and out of girls and gambling for twenty years. But Finley says Stutz is no professor. Mean and competent to an extent but not the smartest. Finley says he's done time but nothing big and he hasn't heard about him for a while."

Fletcher twisted for pad and pencil. "That could be."

"Now what follows is a stray shot. As long as I had the phone in my hand I called an investigator at Manhattan DA. I'll put this on your bill. He's a Knicks fan and I get him in the Garden now and then. So we're talking and I say does he happen to have anything on this Stutz and he says Stutz is a nobody and puts me off. Now this DA guy is not the best liar in the world as his wife's attorneys have discovered and it sounds to me like he just overthrew the cutoff man. So I try him this way. Okay, I say, but my immigration source says Stutz is a comer. I'm telling you, Rush, the silence after that would freeze your margaritas for you. Now he's trying to get off and I'm trying to keep him and he's telling me forget it and he gets pissed and says two words not guaranteed to make me lose interest. 'It's Federal', he says to me. Fine. It's Federal. I'll turn in my press card and go to barber college. So I expect this guy won't return my calls for a while. What's going on? You don't get the Feds worked up about prostitution."

"It might just be drugs," Fletcher said.

"Say that like you mean it, Rush."

Fletcher sat up on the sofa. "I don't know. I had a thought tonight it might be weapons. But that's out of left field."

"That's good. I mean it's bad but it's good."

"I think the girl I've been tracing was from Rhodesia."

"There you go…" There was a pause. "Where am I on this?"

Another pause. "You don't think I can handle it?"

"You know I don't mean that. I'm better positioned for this… if there is anything. You're a weekly. If you've got a paper at all."

"I know, I'm not arguing. You've been in since I called you at six. I'll follow the immigration angle. I'll feed you what I get. How about this: a bar called Clover downtown on Harrison Street closed in the last three months. It did not close due to a lack of clientele."

"Harrison, right. I'll start with the SLA."

"Also a place called Dream Lucky on Desbrosses…"

"Desbrosses? Damn, you do get around."

"Stutz used to socialize there. He doesn't now. I think it might be staked out. If it is they've got a picture of me getting tossed on my ass."

Hickman grunted. "All in a day's work. Dream Lucky, right. I won't take the kids."

"We'll talk tomorrow. Don't call me at the shop."

That pause again. "Rush… when you say something like that it's time to get out. Listen to me. You don't owe that old man anything. He's an original but that mold is broken. And you paid him out, long ago. Duffy's dead, you can't…"

"It isn't anything I don't know, believe me."

"Did you ever call that guy back at the Examiner?"

"I don't want to go out there. I like New York. I don't see myself starting all over again somewhere else."

"You started here once…"

"I was a kid, Bob. I'm too old to fail… to start over. These are newspapers we're talking about, not Nedick's. They're not interchangeable."

"I'm not so sure about that some days but I won't argue the point."

Fletcher did not want to argue about his life now. He needed Logan and Maggie for that. "Nobody knows where this strike is going anyway."

"It won't be pretty. When's the little girl going home?"

"Soon, I hope, but I hate to stick her on the bus. Maybe I'll wait a week and stick us both on the bus. She could use some fun. How much does fun cost?"

Hickman didn't know. Fletcher wrote down the names of three lawyers and hung up. He looked at the floor and went over his mistakes. As the latter promised to take a while he settled for looking at the floor. He ran the night over in his mind until it needed a table of contents and an index. And foot-notes. The first footnote read: should have taken that shower.

The Three Cadillacs

Late Saturday morning Fletcher brought Amanda to the Zeus Brothers coffee shop for bacon and eggs. Harry Zeus, oldest brother, had generous family feeling that he demonstrated by working his relatives to the bone. They flew about while he remained calm after his own fashion. At Amanda Harry clucked and winked, bringing her an additional portion of bacon himself because she was too thin. He was pleased to hear she was from Ohio too. Harry had the idea Ohio was the sort of place where you could keep all the goats you desired. Harry loved goats. Not everyone understood but Harry was accustomed to an ignorance about, not to say a lack of interest in, his special passion. Greenwich Village was good for the coffee shop business because there were customers ordering breakfast at all hours. (Fletcher thought Harry's Breakfast All Day neon sign the finest in Manhattan.) But on the other hand the Village was not so good for goats. If you tried to keep them the police, Harry's mortal enemy, would take them and sell them to the Arabs in Brooklyn. Harry had been told Brooklyn was good country for raising goats due to the mountains and waterfalls they have there. Goats love waterfalls he explained.

Harry did not get on with the police because of their practice of ticketing his Cadillac. He and two of his brothers each had Cadillacs. (Youngest brother Michael did not remember Greece and took the subway.) They parked them on University Place, in a row if possible, and fed dimes into the parking meters every hour. Aside from being frowned on by urban planners and ethicists the world over meter feeding is a violation of New York City traffic regulations. As three consecutive Cadillacs take up a certain amount of room, about the distance from home plate to the pitcher's mound in Yankee Stadium, they were obvious to the naked eye. We are business running here, Harry said to the police. The police did not agree and regarded the three Cadillacs with special disfavor. Sometimes when the coffee shop was busy Harry did not hear the bell of the kitchen timer he had cleverly installed by the cash register to warn him when to feed dimes to the meters. On these occasions the police might ticket one, perhaps two, and on real red letter days all three of the Cadillacs. This brought Harry and his brothers out to the sidewalk like thunderbolts. Howling and tearing their hair, or in Harry's case his toupee, their anguish was appreciated across the street at the *Local*. If he'd been given to tears Fletcher might have wept at the beauty of it all. The meter maids were especially vengeful, as if hatched from the Hellenic subconscious where Furies and Harpies lurk. Whenever they or the police nailed his Cadillac Harry would stand limply by the cash register and say to all: "I work for nothing today". These words called into question all that America stood for. It was as if self-advancement and economic freedom were all a ruse to spirit the hard won dollars, wrung from the frying of innumerable cheeseburgers, into the coffers of city government. The hills are full of bandits, Harry once whispered to Fletcher.

That his brothers had their own Cadillacs did not mean they were free men. Yet for the time it took for them to commute over the Triborough Bridge and down the east side they had this illusion. They had hand-me-down Cadillacs, previous models belonging to Harry to which he retained the titles. (Harry resembled Scanlon in this respect.) Befitting their rank the siblings still wore boiled white aprons from Consolidated Laundries at the coffee shop while Harry dressed in subdued four and five tone suits from Theo & Theo on Steinway Street. The pocket handkerchiefs alone could double as tablecloths. Harry had a threadbare Stalinesque moustache and cufflinks a trifle smaller than his hubcaps. His favorite American expression was: "you're kidding me." He'd say this to Fletcher who was seldom in the habit of kidding anyone. Harry took a shine to Amanda the first time her cousin took her to the coffee shop in June. The Stedmans were darker than the Fletchers, if not quite Mediterranean, and Harry insisted Amanda must be Greek. Fletcher said no. Harry said yes, another Greek could always tell. Fletcher said he knew his own family and there were positively no Greeks in it. You're kidding me, Harry said.

Amanda abandoned the breakfast she found decadent (that word was catching on) and left to go shopping on Fifth Avenue. She was feeling better. From Ohio Mrs. Stedman had signaled her forgiveness in a typically Stedman way. In care of Fletcher, to whom she was not speaking, she sent her daughter a check with instructions to buy mother a raincoat at Bonwit Teller. Additionally daughter, if she so chose, could purchase a back to school outfit, preferably a sturdy sensible tweed as she was presumably done growing. Fletcher was surprised this billet doux did not eat a hole in the coffee table. He chose to see his mother's hand at work in this. She had not called; she was sparing him as she invariably did.

During the night Fletcher awoke thinking of Elke. Thinking of her as a woman made him suddenly afraid that Amanda was afraid she was pregnant. It was possible he supposed and thinking more as gray light appeared in the window (and his wine headache expanded) it became more than possible. She had not told him much about Wayne or how far they had gone, an expression he needed to bring down from the attic, but he was willing to think the worst or the best depending on how you looked at it. One moment she was antic, determined to be restless and questioning. He certainly had never been so young. At other times she could be found stationary in a chair clutching a pair of white socks. Then she seemed as old as he and perhaps he knew the reason. She was pregnant.

She wasn't. On the way to the Zeus Brothers they passed a pharmacy and Amanda said she would stop in there a minute. Her tone implied Fletcher could stick to the sidewalk like flypaper. He did as experience implied she was buying Tampax and when they reached the coffee shop she headed directly for the bathroom with her white drugstore bag. He was relieved, more so than his cousin by the look of it. She probably had not been worried. His own fears seemed to rise from the feeling he was letting Amanda down. She'd come to him after all. He should be asking about Wayne, a name he quickly hated, helping her get over it, but the truth was he didn't want to hear about the Saginaw Bay Romeo all that much. A camp counselor had once told him to "get the lead out" and he'd disliked the breed ever since. Yet Fletcher was looking for an opening and if he had to endure tears on Wayne's behalf and an admission of… well, an admission of whatever it might be, he would. A few cups of Zeus Brothers coffee might have brought it front and center but Harry, the goatherd of University Place, got in the way. Harry did not understand the strike and consequently had it all figured out.

Harry liked having the *Local* across the street and thought of the staff as his newspaper boys. He didn't advertise in the paper, coffee shops don't have to unless they are trying to be something other than a coffee shop, and while he didn't read it either he proudly displayed a mock front page drawing of himself in a Lord Byron Phrygian cap under the headline: You're Kidding Me? This was a gift from Scanlon whose daily bombast could include an ode on what a great guy and American success story Harry was. Scanlon felt this way because Harry adored him and for all his faults Scanlon was not one to turn his back on blind worship. There was something about the aristocratic, well tailored editor that spoke to the Greek coffee shop owner in his four or five tone suits with powerhouse lapels. Scanlon arrived in person each morning for the black coffee and buttered roll he never completely consumed and Harry accepted this as a mark of lordly esteem. Harry would have brought them over in a chafing dish but this was not Scanlon's way. In twelve years Fletcher had never known his editor to send an employee on errands not work related. In the worst of weather if Scanlon needed a cigar to gnaw on he went out and got it.

This though was something of a false front, like a king who sleeps on a cot because it's good for his back. Scanlon's preference was to grant favors, ones sometimes awash with stern morality tales and contradictory testimony. He'd bewail the poorhouse staring them all in the face even as he boasted of rising circulation and the sound financial footing that were due to his shrewd stewardship. If that was too optimistic he'd bellow about taxes. We'd be in the catbird seat, ran a familiar moan, if it wasn't for Uncle Sam. God forbid anyone should think the paper was making money. It was getting along, holding its own, our head is above water but only just, remember that. Any other publisher, he'd insist, would have thrown in the towel long ago. Fletcher had often heard the full throated boast: I'm sixty-something years old and I don't owe a dime. It was a curious affirmation and one in which many of his personnel could not join. Some owed money all over.

Most likely Harry didn't owe a dime either. In the Cadillac hierarchy he'd moved up to an Eldorado. Its leather interior was as tender as braised goat meat. But during that morning chat while the roll was buttered the effusive coffee shop owner never breathed a word of his regard for hollow horned ruminants. The highly urban *Local* editor had probably never seen a goat in his life and Harry may have understood this. In the matter of the Cadillac however Harry's instinct deserted him. Not long after buying the Eldorado he followed Scanlon outside hoping to show it off. Unfortunately he was barking up the wrong noblesse oblige. Scanlon had no appreciation for cars and was such an old fashioned New Yorker he didn't know how to drive. Harry extended his arm towards the windshield as if Miss Greek Independence, draped only in puff pastry, was arranged there. Scanlon's regal eye traversed the arm and Cadillac and looked at the street. He nodded. You're right, he said, we could use a newsstand on this block. Harry was dismayed and then before his very eyes a meter maid with all the viciousness of her kind struck without warning.

After Amanda left for Fifth Avenue Fletcher ate her toast and the glazed doughnut Harry had awarded her for being young. The doughnut was sweet and sticky and he fought the taste with more coffee. Harry brought another carafe and Fletcher resolutely stared out the window. This meant he had to look at the picket line across the street but it was better than again catching the eye of Harry who was patrolling the aisle instead of hovering over the cashier, his sister Maria. (When unfamiliar customers took up a booth to drink only coffee Harry rammed their bill down on the receipt spindle like Van Helsing plunging a stake into Dracula's heart.) The strike befuddled Harry and he said to many: this is kidding me, right? He'd scratched the wine dark cheek he shaved regularly once a week and retreated into Balkan introspection. A strike so close to home like this and against a man like Mr. Scanlon almost threw a shadow across his own existence, Cadillacs and all.

But that was yesterday. After a night's sleep and a reflective drive in the Eldorado Harry's equanimity returned (if his relatives tried to picket him he would ship them home) and with it his special insight into Village affairs. He elbowed his way into the booth and laid out his theory for Fletcher's delectation. It had something to do with communists and something to do with women and something to do with putting too much eggplant in the moussaka. Strangers might be baffled by this last item but Fletcher had been drinking coffee long enough at the Zeus Brothers to know what Harry meant. The moussaka was the *Local* and the eggplant was politics.

Rothberg drifted in. He looked aimless, much as Fletcher felt, but perhaps that was projecton. He was not so close to Rothberg for all the years they'd worked together. Well, yes, he'd had the same thought about Harmon. Who then was the hard one to know? Rothberg swung himself into the booth opposite Fletcher and poured a cup of coffee. His eyes were zig zag, he was stoned. That's how discipline breaks down, Fletcher mumbled, very quickly. Once you became used to Saturday staff meetings, it took a while, it kept carousing in line. Who would even consider a good healthy drunk on Friday night when you had to face the tabloid Tarquinius Superbus the next day.

If Rothberg was stoned he didn't seem very happy about it. "Seen the old man?"

Fletcher shook his head. "Mahaffy says he went up to Luchow's."

"Luchow's... why?"

"We're having Harmon's dinner there next week." "Harmon's dinner?"

A little dense this morning, what could be the reason. "His farewell dinner, remember?"

"I talked to Harmon yesterday," Rothberg said. "He says he's honoring the strike. I wouldn't expect him."

Speaking of discipline, Fletcher was slouching in his booth corner. He sat up. "What's the strike got to do with him? As of next Friday he works for Newsday."

"Yeah, well, what can you do." Rothberg decided on more sugar, stirred it in. "I guess he wants to get off on the right foot."

"What about leaving on the right foot?"

"Listen: he goes to Newsday, he joins the Newspaper Guild. That's a whole new world. Why should he get caught up in choosing sides in this... this I don't know what."

"Fine, stay out of it but he can show up for his own dinner."

"Rush..." Rothberg pushed his coffee away. "Nobody is showing up for this dinner. Get hip, Scanlon is the issue. If you go to the dinner you're in effect saying I'm with the old man and fuck the strike."

"There are people who feel that way."

Rothberg opened his mouth, closed it." Who? The real old ones? You?" "What about you? You've made up your mind?"

He had. "I'm thirty. I like this business." He spoke more slowly. "This paper will change and I want to be here. I'm not tying myself down to Scanlon. I've worked for him, he's paid me. That's as far as our relationship goes. Except I don't want to see him sitting by himself in Luchow's next week. I don't hate the guy."

Fletcher looked out at the picket line. "Harmon should tell him."

"I doubt he will. You'd better." Rothberg didn't wait for a refusal. "You're closest to him, Rush. What do you want? Do you want him sitting there like

Orson Welles at the opera house? Tell him… he'll call it off."

Duffy once said Scanlon was that rare thing in New York, a fight you could not fix. "You think he's already beaten."

"Yeah, I think he is. He's finished." Rothberg seemed straight now. "And if that sounds hard whose fault is it? Who asked him to give an option on his stock to that Wall Street guy?"

"Whatever the reason it was his right to do it."

"The reason is simple, he needs the money. All right, that's his business but how did he get so in debt? Does anybody know? And for once he wasn't as smart as he thinks he is. He couldn't keep stalling those bankers indefinitely."

"I don't think Chemical Bank wants the paper, Ed. What would they do with it? Sure, it makes a profit but that could change in a month if there's chaos like this."

"They could bring in somebody who knows what to do. How many readers do we lose because the old man won't have anything to do with sports or fashion… or sex."

"I've written about sex," Fletcher said.

"Nobody noticed, Rush. You haven't quite got that Valley of the Dolls touch." Rothberg said this lightly but it was not a light conversation. "And don't kid yourself about Scanlon. If they offer him some kind of emeritus position with a paycheck he'll jump at it."

Whatever he was, and all the precincts weren't in yet and never would be, Scanlon was not window dressing. "If there is a deal there. I don't…"

"What choice has he got? He tried to bail himself out with this slumlord and look what happened?" A headshake of genuine woe. "We'll be years getting over this. The SoHo News killed us this week. I mean they creamed us, Rush."

They had, there was no denying it. Balancing a more in anger than in sorrow tone with mordant glee, the SoHo News reported Thursday that Scanlon, strapped for cash and attempting to prevent a bank takeover, had solicited financing from Banner, Quinn. Amongst other dubious assets this real estate firm owned the Barcelona, a midtown welfare hotel said to make the Broadway Central look like a bed and breakfast inn on Cape Cod. Currently involved in a zoning dispute over the height of a projected office tower Banner, Quinn was interested in positive, upbeat publicity and very uninterested in the contrary. According to the SoHo News Scanlon took a fall on the Broadway Central story so as not to rattle the nerves of a man whose money he was courting. F. X. Quinn and Scanlon were on the same Upper East Side dinner circuit and had been romancing at least since the spring. At least since then, hinted the SoHo News, because it was curious that while Banner, Quinn had generously donated to all contenders in the mayoral race the *Local* never mentioned them in its coverage.

"They had help," Fletcher said. Rothberg was looking at a woman settling down on a counter stool. "It was a plant."

"What difference does that make even if it's true?"

"It makes a big difference, Ed. Scanlon has gone outside for money before. It was drugstores that got him going in the first place. Yes, this Banner, Quinn connection smells. Even if we had torn into the Broadway Central the way we should have it still wouldn't look good. But why this week? Why does the SoHo News get it all right now when…"

"Turn it around, Rush. Why not now?"

For a reporter Rothberg was not making much eye contact. "Because the paper gets hit with a strike the same week. A strike some people, like you and me say, didn't know anything about. We're struck, we can't hit back."

"Rush, this isn't a fight between fraternities. We have nothing to hit back with for Christ's sake. Wake up, we're down on the killing floor."

Rothberg quoting Howlin' Wolf cheered Fletcher immensely. "Okay, but when was that piece written? The third paragraph reports a meeting between Scanlon and Quinn for Monday night that even for the SoHo News has a large amount of tense confusion."

"Send them a grammar book; what about it?"

"It's not just a source. They didn't do any legwork on this, they were fed the whole thing. It wasn't even proofread."

"You're dreaming. Who would give it to them? You know it wasn't Quinn. That just leaves you and the old man and that leaves nothing."

Fletcher held up his palm. "Look, the article was prepared beforehand and included a meeting with Quinn that never took place. I've got that far. This was put together to justify the strike. I think Scanlon lost Quinn weeks ago. That's why he's been scrambling. He even tried to work something out with those people his son-in-law works for. Maybe the bank is breathing down his neck but there isn't any arrangement, yet. But that's not good enough. It's not enough to shut down the paper. It looks better, a lot better, if it seems like Quinn is going to be the money guy."

"You've been reading too much Watergate, Rush." Rothberg waved to someone on the sidewalk. "And you're forgetting something. This strike has all the justification it needs."

The wavee was Phillips. She came in and exchanged a rather meaningful soft kiss with Rothberg. She sat beside him, adjusting a strand of hair that had strayed. She nodded at Fletcher. "Isn't this fun? It's like we're playing hooky."

Fletcher suspected Phillips had never played hooky in her life but then neither had he. "I'm famished," she said.

Harry presented himself, obliquely for him. He never knew what to make of Phillips, sharing perhaps in the ancient world's fear of professional women. She might patronize his coffee shop but he would never seek her admiration of the Eldorado. There was no point, she was biologically incapable of appreciating the contours of its classic form. Nonetheless he'd been waiting for the booth to fill. He had a few additional remarks on the strike and hated to waste them on Fletcher alone. Phillips didn't want a menu. Famished as she might be she asked for a small green salad with feta cheese, just a sprinkling, and a Tab. Harry repeated this princely order to one of his relatives and prepared to speak but just as he was transferring his jail keeper's keychain from one loud pocket to another, a maneuver for getting your attention, the parking meter early warning system by the cash register dinged. Harry sighed as duty called and he hurried away to the Cadillacs.

"Gray says there's nothing new," Phillips announced. Thank heaven, they could all rest easy now knowing Gray was on the watch. Rothberg greeted the news, if that's what it was, with impressive gravity. Gray, or Grayson as Fletcher conceived him, was Phillips' stockbroker boyfriend. It seems they had him to thank for blowing the whistle on Scanlon's financial hanky panky and wasn't that just darling of him. Gray was the silent type of course; there was no pea in his whistle, only Phillips could hear it. By her account she and Gray were "apres-theatre" and had stopped at the Brasserie for a "late bite" when "out of the blue" he said he'd been "hearing things down on the Street". Well you know how Gray is, Phillips had said as she related this story, knowing full well that no one at the *Local* had any idea how Gray was as no one had ever met him. They accepted on faith that he was low key and not given to hysteria. At Phillips' request he made some inquiries and it was like the "calvary arriving".

Fletcher was back to looking out the window. She'd meant cavalry he imagined. There was nothing new but she brought Rothberg up to date anyway. This talk about putting a group together to "rescue" the *Local* lacked spontaneity. It rang false, the sour Watergate atmosphere notwithstanding. Fletcher did not believe that his was by nature a suspicious vocation. You asked questions with the expectation of hearing the truth much as we live with the expectation of being understood. When you learned otherwise you might get a story out of it.

"There's a meeting with the strike committee at three," Phillips said. "Very informal; we're just getting together at Nan Bowman's house for coffee. She's close by, she's neutral..."

Why was Nan Bowman neutral? She was on staff, wasn't she? The art designer, the *Local* pretty much looked the way it did because of her. She worked at home, you didn't see her a lot these days but that didn't make her neutral. Strikes are a negotiating tool but so is an ambush sometimes.

"Has Scanlon been invited?"

Phillips received her lunch with delight. Fletcher thought Tab a godawful thing to put in your mouth. "We don't think that would be a good idea."

Not so much an editorial we as a royal one. "Why not?"

"At this juncture his presence would not be constructive."

"I agree," Rothberg said.

What a surprise. "How can we settle this without Scanlon?"

The question was something of a party pooper and Phillips replied by crunching her iceberg lettuce. She was a pale, blondish, flat chested woman Fletcher was beginning to dislike with conviction. He felt the same about her small green salad and sprinkling of feta cheese. She hadn't even put any dressing on it. (On the lazy susan holding the ketchup, mustard and Worcestershire sauce in Harry's booths there was a syrup dispenser of French dressing for all occasions. If no one was looking Fletcher put it on his hamburgers.) They were attempting an end run around Scanlon… Fletcher checked himself. It was an expression the editor would not permit. In some quarters, Scanlon's conciliatory attitude towards the strike had added to the usual resentment he inspired. A press release from the night before, memorable for it's absence of swagger, was nearly mawkish. Scanlon must have written it with a bottle of rye. An old union man himself, he tugged, he could not dispute the hard won rights of labor tra la. He went on for a while about the joys of collective bargaining, it was like a hymn to the Wagner Act. In conclusion he was suspending publication until he had time to review the situation and fire every last son of a bitch involved. That last part was reading between the lines.

"As of right now," Phillips said, chewing, "we have a lockout. John did not have to go that route. It's our task to find a middle way. If there is one. Between ourselves, I don't think he's acting rationally."

He's a newspaper publisher, not Descartes. "Maybe he's wounded," Fletcher said. "And I don't feel locked out. I'm sorry we're shut down but it might be better this way. He's resolved a conflict for us, for me anyway. I won't cross a picket line even if I don't go along with it. And I don't go along with it because I don't know what's going on."

Phillips exchanged a look with her iceberg lettuce. "Frankly, Rush, it doesn't shock me that you would take this line."

"I don't know if I'm taking any line, Paige. Maybe I'm offering one. It's getting a little star chamberish here."

"We all know how you feel about the old man," Rothberg said.

"I'm not feeling one way or the other." Blank stares. "Seriously. I'm trying to keep an open mind and I don't see how we can have a discussion about the future of this newspaper without including its founder. That's Scanlon. He isn't distant corporate ownership. He's right here. I…"

The rest of Fletcher's sentence broke apart like a bubble. He was being ignored and neatly so. Well, someone knew or was reasonably certain how weak Scanlon's position was. Solid as the strike might be it could either be resolved or it couldn't. And if it was more a stalking horse than a strike then it wasn't the real problem. Scanlon might see that and so was not bothering to butt heads with it. Fletcher couldn't say if there was enough loose employee stock around to swing control back to Scanlon. He'd tried to pry this out of Benson but the business manager was non-committal. He did say the paper would have had trouble meeting its payroll without a credit extension from Chemical Bank and they didn't get it. Well, the old man deftly forestalled that by closing down. So much for his gesture of good will. It wasn't in his heart, the touching press release sang, to resume publishing until they were all one happy family again. Yikes. Surely that was a crocodile crying in the wilderness but at least he hadn't shut them out of the newsroom. Still there would be no Saturday staff meeting this week and he had no notion what he would do with the free time.

Additional members of the happy family arrived, Lindquist and the cartoonist Terry

Buckley. Buckley signed himself *Smithereens* and Fletcher liked him.

"I saw Harry outside," Buckley said. "Is that orange piping on his shoulder pads or did he have a fight with the fruit salad again?"

Scanlon professed to love *Smithereens* but did not always get it. Buckley's humor was distinctly post-Beatles and Scanlon sometimes asked Fletcher if that week's cartoon was funny. It usually was. Buckley was mordant and his caricatures crisp and destructive. In a given week he was the best single thing in the paper. On the verge of going national (and greeting cards before long) he was not quite strutting but the aura of success suited him like a single tasteful earring. His girlfriend was a Charlotte Ford model. He'd draw you and leave it on your desk and they were often shocking, like catching yourself in a funhouse mirror. Buckley told Fletcher not to worry. Having no distinguishing features he was more or less caricature proof.

No so Scanlon. Buckley squeezed in next to Phillips and propped a mechanical against the jukebox. It was a mock colonial broadside with Scanlon as King George ranting word balloons at his ministers. Staffers were shown in various degrees of subjection. Fletcher was identified by a prominent cowlick he did not possess.

"Great stuff, Terry," Rothberg approved.

"The lettering is wonderful," Phillips said. "Is that me?"

It wasn't Betsy Ross, that's for sure. "Coming over here," Buckley said, "I realized I forgot Andy Talbot. I'll have to fix it."

Forgetting Talbot was not difficult. The nominal city editor, he took over for Duffy. As no one could replace Duffy, Talbot was doomed from the start. Scanlon had him as a snack several times a day and pretended not to know his name. Talbot had combined vacation with a wedding in California. Fletcher thought he might as well stay there.

"Try not to let Scanlon see that. You made him really old."

Buckley was not mean. "You think so, Rush?"

"What the hell," Lindquist said, "he is old." Lindquist was standing, blocking the aisle with his basketball body. Harry returned, in lunchtime fever, and asked him to sit. Lindquist deflected Harry and leaned over the coffee cups. "Heard the news?" They turned their heads like sheep. "Sirica ordered Nixon to turn over the tapes."

Harry caught Lindquist's arm. As there were no Greeks involved as far as he knew he did not follow Watergate, it was all so much eggplant, but the look of his newspaper friends as they stared at Lindquist was alarming. This, whatever it might be, could be bad for business. "You're kidding me."

Lindquist had very white teeth. He disengaged Harry and shook the coffee carafe. "I have a source," he said.

Rothberg hooted. "Is this source the Associated Press or Reuters by any chance?"

"Go check the wire, turn on WINS. It's not out yet but it's true." The teeth got whiter. "Nixon's had it now."

"So you're familiar with the tapes too?"

"Let's just say I'm a reporter and leave it at that."

Buckley stood halfway. "Keep an eye on this guy, Harry. He says there's something wrong with the meat loaf."

"Nothing wrong with meat loaf," Harry said.

Lindquist pushed Buckley down with the palm of his hand. "We need coffee," he said to Harry. He looked through Phillips to Rothberg. "I've got the front page coming up." "I guess he's the first to find another job," Fletcher said.

"I'm talking about the front page of the *Local*," Lindquist said.

"Yes," Phillips said, "we'll get through this and be all the stronger for it. Maybe you haven't noticed, Rush, but the paper has been drifting. It has no soul now. The strike is a good thing if it wakes some people up. And if it doesn't... well, that might be a good thing too."

"We have to destroy the paper in order to save it?"

Phillips stiffened. "Fine, Rush. If you want to play quotations I've got one for you. If you're not part of the solution you're part of the problem. Okay?" She nudged Buckley who bumped into Lindquist getting out of her way.

"Listen," Rothberg said, "we're all in this together remember."

"It's obvious some of us are more together than others," Phillips said. Her gaze did not include Fletcher. "I'll see you at three. There'll be food, be prepared to stay a while."

"What is Bowman's address?"

Phillips looked at Fletcher. He knew Bowman's address. And she knew he'd only asked to have her say it. "At this point I don't think your presence will be helpful. Rose Agosto is chairing the strike committee and there might be... unnecessary conflict."

"I don't have a problem with Rose."

"That doesn't matter. She has one with you."

Rothberg slid to the end of the booth. "What Paige is trying to say..." "I think it's pretty clear myself."

"Rush," she said, "it's nothing personal."

Fletcher shook his head. "Newspapers are very personal things."

Phillips asked for the check. Harry would not hear of it. He backed up to let Phillips and Rothberg pass. Lindquist and Buckley followed and then Buckley came back for his drawing. Fletcher turned it over. "You make me look defrosted, Terry." He handed it over. "How long did that take you?"

Buckley was boyish. "Maybe twenty minutes. Don't tell anyone."

"You know what the old man says: if it takes more than half an hour it doesn't belong in a newspaper."

"I never heard him say that."

"Maybe I made it up. But it sounds like him."

"Yeah, it does, Rush. That's the scary part... see you."

Harry was left alone with Fletcher again but this was better than nothing. He would sit and rest. The lifts he wore in his shoes made his ankles ache. He sat but the bell dinged once again and he got up wearily but resolute. Stopping at the register for dimes he told Maria to take a break and bus some tables. She rolled a cart down to Fletcher's booth. She was the youngest and like her brother Michael did not remember Greece. "Your cousin is so nice, Mr. Rush."

Fletcher nodded. "She went shopping." He remembered what he'd heard. "Did I hear you're getting married?"

She nodded as she put cups and saucers in the tub. "Next year maybe."

"He's a good guy for you, Maria?"

She nodded again. "Harry likes him." She looked across the street at the picket line. "Don't be sad, Mr. Rush. It will be okay. And you'll still come in please. Everybody likes you here."

"I like it here too," Fletcher said.

Harry was coming back from tending the Cadillacs. Maria moved to the next booth. As Fletcher got up to leave he thought about moving to Greece.

The Asch Building

One day in 1911 when John Scanlon was a boy he walked with his father through Washington Square. They'd been to an oculist on the north side of the park because Austen Scanlon believed he was going blind. This was the case though it would be ten years before his sight was gone completely. This was a Saturday afternoon late in March and as the son recalled afterward he was hopeful of leading his father to a roasted chestnut vendor as they rounded the square at University Place. It was only a hope. Austen Scanlon was an abstracted man at the best of times and marched with a will difficult for an eight year old to emulate. John Scanlon trotted to keep up because his father would not wait for him.

They were headed for the Broadway streetcar to take them home. It was clear and mild. The incense drifting from the chestnut brazier was intoxicating. John Scanlon knew if he could get a few steps ahead between his father and the vendor his hope would be apparent. He could not ask. He never spoke to his father until he was first addressed. His father was a newspaperman, quite a good one, but he was not unkind. He was unimaginative. He needed to see to understand. They crossed to the east side of University and moved rapidly to Washington Place. The moment came but John did not succeed. They passed the vendor who was huskily whispering a frail foreign song. They passed him at a run and John would not have fresh warm chestnuts to eat on the streetcar.

John Scanlon hurried to keep close to his father who was moving so fast his hat flew off. His father did not stop for it. John stooped for the hat but when he looked up his father was gone. There was a crowd at the corner and he could not see into it. The people in the crowd were pointing to the sky and his father's hat was crushed when he tried to push through them. He could not push through until the men in uniform came. As they charged and shouted like Indians in their black and red helmets there was a smell of smoke that was hard to breathe and a sound like the wind blowing. John heard glass shattering and more of that sound like the wind and he was frightened until he saw his father standing on Greene Street.

Austen Scanlon was taking notes. His eyewitness account of the Triangle Shirtwaist fire on the ninth floor of the Asch Building would appear in English language newspapers all over the world. By deadline that night he would file ten thousand words. On Greene Street he put on the hat his son held out. He wrote quickly, stenographically, one glance good for a paragraph. He wrote unmoving, never backing up or bending his knees, as seamstresses trapped by a locked exit door fell the nine stories to the street. Some jumped from the window ledges, some were pushed from behind by others hoping to escape. The fire began at closing time when the girls were dressed to go home. They died in their coats and muffs and hats. They were broken on the concrete or torn by the glass sidewalk skylights as they plunged through them to the cellar. Their torn and broken bodies were in the way of the ladders and fire nets but the ladders were too short and the fire nets useless at that height. The flames spread through the cotton and linens on the factory floor and ninety workers burned to death. Those who reached the windows died on the ground. There were fifty of them. When the dead were totaled 128 were young women. They were Italians, Russians, Hungarians, immigrants and the children of immigrants. Some are buried in a common grave in Brooklyn. The reporter on the scene described two girls who jumped together holding hands. Their clothes on fire they fell embraced like burning swans. They fell a few feet apart. Austen Scanlon led with that.

As John Scanlon told it in later years his father filed his copy that night and followed it to the composing room. It was not unusual with a major story then to stand by and watch it set in type. He paced with his head bowed and arms folded. When the chief compositor was about to signal for the first press run Austen Scanlon asked him to wait. He wanted to change his lead. He removed three sentences about the girls who jumped holding hands and dictated a substitution. The second lead stated the scene and the time of the fire. When that was set in type he returned to the newsroom for his son who was asleep on a bench. It was near midnight and they went home on the last streetcar. At this point in his story John Scanlon would pause. If his audience was young reporters as it often was they asked the obvious question. I don't understand why my father changed his magnificent lead, the son would reply, but I know it was a gutless thing to do.

Sunday morning while Amanda slept, Fletcher went to the laundromat. It was a writing time for him and he felt footloose without work. He didn't like being footloose and attempted a column with no success. An old fear revived, that he was a writer who could produce only for immediate publication. His paper was struck and he was blank. Coffee followed coffee but he could not write as he could not juggle or play the saxophone. He'd read about writers who got themselves going by writing about how they can't write but where that would go in a newspaper he could not say.

He went to the laundromat instead. Bundling Amanda's clothes and his own he went downstairs, hoping to avoid Mrs. Romano who was ever after him to use the washer and dryer that sat luxuriously in her kitchen. I hardly use them, she always said as if the machines were in need of exercise. But from the second floor he heard her on the phone, she spoke to relatives in Italy on Sunday when the rates were lower, and he went safely out where he crossed Sixth Avenue to Carmine Street. The laundromat was dank and cobwebby, just opening as he arrived at seven. The appliances were old and cantankerous and their owner, Mrs. Hoak, pretty much the same. There was a new laundromat on LaGuardia Place, clean and bright as a freshly minted dime, but Fletcher had established a relationship on Carmine Street and did not want to give it up. The new laundromat was killing Mrs. Hoak and she looked it. The washers and dryers were antiseptic on LaGuardia Place but at what cost. You were compelled to buy individual boxes of Tide or All from an aggressively sanitary vending machine. But on Carmine Street you gave Mrs. Hoak a quarter and dipped a cracked ceramic measuring cup in an industrial barrel of ash gray soap powder. And then there was the indispensable personal touch. No matter how busy she was Mrs. Hoak took the time to make sure you didn't take more than you'd paid for.

Fletcher liked washing women's clothes. It was so much more satisfying than only washing his own. He pondered asking Mrs. Hoak for advice on the delicates question but in ten years of biweekly sessions they had not progressed beyond discussing his habit of wandering off during the rinse cycle. Mrs. Hoak had a bulletin board of yellowed Heloise clippings, helpful hints about removing bubble gum with ice cubes and what to do about blood stains. Fletcher had read them all with numb routine but skipped them for once. Heloise was in maybe five hundred papers and he was maybe in none.

He sat on the sorting and folding table and watched his cousin's wash spin passionately round. There were the usual publications you found on sorting and folding tables: *Crossword Puzzle Digest,* a month old *Time* with the cover torn off, newspaper supplements from the previous Sunday, an *American Rifleman* with a Minnesota address label. Why a copy of *American Rifleman* mailed to a guy in Sleepy Eye, Minnesota was on a laundromat sorting and folding table in Greenwich Village was a curiosity probably not worth investigating. Fletcher leafed through a *Crawdaddy* he'd leafed through in the past. He never remembered to bring a book. If he'd put all his hours in the Carmine Street laundromat to good use, like studying astrophysics, he could have built a rocket ship by now and moved to a planet that needs reporters.

The odds of finding romance in a Manhattan laundromat are long and if Fletcher required confirmation of this he had only to ask Mrs. Hoak. Still he would not cease hoping that someday, between the washer and the extractor or the extractor and the dryer, he'd find it. (These are the crucial moments when

172

bending to retrieve a fallen feminine sock you might feel your life turn.) He'd come close a few times he was sure but either because the woman had not noticed him or had noticed him reading *American Rifleman* (or *Betty & Veronica*) the sentiment was not mutual. The gods of love didn't seem to pay much attention to Carmine Street. They'd certainly given short shrift to the hard bitten Mrs. Hoak. (If there was ever a Mr. Hoak he was long gone with the lint.) Poor Mrs. Hoak. She was a joyous and free spirited woman once, along the lines of Isadora Duncan perhaps, but the sixties changed all that. She used to leave her laundromat on the honor system to have strudel in the afternoon with her friend Mrs. Weiner around the corner on Bedford Street. Mrs. Weiner had a small mystifying shop selling china dolls, waffle irons, cookie jars and the sort of cups and saucers movie theatres gave away during the Depression. A junk shop in other words but a more lighthearted environment for a quiet chat than the sudsy swamp on Carmine Street. Mrs. Hoak looked forward to her daily escapade, her sylph like excursion in clamdiggers and sweatshirt to Mrs. Weiner's antique retreat of beaded lampshades and trivets. (Mrs. Hoak wore clamdiggers without regard to season to let her varicose calves breathe.) It was an idyll and like others it ended in 1968. As she once explained to Fletcher she discovered a hippie, or someone who looked like a hippie, taking advantage of her absence. The hippie was, as she put it, bathing his privates in her slop sink. He'd even helped himself to detergent from the industrial barrel. Mrs. Hoak seemed to age after that and didn't leave the laundromat as much.

From time to time Fletcher was tempted to write about Mrs. Hoak but never did. This was either ethics or courtesy or lack of an angle. Mrs. Hoak did not know what he did for a living and as he often as not came in on a weekday morning she perhaps judged him an unemployed bum, if a rather neat and well behaved unemployed bum. He could have changed her name or disguised her moody laundromat at another location but then she wouldn't be who she was but a pale representative of the nether world of wash and dry. That wasn't good enough. It was the real Mrs. Hoak, the orange haired harridan with sciatica and hippies in her slop sink, or nothing. So it was nothing. He was not a spy. He'd told himself that year after year. Mrs. Hoak thought he was crazy for wandering off in the middle of his rinse cycle. She never knew he was thinking about her.

Along with clean clothes Fletcher brought his cousin a Scooter Pie for breakfast. She was awake, listening to Mozart and reading Thoreau, when he came in. The Mozart was plain enough and she emphasized the Thoreau by asking his opinions of the limits of personal freedom before he had his shoes off. Fletcher said he'd have to think about it and produced the Scooter Pie. They had an old joke about them and making a pained face in protest she threw it on the sofa. His mother had called, wanting to know when to expect them. Mrs. Stedman had called her and while this was no skin off Mrs. Fletcher's nose she reckoned it polite to inquire and pass the information on. That was reasonable but Fletcher hesitated calling his mother back. It did not matter now what day they left and that was the problem. His mother in her wise owl observant way would note the pretense in his voice and want to know what was wrong. It was too soon. He was not ready to tell her he was out of work and down to the last two or three scoops in his last can of Maxwell House.

He brewed a pot of very weak coffee, called Hickman, didn't get him, just as well. They'd talked Saturday night while he and Amanda played Scrabble. Fletcher won in a plodding way but she made words like ostrich and jugular. Hickman said the Dream Lucky bar wasn't staked out as far as anyone knew but he wasn't accepting that as definitive. As for Stutz he was a regular Renaissance man of an underling. His name had real resonance when you began to ask around and Hickman was up for it. He had nothing to report on Clover but it was the weekend, he wasn't expecting an egg in his beer. He asked about immigration and Fletcher had to say he had done nothing. He could have said he was involved with the paper but it wasn't true, he was not involved. Hickman mentioned a retired Federal prosecutor he was planning to tap and Fletcher felt tired of the conversation. He'd be a rooting section on this one, following the trail of the girl with the black eye. She was on her way to potter's field and that was the end of it. Simple. She'd done something wrong, maybe, and she'd paid for it. That appealed to the backyard fence and what someone else's kids were getting in trouble about.. There was not much he could do anyway. He didn't have a paper and if he didn't have a paper he didn't care. It was time he was honest about that. When he got off the phone his cousin was grinning at him. She'd spelled NYLOCAL. He challenged it.

All Sunday morning, aquamarine colored sharpie in hand, Amanda wrote a comprehensive letter back home to her best friend. Fletcher, yet in a laundry state of mind, daydreamed about hanging Elke's underwear on a tree branch. The day before when his cousin asked how his date had been he said "all right" and left it at that. A man would conclude he hadn't got laid, Amanda's interpretation was possibly different if equally pessimistic. She wrote on, steadfastly, hardly pausing to reload. Fletcher admired her from his ironing board. He never wrote so easily. Amanda didn't even use the turn of a page as a natural break to get up and look out the window. If the letter was ever finished it might have to go bulk mail. During their Scrabble game Amanda seemed at a confessional boiling point a few times but never quite bubbled. She took refuge on the Scrabble squares spelling anguish and pathos. Fletcher understood. Biting her lower lip it was all going in that therapeutic letter.

He wrote a little story when he was fourteen about a boy, a boy much like himself for who else would it be, who builds a bathysphere to scrape along the furtive bottom of the sea. He only surfaced now and then to spy upon the great skylines, from Babylon to Chicago, of civilization and drift in the tides of femininity and escape. It was a teenage boy's tale, mixing adventure and seclusion, myth and voyeurism along his narrow spit of land. He never wrote an ending. There are only two available and neither was attractive to the adolescent spirit. The boy scuttled clear of a far peninsula and the story stopped like an overwound watch on a bureau top. It went in a drawer and he never wrote like that again.

As he ironed hard on an wobbly shirt collar, Fletcher heard the unmistakable rustle of a Scooter Pie wrapper. He looked over in triumph but Amanda wasn't eating the Scooter Pie, she was holding it in contempt. I'm not a kid anymore, she said, why can't you understand that? He was quite sure he did understand it. Stop mothering me, she said, I can wash my own clothes like I did all summer. Bringing up the summer seemed to hurt her the more. He felt it too. You think it's a big joke, she said, all of you. Fletcher disliked the sound of "all of you". It placed him uncomfortably in the Stedman camp where he had no wish to be. More than that it arraigned him as a double agent, not the most upright calling. Yet he was much older than his cousin and some of his empathy was modified by the harsh curriculum of those years separating them. A reporter was always a man between. He was not her generation he knew. He hoped he was not part of the one pressing down on her.

He was puzzled how this got started. It was only an innocent Scooter Pie after all, he didn't mean to insult her with it. She dropped it on the coffee table and withdrew into her letter like an angry lover behind the Sunday paper. Seeing this Fletcher remembered he hadn't bought the *Times*, an unprecedented lapse. The iron was making him sweat. He left the shirt collar undone and went into his bedroom. Amanda's physical presence there was strong. Her shapeless bathrobe looked as relaxing as a flowerbed. This was like getting away from a fight, the ones that rise up as mysteriously as a volcano in a cornfield. He was familiar with the phenomenon. But out of the steam of the electric iron he felt relief. At his desk he counted the bills in his typewriter fund. He was down below one hundred, the usual dribs and drabs having taken their toll. Feeling rather criminal he put it all in his pocket.

Back to Amanda. He said, loudly, that they had cabin fever. They should go out and spend money until all they had left was the bus fare to Ohio. She didn't think about it very long. Good idea, she said. Fletcher looked for the *Local* to check the listings until he remembered there was no paper that week. It was a grave acknowledgement he had previously ignored. They would, he said, play it by ear. He was dressed to go out. He was always dressed to go out if you were going out to the hardware store for a drill bit or a bag of potting soil. Amanda took some time. He sat on the sofa drinking cold coffee and ate half of the Scooter Pie. It was, in a manner of speaking, a breakfast of champions.

Becker called, sounding upbeat. Fletcher was not in the mood for him but repented when Becker, considerately, offered his car to take to Ohio. Fletcher declined so Becker offered his sympathy about the strike, sort of. Becker said they were so excited down in SoHo about grabbing the *Local*'s classifieds even the dykes were putting out. Fletcher declined the sympathy and asked why he'd left that girl on his doorstep. He knew why but asked anyway. The question brought not an explanation but a grunt of disgust. Becker said when the friend got warmed up she smelled like a garlic bagel in heat. He hadn't enjoyed himself. Fletcher said that was too bad, not meaning it. He wondered if Becker ever ate Scooter Pies. Probably not, he was more the creamsicle type or a lollipop man. So Becker made a few perfunctory comments about the strike but as they say around the outdoor grill he was pussyfooting. Finally he confessed he'd called Mona several times, left messages, but she hadn't called back. Fletcher said he didn't know, Mona was big in the strike, maybe she was busy. Not to mention the boxing lessons. Becker did not know about the boxing lessons, seemed to find the idea provocative. He asked if they were real boxing lessons. Fletcher said they were given in a gym, what were unreal boxing lessons? You know, Becker said, like girls' push-ups in high school. Fletcher shook his coffee. Leave it to Becker to recall the kind of push-ups girls did in high school. He felt like embellishing. He said he'd seen Mona's sparring partner and he was an Adonis at the very least but Becker shouldn't worry, maybe she doesn't like muscles as much as the money guy with the Porsche who's been waiting for her outside the office. I'd tell you more, Fletcher said as he hung up, but my cousin is here and she's only eighteen.

Amanda heard that but her mood had changed. She'd put on fresh blue jeans, still a touch warm from the iron, and one of Fletcher's most weathered Ohio State sweatshirts. He had a varsity jacket too with leather sleeves but never wore it. There are limits, God knows, to these things. As he stood up from the sofa she put her arms around him with her head on his chest. She was the only one in the family who was truly affectionate, demonstrably so. He exchanged rapid hugs with his mother and firm dependable handshakes with his father. Sometimes when he said goodbye to his father he felt like they had just closed a mortgage. Amanda once went through a tomboy phase for the benefit of her older brothers but it made no impression on them. The summer she stayed in Monacacy, when she was eleven, she surprised Fletcher one day by sitting in his lap. She smelled like soap and curled up with her knees in his side she fell asleep. It was late afternoon and from the down the street out of a car being washed came Paint It, Black. One of his legs went numb and his shoulder ached but he didn't move. After an hour, maybe more, she stirred and raised her head and pleased to find him there laughed like a child. He laughed too in feeling for a moment, no larger than the head of a pin, that he was giving birth.

The Village was drowsy. They didn't get far. *Let It Be* and *Yellow Submarine* were at the Bleecker. They caught the rooftop ending of Let It Be and all of Yellow Submarine. Amanda had not seen either. She was not "into the Beatles", they were too popular, too commercialized. And since their breakup they weren't relevant anymore anyway. Fletcher mulled that over. Perhaps his cousin was a harbinger of Beatles revisionism. There might be a column in that, he could ask other young people... he snapped out of it. Amanda enjoyed the animation, what she called the overall effect. She made an effort to give her opinions shape and substance. It was as if she took his mother's instruction more to heart than he possibly could. Whatever you do, Mrs. Fletcher said, don't dither. It was indeed dithering, he believed, that had made him the man he was.

After the movies they walked to Little Italy. Fletcher loved the tenements and storefronts, the way the sound of mothers calling their children seemed to echo. The San Gennaro feast came in September and he spent hours strolling on Mulberry Street, talking and listening, eating sausage and peppers and warm zeppole sprinkled with sugar. It was Maggie's world, the one he had missed. Amanda wanted an ice and they sat in a schoolyard watching two boys do layups. She conceded she would be in school after Labor Day. It was, she said, probably more satisfying in the long run to quit college than not to go at all. He felt emboldened to suggest they leave Tuesday or Wednesday. There were no last minute details to concern him. But waving her lemon ice Amanda had an idea. They should go for a ride on that boat around Manhattan. Fletcher had several reasons why they shouldn't but settled for saying it would be too crowded. Amanda said she liked crowds but maybe the evening cruise wouldn't be. The evening cruise, she sounded like the old man. It was difficult to explain to his cousin that the Circle Line just then was not his fondest desire. He might throw himself overboard though with his recent luck he'd just fall onto another boat. Judiciously he put in a word for the theatre and Amanda's latent stage struck instinct was awakened. Ever so fabulous, she said.

Lemmings was at the Village Gate and they were in time for the early show. If Elke had not slipped away he had planned, devised you might say, to ask her there for their next date. There was a reason. He was so at ease downtown, he might manage affairs with her better on his home turf. At the Gate there would be people he knew. He'd stop, chat, introduce Elke, experience that incendiary expansion of selfhood that comes from being seen with a good looking woman. And a good looking foreign woman to boot. He was far too slowpoke for midtown, that land of dailies and real deadlines. It was shameful to think of her as adornment. He should ask Mrs. Hoak out instead.

Amanda, bless her, laughed out loud at *Lemmings*. Fletcher was ruefully amused. The *National Lampoon's* send up of Woodstock idealism got under his skin (the *Lampoon* was often libertarian ideology posing as the counterculture) but the impressions were first rate. Dylan was done to a turn and the Joe Cocker perfect. It was not every day, it was not any day prior to this, that the left got satirized so trenchantly. He was not used to it and perhaps that was why, for all its good reviews, he hadn't seen *Lemmings* yet. (And the Village Gate did not provide the *Local* with tickets.) He was older than the performers, some were close to Amanda in age, and their burlesque of music he loved struck him as almost insolent. It was more appropriate to attack the callous overlords of society that way than pop culture icons. Unless of course you believed those very icons had achieved overlord status of their own. Fletcher had alluded to this in his cranky evaluation of Watkins Glen, the parallel occurring to him as he made notes on a Village Gate napkin. Not to be a sourpuss he laughed as best he might with his cousin. When they left he threw the napkin away.

They were getting through the day and Fletcher had another fair to middling idea. Amanda had not been to Shipwreck Kelly's yet, an omission he felt obliged to rectify. On Sundays the Chinese cook, Shuggie, by turns morose and uninspired by the weekday menu, mostly soups and sandwiches, bestirred himself to turn out such traditional Cantonese dishes as pot roast and corned beef and cabbage. That is he cooked, he did not actually like to serve. If you were interested you waited at the kitchen door for a pause in the cook's reverie. His reverie consisted of large Scotches, Pall Malls, and a country and western station raised to bowling alley volume. When Shuggie became aware of you, he eventually did, you'd receive a plate of the Sunday special. Almost always you got a little cigarette ash along with it. Logan had a story that Shuggie was a refugee from the Chinatown tong wars of the 1920's. He was taken in at Kelly's and except for food shopping and a little gambling seldom left the bar.

He baked pies too that might have been stamped Made In Ohio. Fletcher thought Shuggie's crust about miraculous though he kept it quiet. It wasn't the sort of thing you wished to be known for saying. Amanda had two pieces of peach pie. Her cousin approved as she'd only picked at her dinner. It was wiener schnitzel, not one of Shuggie's more successful efforts. Fletcher worried he wasn't feeding her enough, that she'd look undernourished by the time they got home. She seemed fragile but girls usually did to him even when he knew they weren't. As he cleared their plates Shuggie looked aggrieved by the uneaten wiener schnitzel but let it pass. He looked older and bent down, a man a world away from his origin. The cook missed Logan and Logan's way of upbraiding him. Fletcher knew that. It was something Fletcher understood.

Amanda ranked Kelly's right up there with the Fulton Fish Market. Most of all she enjoyed the sawdust on the floor and the appreciation of the stand up drinkers as she skated a figure eight through it. After their supper was rung up on the clangorous cash register, a sturdy relic with a brass eagle on its summit, they went up to Washington Square. They took a bench by the Garibaldi statue and not saying much watched night settle down on the park. There was love and subdued riot around them. A trembling murmur was the sound of a shell in Fletcher's ear. In a few days he would sit on his old front porch and hear the last cicadas of the season. That was good but like other things at home it made him fall asleep.

His first year with the paper Duffy told him to go out and find something to write about. Failing that he should talk to people until it became natural to him. That takes a while. So Fletcher would. Describing great arcs around the Village he'd return with not so much as a missing manhole cover. That's all right, Duffy told him, it's good for your ankles, you can't have weak ankles in this business. In the wake of his fruitless wandering Fletcher sat in the park to imagine epic events unfolding before him. Scanlon caught him once one winter afternoon and accused him of woolgathering. It was the same expression his mother would have used. The editor, not quite sixty then, stood staring at a row house on the north side of the square. There was a silence for in those days Fletcher did not speak to his new employer until he was spoken to first. Come, Scanlon finally said, I want to show you something. They crossed the park to University Place and went east on Greene Street. Scanlon took Fletcher's arm. This is the Asch Building, he said, I was here once with my father...

Come, Fletcher said to Amanda, I want to show you something. They left the park and on Greene Street he told her the story Scanlon had told him about the Triangle Shirtwaist fire. He had a memory for facts and quotations, as convenient as his pocket pencil, and he sometimes worked the story over when he stopped before the commemorative plaque on the building wall. Amanda went to the point as he did once. She asked why the fire exits were locked. It was a simple question with a simple answer. He told her that had made it easier to check the girls for stolen cloth before they went home. Amanda looked at the sidewalk. Those girls were the same age as me, she said. The same age as me, she said again, and I've never had a job. She asked what happened to the company, to the owners. They walked, Fletcher said, they walked.

They agreed they were tired and went back to Bleecker Street. At 185 Mrs. Romano was outside on an aluminum lawn chair. She was fanning herself with a damp handkerchief. Usually she called him Mr. Fletcher because Rush made no sense to her as a first name. Sometimes she forgot. "There's Rush," she said, "there he is." Mrs. Romano stood up from her lawn chair, a little breathless. "Mrs. Lucca says it won't stop ringing." Mrs. Lucca lived on Fletcher's floor. When she returned from marketing she pressed his buzzer and he came down and brought her groceries up. "I checked it too," Mrs. Romano said, "two hours now it rings."

Upstairs Mrs. Lucca was watching Bonanza on her portable television set with her front door open so she could tell Fletcher it was she and not Mrs. Romano who first heard his phone ringing. Mrs. Romano was a good woman, she said, but sometimes took credit for things she should not. Mrs. Lucca detained Amanda to go over the details as Fletcher went inside. He picked up his telephone receiver and said hello. There was no response though he could hear the line was open. He felt presentment in his hot living room. "Hello," he said again.

"Is that you lad?" It was Scanlon.

"John?" What's going on? Are you..."

"I was wondering... it won't be too much trouble... could you come up here. I could use a hand here... if it's bad time..."

"No, that's all right. What is it?"

It was a Scanlon with cotton in his mouth. "I could use a hand here for a minute lad. If you could help me up I'll be fine."

"Did you fall, John? Why didn't you call someone?"

The line was silent. Now Fletcher heard water dripping in the background. "I'm calling you lad. If it's not a bad time."

"It's fine, it's fine. I'll be there as soon as I can." Fletcher resisted saying don't worry. "Can you tell the doorman to let me in?"

"He knows," Scanlon said. "Thank you lad."

Fletcher told Amanda where he was going. He also had to tell Mrs. Lucca who was waiting in the hall with one of her sugar cookies that she flavored with anisette. He ate it on Sixth Avenue while waiting for a cab. Traffic was light, it was ten minutes up to Beekman Place. The doorman opened the taxi door while Fletcher was paying the driver. He was an uptown doorman. On a Sunday night, hot and humid, he could easily be mistaken for one of Napoleon's marshals. The gold braid alone looked like he might pay Fletcher's salary for a month. Scanlon was a lavish tipper. The doorman had a porter standing by with a passkey. The elevator operator had braid too but not as much as the doorman. After his last divorce Scanlon moved to Beekman Place from Fifth Avenue. The building was quiet, he said, because the carpet in the lobby was as thick as a Russian novel.

Like Lyndon Johnson, Scanlon had a telephone in his bathroom. Fletcher crossed a parquet floor, it was not a large apartment, to the bedroom. The bathroom was off that. It had a tub and a marble shower stall. Scanlon had fallen between the shower and the toilet. He looked asleep. Fletcher did not recognize the pale strangely naked man who had pulled the phone down by its cord. Scanlon looked the way a tin can does when you strip the label off. He had a mania for air conditioning at home. It was on high. Fletcher shivered and covered Scanlon with a robe. It was monogrammed like all the editor's accessories. "John," Fletcher said, "it's Rush."

He couldn't have died in twenty minutes. Fletcher spoke again, louder. "Ah, that's good lad," Scanlon said, "that's good."

"Can you move? Can I move you?"

Scanlon's eyes opened as he shook his head. They were mostly white. Fletcher did not know if this was shock. "I'll call an ambulance." He reached for the phone but Scanlon clawed at his arm.

"Not like this lad. I want to get dressed."

"I can't dress you, John. You might be really hurt."

The clawing again. It was not the grip it ordinarily would have been. "I don't want them to see me."

"They're doctors, John. It doesn't matter."

"From the paper lad. I don't want them to see me like this."

"There's no one from the paper here, John. Just me."

Scanlon could not keep his head up. "They're outside. I can hear them. I told you not to bring them. You never listen to me."

I've spent twelve years listening to you, Fletcher thought. "I didn't bring anyone, John. I did only what you said."

"You can tell them. You can tell them this comes direct from me. I'm not turning my paper over to a pack of faggots. Got it?" Scanlon clawed the robe off, Fletcher put it back. "Get Duffy to go with you. He'll know how to talk to them. This is all politics, a lot of crap. They can't do anything but think... they think they can run a paper. That's a laugh. I've seen it all my life. Ask Duffy, he'll tell you. Look at what happened to..." Scanlon blinked, swallowed. Fletcher offered water but he wouldn't take it. "You know what I mean lad. Listen to me for Chrissake. I've had time to think. I see it all. You can't let them in. They'll think I'm beaten like this. Finished. It's all money. What's money when you're talking about a newspaper. I told her that. If you're really a newspaperman you don't have to be told. They don't understand that. We should all be Izzy Stone. Write everything yourself. That's the way to do it. I told that little girl... Tom, you were there, you remember. Tell the lad here it's not like she says. I gave her a job. I didn't have to do that. You're a girl, I said, a Puerto Rican, you could do all right. The last thing I do is judge anybody. I never believed this she likes girls stuff either. That's all politics. They get it out of a book." Scanlon laughed, very hoarse. "Tom, tell the lad what Jimmy Walker said. He said no girl was ever ruined by a book. That's right. The Honorable Jimmy Walker said that I don't know forty years ago. Maybe it's different now. It's all politics with young people now. It's like a war with them. I wanted to help her and they turn on me. Listen to that. Listen to them talking about me. Don't let them in. Tell them I'm busy. They couldn't wait. This all would have been settled after Labor Day. I had it all fixed. All set to go. She didn't have to leave like that. I didn't mean her any harm. How could I? I have a daughter myself. We're a tribe. That's what they used to say. We stick together. You got a problem you keep it in the shop. Isn't that right, Tom? Isn't that the first thing? You keep it in the shop. There's a spy in the organization. That's our first problem. Somebody went over to the other side. You must have heard something. Who was it? Remember, this isn't about me. Your first loyalty is to the paper. We'll sit here until we find out who it is. I don't mind. I love this place. I could live in the newsroom. This is the best place for me. I feel young here. She laughed when I said that. You're an old man, she said. That's a fine thing. I didn't mean her any harm. I asked her to have a drink. What is that, a drink? It's nothing. You should see that place where she lives. My God, it was filthy. And this other girl is there, this American girl. She's the bad one, I can tell you that. I could see that right off. I could have helped her but she didn't want my help. She thought I wanted something. Who can understand these people. We'll go back to the beginning. They'll see it's not easy. Whatever they do I'll top them. All I need is time. Where are my clothes? Get my clothes. Nobody reads retractions. Nothing is truer in this business. Nobody. I have to get my story out."

Fletcher's hand was on the telephone. Scanlon was drifting off, talking about Susan, his first wife. Fletcher did not understand most of it. He dialed 911 and asked the operator for an ambulance. Angela and Chuck lived

ten blocks away, maybe less. As for the other daughters and their mother he
didn't know. He called Amanda, said he would be back late. She asked about
Scanlon, more of a legend to the extended clan than a real person. That was
Fletcher's doing. He had always placed his boss in the context of another time.
Maybe that was wrong but maybe it was true. He told his cousin to go to bed,
he wouldn't call again. Scanlon's white eyes were looking but didn't seem
to be seeing much. Fletcher replaced the phone on its shelf and went to the
bedroom dresser for socks, shorts and an undershirt. In the bathroom he wiped
Scanlon off with a washcloth and then saw the bruise running from knee to
hip. The bruise was a color from a medical textbook, from the police blotter.
He stopped trying to dress him and Scanlon had stopped clawing at the robe.
Fletcher called the doorman on the intercom, mentioned the ambulance, then
got a bottle of Heineken from the kitchen. Scanlon liked Heineken. Fletcher
drank it sitting on the edge of the tub. He liked it too.

"Let's not kid ourselves," Scanlon was saying. "They were all bastards."
Fletcher swigging the beer, solemnly agreed. Whoever they were they were
bastards, end of discussion. "Remember this all of you. You can't put the
genie back in the bottle. Go to a daily and see how much they let you get
away with. Go ahead, I don't need you. See the cashier on your way out. You
won't be any good at this. I'll tell you why. You think too much. The hell with
you…"

Fletcher felt he should move up to Heineken from Schlitz and Piel's. Yes,
good to the last drop. There was an old cashier in the sixties they caught taking money. Rosemary was her name. Scanlon told her to leave and said she
should stay home away from temptation. He continued to pay her until her
Social Security started. The doorbell rang. Fletcher put his empty beer bottle
in the sink. For a moment, for the oddest things can be contagious, he thought
it might be someone from the paper or that men with camera and flash would
push in like Weegee and sniff their way to the bathroom. A few questions
please, it won't take long. No, it hadn't taken long and he wouldn't come this
way again. That's all he had to say. He opened the apartment door. It was two
EMS with a gurney. They were both clean and young and as serious as anyone
could ask.

Cold in Hand on Dutch Street

Sunday night from New York Hospital Fletcher found Angela's number in the book and called the apartment. He got the answering service who said she couldn't be reached. That meant they were on Long Island where they shared a summer house with another couple who were, by all accounts, just like them. That must be nice. He said it was an emergency and was told the service did not have a forwarding number. Perhaps. Why go to the expense of a summer rental if you could not escape annoying news such as your distant, unpleasant father was hurt and off his silver haired inaccessible nut. Scanlon had been admitted and x-rays ordered. Fletcher left concise details with the service and went down to the hospital newsstand.

There was a gap on the newsstand bench where the *Local* should have been. If that gap remained long enough the sides would cave in like a hole in the sand. They had the bulldog *Times* and *News* but anticipating a wait Fletcher looked over the paperbacks. Aside from Michener and Robbins and Updike there were the usual cops and robbers: Ed McBain, Chester Himes, Iceberg Slim. He'd read many of them. His specialty was police procedurals where cops plodded through their days and nights drinking bad coffee and complaining to their partners about their wives while gathering clues. These books piled up on his night table during winter when his detective story consumption hummed like a pulp mill. The newsstand carousel had a likely specimen with a Georgia setting. Something about a body turning up in a shipment of Vidalia onions. That was topical, Vidalia onions were turning up on everything from pizza to hot chocolate.

Back upstairs Fletcher read standing for a while with one foot raised like a flamingo. His mother kept hundreds of mystery paperbacks in crates on her sleeping porch. Some were old enough to have war bond advertisements on their endpapers. Mysteries, his mother insisted, could be used again and again like a good muffin pan. They formed a two member club and exchanged authors and titles. Mrs. Fletcher did not care for anything too violent, leaning towards the drawing room or English country garden school. She preferred detectives as knowledgeable about botany as they were about crime. Her son liked a bit more grit with pursuers as morally compromised as the pursued. Slayings for example should be as baroque as possible. Mrs. Fletcher found this distasteful. In her mind everyone should be poisoned, every victim that is, quietly. She said it did not detract from the story if the murderer was well brought up.

Fletcher looked around the ward. It was curious to be surrounded by night creatures. These nurses and orderlies worked while the city slept. About half past midnight Angela and Chuck, looking Caribbean, came down the morbid yellow hall at a trot. Driving back late to beat the traffic they hadn't changed after picking up the message. Fletcher was pleased to see Chuck's usual sartorial expertise did not extend to leisure wear. Chuck looked terribly concerned in pink shorts and a striped terry cloth sweater. Angela was snippy. After the briefest pleasantry she wanted to know why Fletcher hadn't ordered a private ambulance and taken her father to Lenox Hill or Flower Fifth Avenue for heaven's sake. It was obvious she considered New York Hospital but a step above a leper colony. Fletcher, unfamiliar with the social distinctions of Upper East Side medical care, had no excuse but Angela let the matter drop. She demanded to see her father immediately, her manner suggesting Fletcher was concealing the old man for dubious purposes of his own. He fetched an inward sigh. Angie was adopting a crisis attitude and he might as well get used to it. He pointed to the room and she went in, signing to her husband to stay outside.

Making small talk, it perhaps could not come smaller, Fletcher asked Chuck if he knew much about Vidalia onions. Chuck didn't. He was more interested in hearing about this "mess down at the paper". They're sweet and mild, Fletcher told him, and fry up beautifully. Chuck appeared to think this "mess down at the paper" was the staff's doing and that Fletcher, as oldest staff member, was at the bottom of it. Let's face facts, Chuck said, they didn't need a doctor to tell them there was nothing physically wrong with the old boy. Yes, it was this mess down at the paper laying him low. Fletcher nodded agreeably. As the old boy in question had a broken hip and a sweet little buttercup of a concussion he deemed Chuck's argument overstated but not worth contesting. Chuck and Angela were entitled to their own view of life; Fletcher had his after all. You can bet on it, he told Chuck, Vidalia onions will be in every turkey stuffing recipe this Thanksgiving.

In the fluorescence and disinfectant Chuck wouldn't bite. The mess down at the paper was too tempting. He kept at it even as Fletcher remained silent. Fletcher didn't want to talk to Chuck about the paper. It would be like telling a bartender your girlfriend left and took all your records, including the Carl Perkins and the Charlie Parker on Dial. It was unnecessary and could do no good. Angela put an end to it. Her father was not given to illness, likely she had never seen him unwell. She came softly out of the room like a girl sneaking from the house and to Fletcher's surprise, ignoring her husband, put her arms around him. She smelled divinely of suntan lotion and gin. They did not know each other really but shared a mute appreciation of endurance. She put up with her father and so did he but there was a difference. He could quit. She was crying and the tears wet his shirt. The sympathy drained away by Chuck's pink shorts and general obtuseness flowed back. Angela only wanted love and would have settled for scraps. Her sadly alcoholic mother could barely be spoken to on the phone. Her father dismissed her like the school alarm ringing at three o'clock. She married a dumbbell in the belief that a dumbbell would need her and tell her she was special. Her tears became sobs.

"It's hard to see him like this," she said. "I just talked to him last week."

"He'll be fine," Fletcher said. It wasn't enough, not nearly enough. "You know better than anyone, he's the toughest old bird on the block."

"I know, I know…"

"It's amazing what they do with broken hips now, Angie. They stick a pin in it and he'll be jogging around the reservoir in no time."

After a moment, simultaneously, the image of her father in Pierre Cardin slacks and a Gucci sweater jogging around the reservoir in Central Park made them laugh. It seemed so loud in the corridor they stopped and were reduced to smiling. Over her shoulder Fletcher saw Chuck looking for something to do. "You'd better call at least one of your sisters," he said.

"I'd better…"

Fletcher wanted no part of that. Angie broke away and walked over to the phones by the elevator. Chuck was still motionless. "She needs you," Fletcher said.

Chuck looked up. "Right, absolutely." He hurried after his wife. Fletcher leaned back against the wall and took out his mystery. That was the first decent thing he'd said to another human being in months.

Fletcher called selected staff members Monday morning. As sentimentality is fatal to newspaper work he tried not to be. Yet he was willing to expect some expression of regret and a hint of reaching out, of cancelling the strike if it could be done until Scanlon was back on his feet. Sleepless and out of touch Fletcher was prone to pollyanna moments of pure wishfulness. He assumed it was something in the milk he drank as a boy. These moments passed. On the phone he heard some cynicism and indications it was as useful to have Scanlon out of the picture this way as another. By the fifth or sixth call he knew he need not worry too much about sentimentality. There was not a shot glass full at either end.

Mona made that clear. Amanda, Fletcher's private secretary, logged a call from her while he was showering. He reluctantly called the saleswoman back. She was tired of the strike. That did not surprise him. The humdrum mechanics of it, the politics and politesse, were not to her liking. She enjoyed selling and had nothing to do but keep her accounts from getting too warm at the *SoHo News*. She said she wanted to brief him but Fletcher resisted. He had no desire to be briefed. If he was out in no man's land, precisely where he believed he was, he would as soon be out there in the dark. Simplicity of outlook was his compass. His concern, his self-interest, was a paper he wanted to write for. A new regime might pay him more, they couldn't possibly pay him less. If they kept him on. When all was done there might be no *Local* at all, or something unrecognizable with its name. And in that case there would be no decision for him. He could ask his good friend Chuck for a job. Maybe they would send him to Paraguay to do music reviews for the General.

Mona said the strike was breeding power plays, not pretty to see. Fletcher contained his shock as he felt none. He'd seen the same happen to other organizations, seemingly close knit, when a leadership vacuum invited everyone to jump in the pool. Mona told him there was talk of running the paper cooperatively if they could get the backing. Fletcher rejected that as lunacy. Against his will he was being briefed but hearing of a New York *Local* run like a community vegetable garden was worth it. Scanlon's brand of now-you-feel-it-now-you-don't autocracy was most of the time, perhaps all of the time, an interfering nuisance but Fletcher never doubted its essential legitimacy. A democratically run newspaper was of no use to anyone, least of all democracy. You need a strong editor to take out the trash. If you liked him too much you most likely had a fool for a boss. But Scanlon had been a fool, it could not be said too plainly. For reasons unknown the editor had banished, beyond recall it might be, the only fulfilling part of his life. If there was ever another boat ride he would not be on it.

Fletcher said another time to an invitation to lunch, he had to outfit the wagon train for Ohio. A dissatisfied Mona said he should not wall himself in. He might have said it was a matter of being walled out but didn't. If they met they would argue, they would get nowhere. Or Mona might win. She believed it would all sift down pretty soon, the country pie expression ringing as trite as the prediction. As far as Mona knew the midwest was populated by near relations of Elsie and Elmer. He wondered if she was patronizing him for being so aw shucks. *The Local*'s difficulties were not about to break up like a few lumps in the flour unless... how big a player was she? He had now no other real contact at the paper and that, he was sure, did not say much in his favor. The others did not trust him, maybe with good reason. But as for trusting Mona it might be better not to try. No doubt that said even less for him. It stank, there was no other word. These things shouldn't happen for eighty-five bucks a week take home.

Monday afternoon Fletcher went over to University Place to clean out his desk. It was not as wrenching as his mood required. He left his files alone and packed notebooks and the choicer bits of memorabilia from his top drawer. Some of that, out of their setting, immediately entered the realm of junk. His chipped Muddy Waters guitar pick in the paper clip dish would not amount to much at the bottom of a briefcase. It did not amount to much right now.

Likewise the broken pocket watch an admirer sent to indicate his time was not long. ("Even you can understand this. Look out!") How could you justify that somewhere else? The buttons, bar coasters, ticket stubs and postcards had no significance beyond this terrarium. They were devalued, their spirit lost because indeed he had not looked out.

Certain photographs and drawings were another matter. They were on a mural sized bulletin board by the stairs by decree were community property. Boat rides, staff picnics, the softball games. Happy subjects all, some with faces only Fletcher recalled. The centerpiece, it had been since 1968, was a black & white of Fletcher at the Chicago Convention. His head slugged open, blood streaming from his face to his press card, he stood erect with arm raised, almost like rock and roll as the crowd surrounds him. Mahaffy took it, Scanlon ran it on the front page. In twelve years it was the only time Fletcher's face appeared in the paper. It was his skull, his blood, his need to be there and get the story out. The image belonged to him and they couldn't have it. But who "they" were he couldn't say. If the paper became a dining guide and job lot, a boy meets girl gazette, it would be his for the asking or taking. It probably was anyway. The past gets deeper every day. It was a year, maybe more, since anyone had mentioned Chicago.

He wouldn't be before long; not without a place to mention it. Fletcher shut the briefcase, sat back in his chair. It was Duffy's swivel chair, a very good one. He appropriated it after the funeral, feeling it was his right to do so. Duffy would have wanted him to and so forth. It was that sort of thing, an embrace of small things deserved, of deference even, that had him betwixt and between. Resentment is one of the last emotions we decipher in others. Did they really think he was kissing the old man's ass? Did they? That he was breathless in the wings to be the anointed successor? What a joke. Didn't they hear how he talked back to Scanlon? He alone did. Or did they think he was the one allowed to? So it was true. A group, pick one, believe they are like a family when they don't like one another enough to be friends. He didn't want to think about it. He was thinking too much. Other people had jobs, they changed them sometimes. But that was other people, the trifling, non-newspaper billions. Everything he was came through the *Local*. If you took it away, if you pulled the plug, he might not be there at all.

She wasn't, not now. Her resume was under his desk blotter. He'd left Vix at the newspaper because she had no personal role in his life. If he brought her home like a girl at the stage door after a show, he'd get involved the way he always did and forget it was not meant to be real. She was too young for him anyway. He was a slowpoke thirty-three and she was as much as she'd ever be, twenty or so. They never had much to say after the passion was gone. If it was not for this cloudy Polaroid he could put her out of his mind. She wasn't his girl. It made no sense to get hung up on her like that. He meant all the things he said at the time he said them. Wasn't that enough? Another few months in the city and she'd be like everyone else. She'd think he was too square for words, strictly rhomboid.

Fletcher felt tense, as if the newsroom itself was a malevolent spirit. He thought about that. A psychotic editor dies, horribly with any luck, and his evil essence infests the newsroom like a catfish fry. Fresh young cubs from the cowlands seeking justice for all and a by-line grow corrupt under its influence. They drink and smoke and no longer believe prostitutes have hearts of gold. They become… newspaper reporters. Fletcher did not bother writing this down, having achieved anti-climax before he'd begun. His newsroom, their newsroom, was no more malevolent than the automat, if not as tolerant or understanding. It was all out in the open. They didn't have any secrets worth keeping, it all went in the paper every week.

Reflections on the automat were not good, bringing Elke too sharply to mind. In Fletcher's flawed conception of romance, rainy day coffee and conversation at the automat should bind a man and woman together like rubber cement. It hadn't and this seemed unfair. Yet another of life's cherished constructions was under siege. You only have so many in the long surrender. Briefcase zippered he contrarily, petulantly, dropped it in his bottom drawer. The hell with the Muddy Waters guitar pick and all the rest, he didn't want any of it. He put Vix in his shirt pocket and crossed the newsroom, taking the stairs to the lobby. Rothberg was waiting at the elevator. If he keeps that up, Fletcher told himself sourly, he'll be fat in a few years. They exchanged a few words, Scanlon's name not coming up. Rothberg grumbled about Lindquist, he'd been right about the Nixon tapes. No one knew how he got such an advance word. Fletcher was generous. Lucky guess, he said. Rothberg hovered close to saying something about the strike but Fletcher froze him out. If he wasn't interested, if he didn't care, serenity would follow.

Serenity did not follow him to Washington Square. He got that far and stopped by the fountain. The end of August was squatting on the park and squirming out through the exits. NYU students were arriving for the fall and the added degree of youthfulness tinkled like a bell. Another worry. The schools were producing journalism majors with missionary zeal. The graduates were of every race and creed but united in their mission to keep Fletcher from finding another job. One fifteen a week would strike them as a princely sum and if you threw in Duffy's swivel chair they'd never complain. Paige Phillips was on the other side of the fountain moving towards the arch. In their small town world this was Main Street. If she was heading for the paper there must be another meeting he didn't know about. Even Paranoids Have Enemies the graffiti once declared. Maybe they were plotting their first issue by general acclamation. Good luck. They should keep in mind even The Daily Worker has an editor.

Never rising above second gear Fletcher strolled a handsome stroll to Foley Square and the Civic Center. Chinatown makes it slower so he went that way. He loved Chinatown, there wasn't anything down that way to remind you of Monacacy Court House. He bottomed out at the County Courthouse and took Worth Street to Broadway and then to Chambers. Hickman's first immigration address was above the Cheese of All Nations store in a nineteenth century building with glass doors and transoms. You could throw a banana and hit lawyers making less than traffic cops. And they had to scratch for that. Duffy called them hummingbirds because they were so fascinating to study up close. There were hummingbirds all around City Hall and environs, their slightly shady wings in each other's way. This guy was a Schliemann, the same name as the archaeologist who dug up Troy. He had about ten people in his outer office, all of them dark skinned and in work clothes. His office smelled like the cheese from downstairs with an undercurrent of marsh gas. There was no receptionist or secretary but the transom was open so the flies didn't asphyxiate and fall on the floor.

Schliemann did not want to talk to Fletcher. He kept his jacket on so when he said he was on his way to see a judge when he was really heading to the donut shop it did not seem implausible. He did not want to talk to Fletcher because Fletcher was so obviously not a future client. He might even be a process server though when Schliemann discovered Fletcher was a reporter he wished he was a process server. He said he was busy. It was not a lie exactly so there was no reason to be insulted. Fletcher stuck his foot in the closing inner door and said he had a couple of questions, it wouldn't take a minute. Schliemann said through the crack he didn't have a minute. Fletcher said he could come back with a photographer if that would help and Schliemann said one minute, that's all.

Fletcher didn't get much out of him. Schliemann said he didn't know from Rhodesians. He dealt in Filipinos and it wasn't bad. This was standard hummingbird guff. Duffy said hummingbirds told you their line wasn't bad even when it was terrible. If they said it was pretty good that meant it couldn't get any worse. If they told you it was like money in the bank you knew they were really starving. Schliemann said Filipinos and Pakistanis were like money in the bank any day of the week. He looked hungry. Fletcher asked who had Rhodesians and Schliemann pretended the minute was up. It wasn't. Fletcher had nothing to lean on him with so he waved the picture of Vix. He said murder is messy and sometimes all sorts of people get involved who would rather not. If this approach worked you sounded tough, if it didn't you sounded like an idiot. Fletcher sounded like an idiot. He was quoting about verbatim from the Vidalia onions book that was squashed in his back pocket. A deputy talks that way to a suspect and it was pretty effective. But that was fiction and relatively crummy fiction at that. Maybe Schliemann read mysteries and knew the material. In any case he was not impressed. He said he didn't know anything about anything, he learned that in law school. The minute was up anyway. When Fletcher was back on the street and didn't smell cheese anymore it was like dancing with a girl who had attar of roses behind her ear.

Next stop was Elk Street, not one of the more prominent thoroughfares around the mayor's business address. This lawyer was Brody, the same name as the guy who became famous for jumping off the Brooklyn Bridge when in fact he did not. Duffy would say somebody took a brody when they jumped off a building. All his professional life Duffy took a lighthearted interest in suicide. He liked them lurid. Double suicides were that rare day in June and if an aged dowager bumped off her philandering lover with Drano before taking a dose herself Duffy was prone to cartwheels. Something like that, he said, restores your faith in human nature. It did not help him later when he was ill. I'm a newspaper reporter, he told Fletcher, I shouldn't be afraid to die.

Attorney Brody was passing a quiet afternoon sucking cold chop suey out of a waxed container. His office, one room with a sink, was thinly furnished but there was an umbrella stand under a medicine cabinet and two light fixtures without globes. It was homey. Fletcher surmised Brody was one of those advocates who meet their clients under a lamppost after dark. He felt warm towards Brody when he saw a month old *Local* folded on a chair. He felt less warm when he saw the library subscription label on it. Always keep this time free, Brody said brightly, to write my briefs. (Duffy revealed that even as their wings beat one hundred times per second hummingbirds can still pick loose dimes from pay phones.) The brief Brody was working on was the *Daily News* crossword. Not much was filled in but Fletcher didn't like to work when he was eating either.

Fletcher asked about Rhodesians and Brody said he did South Americans exclusively and it wasn't bad. They were good payers, he said. This meant Brody operated on a cash basis and still got stiffed. Duffy's field research revealed that the sound disappointed hummingbirds make when you squeeze them is like a kewpie doll crying mommy. Once heard it is never forgotten. But there was no point in squeezing Brody who had dried shaving cream in his ear and mold on his chop suey. There was a framed family photograph on the desk, a wife and two daughters. Fletcher hoped the kids had rich aunts and uncles. If Brody had made an illegal dollar lately it hadn't come from Stutz.

Fletcher had one other name on his list from Hickman. It sounded good, Creakey. There was a man with that name back home who went to the penitentiary. He was a forger of some kind and it was said of him in the barber shop that he might have made something of himself if he had not turned to crime. Fletcher's father said this was not so. Forgers are no smarter than stick-up men, he said, and maybe less smart than hijackers who need to read a road map. Mr. Fletcher made no allowance for thieves from a good background. It offended against his sense of place. So Creakey sounded good to Fletcher but turned out too good. The address on Church Street was now a messenger service. Inquiries at another law office across the hall revealed that Creakey was no longer practicing due to disbarment. Only a matter of time, this attorney said, not sounding sorry. Fletcher asked if he did any immigration work and the man looked disgusted and said he didn't.

Outside City Hall Fletcher had a hot dog and washed it down at a water fountain. He should have had a knish. He had onions on the hot dog instead of sauerkraut and that was a mistake too. He couldn't even get his lunch right. He considered stopping in Room 9, the press room in City Hall and asking around but someone might ask him about the *Local*. The Yellow Pages were a better idea. Over at Pace College he borrowed a copy at the security desk. There were ads for expediters and the like, promising green card assistance. He was proud of himself, not every reporter had a source like the Yellow Pages. It was two-thirty, another few lawyers wouldn't kill him he hoped. The receptionist at a place on Duane Street told him to come back in an hour. Another office on Murray said they couldn't help him, they were closing early to change the locks. Another was so crowded Fletcher felt he was in the middle of the Marx Brothers' stateroom scene. So much for the Yellow Pages. And that hot dog had too much mustard.

Immigration and Naturalization was nearby. Federal, they were still on a wartime alert, such as it was, and Fletcher could not get past the lobby checkpoint. Not having a destination he didn't try very hard. He succumbed to a phone booth with the door open and called the News. Hickman was out, Fletcher was relieved. He had nothing to say and that was putting it graciously. He felt like a door to door salesman, not a reporter. Amanda was out too, he was saving dimes at least. Lethargy set in, leaving that phone booth might be hard. He'd overslept that morning, it was all part of the inexorable quicksand. Once you lost your work habits that was just the beginning. Maybe he'd stop shaving next and shining his shoes. The question was: how low would he go? Could he possibly stay home and spend the day in his bathrobe? No, his mother would sense it. If he still had his bathrobe on at lunchtime the phone would ring and she'd tell him to get dressed. Fletcher wasn't making any friends in immigrations circles using a phone booth as a park bench. And to make it the more objectionable he folded his arms and stuck his legs out. He was a snotty nosed punk at last. The lobby was busy. Men in turbans, women in saris, untold languages. It was the rest of the world on your doorstep. There wasn't anyone there who had marched against the war. They wanted in too much. They'd work themselves to death so their kids could smoke the dean's cigars.

Well, now, Duffy would have loved this guy over there. Slumped against the opposite wall he looked like Mr. Potato Head when you still had to use a real potato. The lumpy file folder under his arm probably held a Blimpie and a change of shorts. If he had any clients, God forbid, they should have stayed home. Lawyers like that make you suspect the bar exam must be no more exacting than applying for a library card. The guy nodded to passersby who ignored him and made a notation on his file folder that was possibly a reminder to pick up his other shirt at the laundry. Due to waistline expansion Fletcher had a good view of the leather pipe holder attached to his belt. It was a touch Duffy would have esteemed. Vestiges of former domesticity, wrote the Herodotus of hummingbirds, cling to members of the bund like a milk moustache. This is especially so if the object has no pawn value. Duffy once knew a theatre district shyster who always carried a suburban train schedule for sentimental reasons. Most likely you couldn't hock a leather pipe holder on the Bowery.

Fletcher could not have watched Fred Astaire with more pleasure than the lawyer with the pipe holder but he was compelled by public opinion to give up his seat. As he stood a tall and very broad and muscular sports coat came in from the street and covered the short porky lawyer like an eclipse. They talked. Fletcher never took a step forward. He took three steps sideways that put him out of sight beside the bank of phone booths because the sports coat was Marvin, the door moose from the Dream Lucky bar. There couldn't be another pair of shoulders like that in North America. The conference was short. The door moose tendered an envelope, not a thick one, hummingbirds never receive thick envelopes unless they're filled with phony money, and left. It was not an especially nefarious encounter but it would do. The lawyer deposited the envelope in a saggy outer pocket and did what Fletcher hoped he would. He beat it, pipe in mouth, a whole lot faster than you'd think possible.

On the sidewalk no sign of Marvin. The lawyer started south, dropping a *Post* from his file folder into a trash can. Fletcher followed. They took Vesey Street to Broadway, then down to Fulton. Waiting for the light the lawyer tapped out his pipe on a mailbox. Lower Manhattan is a harsh mistress for the web footed and this waddler was nearly nailed by a taxi as he crossed to the east side of Broadway. That envelope meant he could eat for maybe a week and he was already thinking about it too much. Fletcher followed to what looked like an alley between Nassau and William. It was a through street, running one block to John. Dutch Street it was called. Fletcher had never heard of it.

Duffy used to kid him: you're not as big a hick as you think you are, they got a street down there around Wall Street named for you. It was true. There was a Fletcher Street below the fish market. It was short and narrow but had Dutch Street beat. In terms of office space Dutch Street was the bottom of a well. Even on a dry day its cobblestones were slippery and there was a reek like stale refrigerator to the pavement. It was the sort of street where you'd take a leak without looking over your shoulder. If you did look you'd only see somebody else pissing too. At the moment there was just a drip from a rooftop gutter hitting a bag of garbage something with teeth had torn open. The lawyer was not taking a shortcut. He went into a three story brick warehouse with the look of a converted stable. Number 9 Dutch Street told a client all they needed to know: deportation might be better than this. Fletcher waited on the other sidewalk and then feeble light appeared at a top floor window. Home is the hunter so to speak. Fletcher looked at his watch, three fifteen, looked at it again. He could think of no plausible explanation for showing up above. That is he was at a loss for a good lie. Hummingbirds have not only heard them all, they've used most of them. You did not turn up on Dutch Street without cause and Fletcher was fresh out.

In the building there were antique stairs and a rambunctious freight elevator. The directory listed six tenants, showing how much you should believe directories. There was a chiropractor and a rare coin dealer, two locksmiths and a flower arranger. Rare coin dealer was right out of Raymond Chandler and as for the flower arranger his customers must be select. B. Hummel had the penthouse. That Mr. Hummel Esq. declined to announce his profession testified to his bona fides and reputation. Fletcher tried the stairs. They creaked as much as they looked like they would. Hummel would hear him and there was still no excuse at hand for being there. Fletcher backed down the stairs and examined a niche on the other side of the elevator. It might have smelled worse. Beside a roach motel and a crushed pack of Winstons there was a bucket placed for the comfort of snoops. He turned it over and sat on it. Not bad. Leaning his shoulder to the wall he was glad he'd come equipped. There was about half of the Georgia mystery left.

Fletcher read for an hour. There was little activity. A man, maybe a locksmith, came in grunting a heavy load and used the elevator. It shook the building and gave Fletcher a good rattle too. The sheriff in Vidalia had more worldly wisdom than normal for law enforcement but the plot wasn't bad and the location and dialogue were scenic. Fletcher was absorbed enough to forget the time, to nearly forget where he was. In truth he did not know what he was doing. In two days he would be in Ohio and though this day's work might give him a sleepless turn on Maple Avenue what of it? Getting the story, Duffy said, is what counts. That man from the Bronx meant it, that's why he was so good.

A lawyer whistling had to mean trouble for someone somewhere. Hummel used the stairs and having heard the elevator Fletcher didn't blame him. Rising from his bucket Fletcher peeked around the wall. Hummel came out of the stairwell looking like bowling night in a windbreaker and jeans. No bothersome file folder either, he was homeward bound and happy to be alive. That envelope must have been thick enough for him. Fletcher followed to the door, watching him down to John Street. That was all right. If the lawyer came back there wasn't any way Fletcher wouldn't hear him.

Duffy said tell them you're there to check the fire extinguisher. Too bad the top floor didn't seem to have one. Hummel's name was on an attorney-at-large business card thumbtacked to his door. The door was wood, only one lock. He tried the knob twice. There was something of a cafe argument at one time that crime required more commitment than art. Fletcher never thought much of the debate but now he wasn't so sure. Maybe the trick was not to think about it.

Well, there was generally a lot not to think about. He looked around once and then with a demure aw, fuck it spoken under his breath he kicked the door in.

It was a good kick, worthy of Ohio State and those Saturday afternoons when he had listlessly cheered for a sport he found unbearable. He caught the door as it bounced back. The office was small, stuffy, a strong poke in the nose of Sir Walter Raleigh. A flashlight would have helped, he'd keep that in mind when next breaking and entering. He switched on a desk lamp, went through the drawers. Hummel was more than a slob, he was a health hazard. Never mind the flashlight, bring a surgical mask in the future. As he rifled Fletcher recalled the government had his fingerprints but didn't care. Hummingbirds never called the cops unless they were being mugged and not before giving the mugger their card. The desk had little but court debris and Dixie cups for the empty water cooler. Fletcher squealed Hummel's chair across to a file cabinet. It was letter size, the carefree Hummel had legal size folders bent into it. Their condition was dog-eared evidence of a practice not quite flourishing. Whatever order they were in would never be duplicated so Fletcher didn't try. He ditched papers like a speed reader as he went through them. There wasn't much, blank forms, tax returns, evidence of a little landlord-tenant work.

Fletcher was nostalgic for alphabetical order. It wouldn't have helped, he didn't have a name, but it appealed to his love of classification. Hummel had none. His filing system presumed retirement or perhaps time in a minimum security institution. What had the man been doing lately? There was nothing on the wall from a law school or bar association, nothing to indicate he was li-censed to make your will or pull your teeth. Was it a set up? But the street, the office, who would fall for it? The desperate? Maybe they'd think Hummel was so cash and carry he had to be legitimate. And maybe the girls never saw this place, maybe Hummel made house calls. The elevator started. Fletcher felt an electric shock. At the door he heard the elevator going down. It stopped, started up again. Fletcher looked to the stairs, towards escape, but the elevator cranking stopped at the floor below. Feet down a hall, a door opened, a pause, the door closing with a slam. Fletcher's shoulders came down a notch and he breathed again.

But short of attacking the floorboards with a crowbar he didn't know where else to look. Vix may have given Hummel money to expedite a visa application he was not to any degree expediting. Maybe there was more due and that was the three hundred Cheryl at Dream Lucky promised her. If he got his business from Stutz that made sense. Stutz was not interested in making Vix legal. The more he had on her the better for him. Hummel had left his Mr. Coffee coffee maker on and Fletcher shut it off. That did not make him feel better about making a mess. There was a bookcase with law books, mounds of newspapers, an A & P bag with cans of chili and beefaroni, some loose *Pent-houses* and *Playboys*, a box of *National Geographics*. The Geographics might have been useful in a waiting room if Hummel had one. He didn't. Fletcher knelt down. He had a soft spot for *National Geographic*. Like other men his age he had seen his first image of a naked female breast in one. Hummel had a fair selection and behind them in the box was an accordion file. Its string was neatly tied, there was even a bow. Fletcher undid it. There were legal folders inside, each with an index card stapled to the flap. The names typed on the index cards were women's names, many had a foreign sound. There were twelve, fifteen, Fletcher counted, twenty-one. The second time he flipped through them he stopped at Victoria Grey. The forms were filled in but none of the forms were stamped. The papers had not been processed. There was a passport photo and a biographical essay. Fletcher read it twice, Vix wrote pretty well, good handwriting. She was twenty, she'd had a birthday since she'd been dead, the tenth of August. Her parents were Leonard and Jean, they lived in Salisbury. She wanted to attend school at…

Fletcher tidied up the room and left the office like he worked there every day. Down on the street the financial district was on its way home. On Broadway he bought a *Post* to hold Vix's file. The headline was Abbie Hoffman Busted. Across from the Brooklyn Bridge he sat on the same bench where he'd eaten the hot dog and read about Abbie Hoffman. It was drugs, cocaine, what was the expression, weight. If it was true it was too bad. If it was not true it was too bad too. Either way some part of you didn't win. He didn't want to read about it. Inside there was a deaf mute girl on page three with facial injuries and broken teeth. Somebody shoved her from behind into a subway exit turnstile in Washington Heights for the change in her pocket. Fletcher hated those enclosed exit turnstiles and would walk a long way to an open staircase. The girl was one of the deaf who hand out sign language cards on the train for a contribution. Fletcher used them as bookmarks. He supposed she couldn't cry out but wasn't sure. It was stupid not to know if she could cry out. Every day there was something making you feel stupid. He put Vix's file into the Post. The best thing to do was… good question. The best thing to do didn't exist. If it did he would have heard about it by now. But he could tell them. He could tell them so they wouldn't read about it in the newspaper. Fletcher got up and went home with Vix. He'd always meant to. All things being equal, though they are not, it would be easier to call her mom and dad from Ohio.

NYC 1998

Made in the USA
Las Vegas, NV
01 April 2021